The Truth
about the World

Basic Readings in Philosophy

THIRD EDITION

EDITED BY JAMES RACHELS
AND STUART RACHELS

Connect
Learn
Succeed™

THE TRUTH ABOUT THE WORLD

Published by McGraw-Hill, an imprint of The McGraw-Hill Companies, Inc., 1221 Avenue of the Americas, New York, NY 10020. Copyright © 2012, 2008, 2005. All rights reserved. No part of this publication may be reproduced or distributed in any form or by any means, or stored in a database or retrieval system, without the prior written consent of The McGraw-Hill Companies, Inc., including, but not limited to, in any network or other electronic storage or transmission, or broadcast for distance learning.

This book is printed on acid-free paper.

1 2 3 4 5 6 7 8 9 0 DOC/DOC 1 0 9 8 7 6 5 4 3 2 1

ISBN: 978-0-07-803830-3
MHID: 0-07-803830-8

Sponsoring Editor: *Meredith Grant*
Marketing Manager: *Tara Culliney*
Developmental Editor: *Meghan Campbell*
Production Editor: *Ruth Sakata Corley*
Production Service: *Scratchgravel Publishing Services*
Cover Designer: *Preston Thomas*
Buyer II: *Tandra Jorgensen*
Composition: *10/12 Baskerville by Laserwords Private Limited*
Printing: *45# New Era Matte, R. R. Donnelley & Sons*

Vice President Editorial: *Michael Ryan*
Publisher: *Mike Sugarman*

Cover Image: *Non-Objective Painting no. 80 (black on black), 1918 by Alexander Rodchenko. Cover Art © Estate of Alexander Rodchenko/RAO, Moscow/VAGA, New York/Digital Image © The Museum of Modern Art/Licensed by SCALA/Art Resource, NY*

Library of Congress Cataloging-in-Publication Data
The truth about the world : basic readings in philosophy / edited by James Rachels and Stuart Rachels. — 3rd ed.
    p. cm.
  ISBN 978-0-07-803830-3
  1. Philosophy. I. Rachels, James, 1941–2003. II. Rachels, Stuart, 1969–
B72.T78 2012
100—dc23

                                                                    2011017229

www.mhhe.com

Contents

FREEDOM

KNOWLEDGE

ETHICS

Preface

This book is a collection of essays about some of the most important topics in philosophy—God, the mind, freedom, knowledge, and ethics. It is a companion to James Rachels' and Stuart Rachels' book, *Problems from Philosophy*, but neither book presupposes knowledge of the other.

This new edition contains some changes:

- Some figures have been updated in James Rachels' "Introduction."
- In the section on God, Michael Peterson's essay on the Problem of Evil has been replaced by Peter van Inwagen's more substantial defense of religious belief.
- In the section on Freedom, Jean-Paul Sartre's "Existentialism Is a Humanism" has been replaced by Derk Pereboom's vigorous rejection of free will. Sartre's essay, I felt, was a bit light on argumentation; Pereboom's essay is not.
- In the section on Knowledge, I removed a beautiful but dated piece by J. L. Austin.
- In the section on Ethics, I replaced James Rachels' and Stuart Rachels' chapter on Utilitarianism with an updated version, and I added two new selections:
  - Immanuel Kant, "Four Applications of the Categorical Imperative," and
  - Robert Nozick, "The Experience Machine."

The book's content has been improved, but the page count remains the same.

For their help, I thank Torin Alter, Heather Elliott, Carol Enns, Kelly Carver Finn, Daniel Hollingshead, Michael Huemer, Derk Pereboom, Carol Rachels, and Chase Wrenn. I would also like to thank (belatedly!) David Blatty, who did a superb job as the production editor of the second edition of this book.

—Stuart Rachels

About the Authors

James Rachels (1941–2003) wrote *The End of Life: Euthanasia and Morality* (1986), *Created from Animals: The Moral Implications of Darwinism* (1990), *Can Ethics Provide Answers? And Other Essays in Moral Philosophy* (1997), *The Elements of Moral Philosophy* (editions 1–4), and *The Legacy of Socrates: Essays in Moral Philosophy* (2007). His website is www.jamesrachels.org.

Stuart Rachels is Associate Professor of Philosophy at the University of Alabama. He has revised several of James Rachels' books, including *The Elements of Moral Philosophy* (sixth edition, 2010) and Rachels' introduction to philosophy, *Problems from Philosophy* (third edition, 2012), which is the companion to this book. Stuart won the United States Chess Championship in 1989 at the age of 20, and today he is a Bronze Life Master at bridge. His website is www.jamesrachels.org/stuart.

CHAPTER 1

Introduction

James Rachels

Most Americans believe in God. In fact, according to a recent Gallup poll, 56 percent of Americans say that religion plays a "very important" role in their lives. And when the Pew Research Center conducted polls in different countries, it found the United States to be much more religious than other developed Western nations. In France, only 14 percent say that religion is very important to them. In Great Britain, the figure is 18 percent; in Spain, 21 percent; and in Canada and Germany, 27 percent. However, Indonesians, Pakistanis, and Indians are even more religious than Americans. Thus, in terms of professed religious faith, Americans are "closer to people in developing nations than to the publics of developed nations."

What accounts for the decline in religious faith in the developed nations? No doubt the explanation is complicated, and no one knows the whole story for sure. But one factor may be the prestige of science and the increasing prevalence of the scientific view of the world. There was a time, not very long ago, when belief in God did not seem to be a mere matter of "faith." Then, it seemed necessary to believe that God had designed and created the world—otherwise, there was no good way to understand the natural order. Today, however, the situation seems to have changed. Modern science gives us a picture of what the world is like in which God plays no part. We may begin by looking briefly at these two conceptions.

The Traditional Religious Understanding of the World. While he was awaiting death, Socrates told his friends the story of his development as a philosopher. This story is recounted in Plato's *Phaedo.* When he was a young man, Socrates said, he wanted to pursue natural science. He wanted to understand such things as how living creatures come to be and the physical basis of thought. ("Is it with the blood that we think," he wondered, "or with the air or the fire that is in us?") But he was frustrated because he could not imagine how to answer such questions. Then he had an epiphany:

> I heard someone reading from a book (as he said) by Anaxagoras, and asserting that it is Mind that produces order and is the cause of everything. This explanation pleased me. Somehow it seemed right that Mind should be the cause of everything; and I reflected that if this is so, Mind in producing order sets everything in order and arranges each individual thing in the way that is best for it. Therefore if anyone wished to discover the reason why any given thing came or ceased or continued to be, he must find out how it was best for that thing to be, or to act or be acted upon.

Thus Socrates began to conceive of the world as governed by principles of good and evil. On this way of thinking, the "natural laws" that explain how things are do not just refer to physical causes and effects. In addition, the laws of nature say *how things ought to be*. This idea is so unlike the modern way of thinking that it takes effort for us to grasp it. The idea is that things in the world arrange themselves in a certain way *because it is for the best*. It is as though the value structure of the world were a force, like gravity, that causes things to move. It is hard for us to conceive of how this could be. But to Socrates, "it seemed right." Plato agreed.

Aristotle, who lived a few decades later, made this idea a centerpiece of his philosophy. Everything in nature has a purpose, he said, and natural occurrences take place so that those purposes can be realized. Why does it rain? Aristotle's answer is that it rains so that plants can grow. He considered other alternatives, such as that the rain falls "of necessity" and that this helps the plants by "coincidence," but he rejected them. "Nature," he said, "belongs to the class of causes which act for the sake of something."

The world, therefore, is an orderly, rational system, with each thing having its own proper place and serving its own special purpose. There is a neat hierarchy: The rain exists for the sake of the plants, the plants exist for the sake of the animals, and the animals exist for the sake of people, whose well-being is the point of the whole arrangement. In the *Politics* Aristotle wrote:

[W]e must believe, first that plants exist for the sake of animals, second that all other animals exist for the sake of man, tame animals for the use he can make of them as well as for the food they provide; and as for wild animals, most though not all of these can be used for food or are useful in other ways; clothing and instruments can be made out of them. If then we are right in believing that nature makes nothing without some end in view, nothing to no purpose, it must be that nature has made all things specifically for the sake of man.

For Aristotle, these thoughts had nothing to do with religion. They were just a description of how things are.

Thus, these philosophers believed, on more or less secular grounds, that the cosmos, with the earth at its center, is a realm of values and purposes, and that human beings have a special place in it. For them, this was simply the most reasonable way to understand the nature of things. It was the best available theory of what the world is like. This theory was to prevail for more than two thousand years. But the theory seemed incomplete. What was the origin of the world, and why does it have this character? The Christian thinkers who came later adopted the Greek cosmology, and, to complete the picture, they added God. The fact that the world was created by God, according to a divine plan, explains why the world exists and why it has the structure it has. The laws of nature are God's laws.

Today, vast numbers of people continue to think of the world in these terms. But thoughtful people are uneasy because this way of thinking seems out of step with modern science.

The Worldview of Modern Science. The world as described by Galileo, Newton, and Darwin is not governed by principles of right and wrong. What happens just happens, fortuitously, in consequence of the laws of cause and effect. The rain does not fall so plants can grow. Instead, rainfall is explained by the principles of modern meteorology. If the rain benefits the plants, it is only because the plants have evolved by natural selection in a rainy climate. And as for Aristotle's idea that "nature has made all things specifically for the sake of man," that is only human vanity. From a biological point of view, human beings are just one species among many.

Thus, we have a second, radically different way of understanding what the world is like. It is so familiar that it needs little comment. In this view, the universe is unimaginably vast. It began with the "Big Bang" about 13.7 billion years ago. It operates by physical laws that have nothing to do with right or wrong—indeed, the whole idea of "right and wrong" is a human invention. The earth, an insignificant speck, was formed about 4.5 billion years ago. The development of life on earth was a slow, quirky process governed by natural selection, and the emergence of human beings was an unlikely evolutionary accident. There are no "immortal souls"—our thoughts and feelings are products of our brains. Other animals also have thoughts and feelings, but theirs are in many ways unlike ours. Moreover, "free will" is a dubious notion, because our personalities and behavior are shaped by our genes and environment. And much as we may regret it, death is the permanent end of our existence.

In the worldview of modern science, there is no mention of God. He is simply absent from the picture. As Laplace supposedly said to Napoleon, "Sire, I have no need of that hypothesis."

A thoughtful person is apt to feel the pull of both these ways of thinking. Few of us will want to swallow either outlook whole. Instead, we will probably want to accept some parts of each view. The main problems of philosophy arise from the effort to decide what, exactly, we should believe.

*P*lato

CHAPTER 2

Socrates' Trial

Plato

The first great philosophers of the Western tradition were Plato (427–347 B.C.) and his teacher Socrates (c. 470–399 B.C.). Socrates is the star of Plato's books, which were written in the form of dialogues, or conversations.

It is something of a mystery why Socrates was put on trial for his life and then condemned to death by the Athenian court. The Athenians, after all, were proud of their intellectual achievements and democratic institutions. In the *Apology*, reprinted here in full, we have Plato's account of the trial, or at least of Socrates' defense. Plato does not give us the accusers' case.

I do not know what effect my accusers have had upon you, gentlemen, but for my own part I was almost carried away by them; their arguments were so convincing. On the other hand, scarcely a word of what they said was true. I was especially astonished at one of their many misrepresentations: I mean when they told you that you must be careful not to let me deceive you—the implication being that I am a skilful speaker. I thought that it was peculiarly brazen of them to tell you this without a blush, since they must know that they will soon be effectively confuted, when it becomes obvious that I have not the slightest skill as

Source: This selection, Plato's *Apology,* is reprinted from *The Last Days of Socrates* by Plato, trans. Hugh Tredennick and Harold Tarrant (London: Penguin, 1954), pp. 45–76. Copyright © 1954, 1959, 1969 Hugh Tredennick. Reproduced by permission of Penguin Books Ltd.

a speaker—unless, of course, by a skilful speaker they mean one who speaks the truth. If that is what they mean, I would agree that I am an orator, though not after their pattern.

My accusers, then, as I maintain, have said little or nothing that is true, but from me you shall hear the whole truth; not, I can assure you, gentlemen, in flowery language like theirs, decked out with fine words and phrases; no, what you will hear will be a straightforward speech in the first words that occur to me, confident as I am in the justice of my cause; and I do not want any of you to expect anything different. It would hardly be suitable, gentlemen, for a man of my age to address you in the artificial language of a schoolboy orator. One thing, however, I do most earnestly beg and entreat of you: if you hear me defending myself in the same language which it has been my habit to use, both in the open spaces of this city (where many of you have heard me) and elsewhere, do not be surprised, and do not interrupt. Let me remind you of my position. This is my first appearance in a court of law, at the age of seventy; and so I am a complete stranger to the language of this place. Now if I were really from another country, you would naturally excuse me if I spoke in the manner and dialect in which I had been brought up; and so in the present case I make this request of you, which I think is only reasonable: to disregard the manner of my speech—it may be better or it may be worse—and to consider and concentrate your attention upon this one question, whether my claims are fair or not. That is the first duty of the juryman, just as it is the pleader's duty to speak the truth.

The proper course for me, gentlemen of the jury, is to deal first with the earliest charges that have been falsely brought against me, and with my earliest accusers; and then with the later ones. I make this distinction because I have already been accused in your hearing by a great many people for a great many years, though without a word of truth; and I am more afraid of those people than I am of Anytus and his colleagues, although they are formidable enough. But the others are still more formidable; I mean the people who took hold of so many of you when you were children and tried to fill your minds with untrue accusations against me, saying, 'There is a clever man called Socrates who has theories about the heavens and has investigated everything below the earth, and can make the weaker argument defeat the stronger.' It is these people, gentlemen, the disseminators of these rumours, who are my dangerous accusers; because those who hear them suppose that anyone who inquires into such matters must be an atheist. Besides, there are a great many of these accusers, and they have been accusing me now for a great many years; and what is more, they approached you at the most impressionable age, when some of you were children or adolescents; and they literally won their case by default, because there was no one to defend me. And the most fantastic thing of all is that it is impossible for me even to know and tell you their names, unless one of them happens to be a playwright. All these people, who have tried to set you against me out of envy and love of slander—and some too merely passing on what they have been told by others—all these are very difficult to deal with. It is impossible to bring them here for cross-examination; one simply has to conduct one's defence and argue one's case against an invisible opponent, because there is no one to answer. So I ask you to accept my statement that my critics fall into two classes: on the one hand my immediate accusers, and on the other those earlier ones whom I have mentioned; and you must suppose that I have first to defend myself against the latter. After all, you heard them abusing me longer ago and much more violently than these more recent accusers.

Very well, then; I must begin my defence, gentlemen, and I must try, in the short time that I have, to rid your minds of a false impression which is the work of many years. I should like this to be the result, gentlemen, assuming it to be for your advantage and my own; and I should like to be successful in my defence; but I think that it will be difficult, and I am quite aware of the nature of my task. However, let that turn out as God wills; I must obey the law and make my defence.

Let us go back to the beginning and consider what the charge is that has made me so unpopular, and has encouraged Meletus to draw up this indictment. Very well; what did my critics say in attacking my character? I must read out their affidavit, so to speak, as though they were my legal accusers. 'Socrates is guilty of criminal meddling, in that he inquires into things below the earth and in the sky, and makes the weaker argument defeat the stronger, and teaches others to follow his example.' It runs something like that. You have seen it for yourselves in the play by Aristophanes, where Socrates goes whirling round, proclaiming that he is walking on air, and uttering a great deal of other nonsense about things of which I know nothing whatsoever. I mean no disrespect for such knowledge, if anyone really is versed in it—I do not want any more lawsuits brought against me by Meletus—but the fact is, gentlemen, that I take no interest in it. What is more, I call upon the greater part of you as witnesses to my statement, and I appeal to all of you who have ever listened to me talking (and there are a great many to whom this applies) to clear your neighbours' minds on this point. Tell one another whether any one of you has ever heard me discuss such questions briefly or at length; and then you will realize that the other popular reports about me are equally unreliable.

The fact is that there is nothing in any of these charges; and if you have heard anyone say that I try to educate people and charge a fee, there is no truth in that either. I wish that there were, because I think that it is a fine thing if a man is qualified to teach, as in the case of Gorgias of Leontini and Prodicus of Ceos and Hippias of Elis. Each one of these is perfectly capable of going into any city and actually persuading the young men to leave the company of their fellow-citizens, with any of whom they can associate for nothing, and attach themselves to him, and pay money for the privilege, and be grateful into the bargain. There is another expert too from Paros who I discovered was here on a visit. I happened to meet a man who has paid more in sophists' fees than all the rest put together—I mean Callias the son of Hipponicus; so I asked him (he has two sons, you see): 'Callias,' I said, 'if your sons had been colts or calves, we should have had no difficulty in finding and engaging a trainer to perfect their natural qualities; and this trainer would have been some sort of horse-dealer or agriculturalist. But seeing that they are human beings, whom do you intend to get as their instructor? Who is the expert in perfecting the human and social qualities? I assume from the fact of your having sons that you must have considered the question. Is there such a person or not?' 'Certainly,' said he. 'Who is he, and where does he come from?' said I, 'and what does he charge?' 'Evenus of Paros, Socrates,' said he, 'and his fee is 500 drachmae.' I felt that Evenus was to be congratulated if he really was a master of this art and taught it at such a moderate fee. I should certainly plume myself and give myself airs if I understood these things; but in fact, gentlemen, I do not.

Here perhaps one of you might interrupt me and say, 'But what is it that you do, Socrates? How is it that you have been misrepresented like this? Surely all this talk and gossip about you would never have arisen if you had confined yourself to ordinary activities, but only if your behaviour was abnormal. Tell us the explanation, if you do not want us to invent it for ourselves.' This seems to me to be a reasonable request, and I will try to explain to you what it is that has given me this false notoriety; so please give me your attention. Perhaps some of you will think that I am not being serious; but I assure you that I am going to tell you the whole truth.

I have gained this reputation, gentlemen, from nothing more or less than a kind of wisdom. What kind of wisdom do I mean? Human wisdom, I suppose. It seems that I really am wise in this limited sense. Presumably the geniuses whom I mentioned just now are wise in a wisdom that is more than human; I do not know how else to account for it. I certainly have no knowledge of such wisdom, and anyone who says that I have is a liar and wilful slanderer. Now, gentlemen, please do not interrupt me if I seem to make an extravagant claim; for what I am going to tell you is not my own opinion; I am going to refer you to an unimpeachable authority. I shall call as witness to my wisdom (such as it is) the god at Delphi.

You know Chaerephon, of course. He was a friend of mine from boyhood, and a good democrat who played his part with the rest of you in the recent expulsion and restoration. And you know what he was like; how enthusiastic he was over anything that he had once undertaken. Well, one day he actually went to Delphi and asked this question of the god—as I said before, gentlemen, please do not interrupt—he asked whether there was anyone wiser than myself. The priestess replied that there was no one. As Chaerephon is dead, the evidence for my statement will be supplied by his brother, who is here in court.

Please consider my object in telling you this. I want to explain to you how the attack upon my reputation first started. When I heard about the oracle's answer, I said to myself, 'What does the god mean? Why does he not use plain language? I am only too conscious that I have no claim to wisdom, great or small; so what can he mean by asserting that I am the wisest man in the world? He cannot be telling a lie; that would not be right for him.'

After puzzling about it for some time, I set myself at last with considerable reluctance to check the truth of it in the following way. I went to interview a man with a high reputation for wisdom, because I felt that here if anywhere I should succeed in disproving the oracle and pointing out to my divine authority, 'You said that I was the wisest of men, but here is a man who is wiser than I am.'

Well, I gave a thorough examination to this person—I need not mention his name, but it was one of our politicians that I was studying when I had this experience—and in conversation with him I formed the impression that although in many people's opinion, and especially in his own, he appeared to be wise, in fact he was not. Then when I began to try to show him that he only thought he was wise and was not really so, my efforts were resented both by him and by many of the other people present. However, I reflected as I walked away: 'Well, I am certainly wiser than this man. It is only too likely that neither of us has any knowledge to boast of; but he thinks that he knows something which he does not know, whereas I am quite conscious of my igno-rance. At any rate it seems that I am wiser than he is to this small extent, that I do not think that I know what I do not know.'

After this I went on to interview a man with an even greater reputation for wisdom, and I formed the same impression again; and here too I incurred the resentment of the man himself and a number of others.

From that time on I interviewed one person after another. I realized with distress and alarm that I was making myself unpopular, but I felt compelled to put my religious duty first; since I was trying to find out the meaning of the oracle, I was bound to interview everyone who had a reputation for knowledge. And by Dog, gentlemen! (for I must be frank with you) my honest impression was this: it seemed to me, as I pursued my investigation at the god's command, that the people with the greatest reputations were almost entirely deficient, while others who were supposed to be their inferiors were much bet-ter qualified in practical intelligence.

I want you to think of my adventures as a sort of pilgrimage undertaken to establish the truth of the oracle once for all. After I had finished with the politicians I turned to the poets, dramatic, lyric, and all the rest, in the belief that here I should expose myself as a comparative ignoramus. I used to pick up what I thought were some of their most perfect works and question them closely about the meaning of what they had written, in the hope of incidentally enlarg-ing my own knowledge. Well, gentlemen, I hesitate to tell you the truth, but it must be told. It is hardly an exaggeration to say that any of the bystanders could have explained those poems better than their actual authors. So I soon made up my mind about the poets too: I decided that it was not wisdom that enabled them to write their poetry, but a kind of instinct or inspiration, such as you find in seers and prophets who deliver all their sublime messages without knowing in the least what they mean. It seemed clear to me that the poets were in much the same case; and I also observed that the very fact that they were poets made them think that they had a perfect understanding of all other subjects, of which they were totally ignorant. So I left that line of inquiry too with the same sense of advantage that I had felt in the case of the politicians.

Last of all I turned to the skilled craftsmen. I knew quite well that I had practically no technical qualifications myself, and I was sure that I should find them full of impressive knowledge. In this I was not disappointed; they understood things which I did not, and to that extent they were wiser than I was. But, gentlemen, these professional experts seemed to share the same failing which I had noticed in the poets; I mean that on the strength of their technical proficiency they claimed a perfect understanding of every other subject, however important; and I felt that this error more than outweighed their positive wisdom. So I made myself spokesman for the oracle, and asked myself whether I would rather be as I was—neither wise with their wisdom nor stupid with their stupidity—or possess both qualities as they did. I replied through myself to the oracle that it was best for me to be as I was.

The effect of these investigations of mine, gentlemen, has been to arouse against me a great deal of hostility, and hostility of a particularly bitter and persistent kind, which has resulted in various malicious suggestions, including the description of me as a professor of wisdom. This is due to the fact that whenever I succeed in disproving another person's claim to wisdom in a given subject, the bystanders assume that I know everything about that subject myself. But the truth of the matter, gentlemen, is pretty certainly this: that real wisdom is the property of God, and this oracle is his way of telling us that human wisdom has little or no value. It seems to me that he is not referring literally to Socrates, but has merely taken my name as an example, as if he would say to us, 'The wisest of you men is he who has realized, like Socrates, that in respect of wisdom he is really worthless.'

That is why I still go about seeking and searching in obedience to the divine command, if I think that anyone is wise, whether citizen or stranger; and when I think that any person is not wise, I try to help the cause of God by proving that he is not. This occupation has kept me too busy to do much either in politics or in my own affairs; in fact, my service to God has reduced me to extreme poverty.

There is another reason for my being unpopular. A number of young men with wealthy fathers and plenty of leisure have deliberately attached themselves to me because they enjoy hearing other people cross-questioned. These often take me as their model, and go on to try to question other persons; whereupon, I suppose, they find an unlimited number of people who think that they know something, but really know little or nothing. Consequently their victims become annoyed, not with themselves but with me; and they complain that there is a pestilential busybody called Socrates who fills young people's heads with wrong ideas. If you ask them what he does, and what he teaches that has this effect, they have no answer, not knowing what to say; but as they do not want to admit their confusion, they fall back on the stock charges against any philosopher: that he teaches his pupils about things in the heavens and below the earth, and to disbelieve in gods, and to make the weaker argument defeat the stronger. They would be very loath, I fancy, to admit the truth: which is that they are being convicted of pretending to knowledge when they are entirely ignorant. So, jealous, I suppose, for their own reputation, and also energetic and numerically strong, and provided with a plausible and carefully worked out case against me, these people have been dinning into your ears for a long time past their violent denunciations of myself. There you have the causes which led to the attack upon me by Meletus and Anytus and Lycon, Meletus being aggrieved on behalf of the poets, Anytus on behalf of the professional men and politicians, and Lycon on behalf of the orators. So, as I said at the beginning, I should be surprised if I were able, in the short time that I have, to rid your minds of a misconception so deeply implanted.

There, gentlemen, you have the true facts, which I present to you without any concealment or suppression, great or small. I am fairly certain that this plain speaking of mine is the cause of my unpopularity; and this really goes to prove that my statements are true, and that I have described correctly the nature and the grounds of the calumny which has been brought against me. Whether you inquire into them now or later, you will find the facts as I have just described them.

So much for my defence against the charges brought by the first group of my accusers. I shall now try to defend myself against Meletus—high-principled and patriotic as he claims to be—and after that against the rest.

Let us first consider their deposition again, as though it represented a fresh prosecution. It runs something like this: 'Socrates is guilty of corrupting the minds of the young, and of believing in deities of his own invention instead of the gods recognized by the State.' Such is the charge; let us examine its points one by one.

First it says that I am guilty of corrupting the young. But I say, gentlemen, that Meletus is guilty of treating a serious matter with levity, since he summons people to stand their trial on frivolous grounds, and professes concern and keen anxiety in matters about which he has never had the slightest interest. I will try to prove this to your satisfaction.

Come now, Meletus, tell me this. You regard it as supremely important, do you not, that our young people should be exposed to the best possible influence? 'I do.' Very well, then; tell these gentlemen who it is that influences the young for the better. Obviously you must know, if you are so much interested. You have discovered the vicious influence, as you say, in myself, and you are now prosecuting me before these gentlemen; speak up and inform them who it is that has a good influence upon the young.—You see, Meletus, that you are tongue-tied and cannot answer. Do you not feel that this is discreditable, and a sufficient proof in itself of what I said, that you have no interest in the subject? Tell me, my friend, who is it that makes the young good? 'The laws.' That is not what I mean, my dear sir; I am asking you to name the *person* whose first business it is to know the laws. 'These gentlemen here, Socrates, the members of the jury.' Do you mean, Meletus, that they have the ability to educate the young, and to make them better? 'Certainly.' Does this apply to all jurymen, or only to some? 'To all of them.' Excellent! a generous supply of benefactors. Well, then, do these spectators who are present in court have an improving influence, or not? 'Yes, they do.' And what about the members of the Council? 'Yes, the Councillors too.' But surely, Meletus, the members of the Assembly do not corrupt the young? Or do all of them too exert an improving influence? 'Yes, they do.' Then it would seem that the whole population of Athens has a refining effect upon the young, except myself; and I alone demoralize them. Is that your meaning? 'Most emphatically, yes.' This is certainly a most unfortunate quality that you have detected in me. Well, let me put another question to you. Take the case of horses; do you believe that those who improve them make up the whole of mankind, and that there is only one person who has a bad effect on them? Or is the truth just the opposite, that the ability to improve them belongs to one person or to very few persons, who are horse-trainers, whereas most people, if they have to do with horses and make use of them, do them harm? Is not this the case, Meletus, both with horses and with all other animals? Of course it is, whether you and Anytus deny it or not. It would be a singular dispensation of fortune for our young people if there is only one person who corrupts them, while all the rest have a beneficial effect. But I need say no more; there is ample proof, Meletus, that you have never bothered your head about the young; and you make it perfectly clear that you have never taken the slightest interest in the cause for the sake of which you are now indicting me.

Here is another point. Tell me seriously, Meletus, is it better to live in a good or in a bad community? Answer my question, like a good fellow; there is nothing difficult about it. Is it not true that wicked people have a bad effect upon those with whom they are in the closest contact, and that good people have a good effect? 'Quite true.' Is there anyone who prefers to be harmed rather than benefited by his associates? Answer me, my good man; the law commands you to answer. Is there anyone who prefers to be harmed? 'Of course not.' Well, then, when you summon me before this court for corrupting the young and making their characters worse, do you mean that I do so intentionally or unintentionally? 'I mean intentionally.' Why, Meletus, are you at your age so much wiser than I at mine? You have discovered that bad people always have a bad effect, and good people a good effect, upon their nearest neighbours; am I so hopelessly ignorant as not even to realize that by spoiling the character of one of my companions I shall run the risk of getting some harm from him? because nothing else would make me commit this grave offence intentionally. No, I do not believe it, Meletus, and I do not suppose that anyone else does. Either I have not a bad influence, or it is unintentional; so that in either case your accusation is false. And if I unintentionally have a bad influence, the correct procedure in cases of such involuntary misdemeanours is not to summon the culprit before this court, but to take him aside privately for instruction and reproof; because obviously if my eyes are opened, I shall stop doing what I do not intend to do. But you deliberately avoided my company in the past and refused to enlighten me, and now you bring me before this court, which is the place appointed for those who need punishment, not for those who need enlightenment.

It is quite clear by now, gentlemen, that Meletus, as I said before, has never shown any degree of interest in this subject. However, I invite you to tell us, Meletus, in what sense you make out that I corrupt the minds of the young. Surely the terms of your indictment make it clear that you accuse me of teaching them to believe in new deities instead of the gods recognized by the State; is not that the teaching of mine which you say has this demoralizing effect? 'That is precisely what I maintain.' Then I appeal to you, Meletus, in the name of these same gods about whom we are speaking, to explain yourself a little more clearly to myself and to the jury, because I cannot make out what your point is. Is it that I teach people to believe in some gods (which implies that I myself believe in gods, and am not a complete atheist, so that I am not guilty on that score), but in different gods from those recognized by the State, so that your accusation rests upon the fact that they are different? Or do you assert that I believe in no gods at all, and teach others to do the same? 'Yes; I say that you disbelieve in gods altogether.' You surprise me, Meletus; what is your object in saying that? Do you suggest that I do not believe that the sun and moon are gods, as is the general belief of all mankind? 'He certainly does not, gentlemen of the jury, since he says that the sun is a stone and the moon a mass of earth.' Do you imagine that you are prosecuting Anaxagoras, my dear Meletus? Have you so poor an opinion of these gentlemen, and do you assume them to be so illiterate as not to know that the writings of Anaxagoras of Clazomenae are full of theories like these? and do you seriously suggest that it is from me that the young get these ideas, when they can buy them on occasion in the marketplace for a drachma at most, and so have the laugh on Socrates if he claims them for his own, to say nothing of their being so silly? Tell me honestly, Meletus, is that your opinion of me? do I believe in no god? 'No, none at all; not in the slightest degree.' You are not at all convincing, Meletus; not even to yourself, I suspect. In my opinion, gentlemen, this man is a thoroughly selfish bully, and has brought this action against me out of sheer wanton aggressiveness and self-assertion. He seems to be devising a sort of intelligence test for me, saying to himself, 'Will the infallible Socrates realize that I am contradicting myself for my own amusement, or shall I succeed in deceiving him and the rest of my audience?' It certainly seems to me that he is contradicting himself in this indictment, which might just as well run, 'Socrates is guilty of not believing in the gods, but believing in the gods.' And this is pure flippancy.

I ask you to examine with me, gentlemen, the line of reasoning which leads me to this conclusion. You, Meletus, will oblige us by answering my questions. Will you all kindly remember, as I requested at the beginning, not to interrupt if I conduct the discussion in my customary way?

Is there anyone in the world, Meletus, who believes in human activities, and not in human beings? Make him answer, gentlemen, and don't let him keep on making these continual objections. Is there anyone who does not believe in horses, but believes in horses' activities? or who does not believe in musicians, but believes in musical activities? No, there is not, my worthy friend. If you do not want to answer, I will supply it for you and for these gentlemen too. But the next question you must answer: Is there anyone who believes in supernatural activities and not in supernatural beings? 'No.' How good of you to give a bare answer under compulsion by the court! Well, do you assert that I believe and teach others to believe in supernatural activities? It does not matter whether they are new or old; the fact remains that I believe in them according to your statement; indeed you solemnly swore as much in your affidavit. But if I believe in supernatural activities, it follows inevitably that I also believe in supernatural beings. Is not that so? It is; I assume your assent, since you do not answer. Do we not hold that supernatural beings are either gods or the children of gods? Do you agree or not? 'Certainly.' Then if I believe in supernatural beings, as you assert, if these supernatural beings are gods in any sense, we shall reach the conclusion which I mentioned just now when I said that you were testing my intelligence for your own amusement, by stating first that I do not believe in gods, and then again that I do, since I believe in supernatural beings. If on the other hand these supernatural beings are bastard children of the gods by nymphs or other mothers, as they are reputed to be, who in the world would believe in the children of gods and not in the gods themselves? It would be as ridiculous as to believe in the young of horses or donkeys and not in horses and donkeys themselves. No, Meletus; there is no avoiding the conclusion that you brought this charge against me as a test of my wisdom, or else in despair of finding a genuine offence of which to accuse me. As for your prospect of convincing any living person with even a smattering of intelligence that belief in supernatural and divine activities does not imply belief in supernatural and divine beings, and *vice versa*, it is outside all the bounds of possibility.

As a matter of fact, gentlemen, I do not feel that it requires much defence to clear myself of Meletus' accusation; what I have said already is enough. But you know very well the truth of what I said in an earlier part of my speech, that I have incurred a great deal of bitter hostility; and this is what will bring about my destruction, if anything does; not Meletus nor Anytus, but the slander and jealousy of a very large section of the people. They have been fatal to a great many other innocent men, and I suppose will continue to be so; there is no likelihood that they will stop at me. But perhaps someone will say, 'Do you feel no compunction, Socrates, at having followed a line of action which puts you in danger of the death-penalty?' I might fairly reply to him, 'You are mistaken, my friend, if you think that a man who is worth anything ought to spend his time weighing up the prospects of life and death. He has only one thing to consider in performing any action; that is, whether he is acting rightly or wrongly, like a good man or a bad one. On your view the heroes who died at Troy would be poor creatures, especially the son of Thetis. He, if you remember, made so light of danger in comparison with incurring dishonour that when his goddess mother warned him, eager as he was to kill Hector, in some such words as these, I fancy, "My son, if you avenge your comrade Patroclus' death and kill Hector, you will die yourself; Next after Hector is thy fate prepared,"—when he heard this warning, he made light of his death and danger, being much more afraid of an ignoble life and of failing to avenge his friends. "Let me die forthwith," said he, "when I have requited the villain, rather than remain here by the beaked ships to be mocked, a burden on the ground." Do you suppose that he gave a thought to death and danger?'

The truth of the matter is this, gentlemen. Where a man has once taken up his stand, either because it seems best to him or in obedience to his orders, there I believe he is bound to remain and face the danger, taking no account of death or anything else before dishonour.

This being so, it would be shocking inconsistency on my part, gentlemen, if, when the officers whom you chose to command me assigned me my position at Potidaea and Amphipolis and Delium, I remained at my post like anyone else and faced death, and yet afterwards, when God appointed me, as I supposed and believed, to the duty of leading the philosophic life, examining myself and others, I were then through fear of death or of any other danger to desert my post. That would indeed be shocking, and then I might really with justice be summoned into court for not believing in the gods, and disobeying the oracle, and being afraid of death, and thinking that I am wise when I am not. For let me tell you, gentlemen, that to be afraid of death is only another form of thinking that one is wise when one is not; it is to think that one knows what one does not know. No one knows with regard to death whether it is not really the greatest blessing that can happen to a man; but people dread it as though they were certain that it is the greatest evil; and this ignorance, which thinks that it knows what it does not, must surely be ignorance most culpable. This, I take it, gentlemen, is the degree, and this the nature of my advantage over the rest of mankind; and if I were to claim to be wiser than my neighbour in any respect, it would be in this: that not possessing any real knowledge of what comes after death, I am also conscious that I do not possess it. But I do know that to do wrong and to disobey my superior, whether God or man, is wicked and dishonourable; and so I shall never feel more fear or aversion for something which, for all I know, may really be a blessing, than for those evils which I know to be evils.

Suppose, then, that you acquit me, and pay no attention to Anytus, who has said that either I should not have appeared before this court at all, or, since I have appeared here, I must be put to death, because if I once escaped your sons would all immediately become utterly demoralized by putting the teaching of Socrates into practice. Suppose that, in view of this, you said to me, 'Socrates, on this occasion we shall disregard Anytus and acquit you, but only on one condition, that you give up spending your time on this quest and stop philosophizing. If we catch you going on in the same way, you shall be put to death.' Well, supposing, as I said, that you should offer to acquit me on these terms, I should reply, 'Gentlemen, I am your very grateful and devoted servant, but I owe a greater obedience to God than to you; and so long as I draw breath and have my faculties, I shall never stop practising philosophy and exhorting you and elucidating the truth for everyone that I meet. I shall go on saying, in my usual way, "My very good friend, you are an Athenian and belong to a city which is the greatest and most famous in the world for its wisdom and strength. Are you not ashamed that you give your attention to acquiring as much money as possible, and similarly with reputation and honour, and give no attention or thought to truth and understanding and the perfection of your soul?"' And if any of you disputes this and professes to care about these things, I shall not at once let him go or leave him; no, I shall question him and examine him and test him; and if it appears that in spite of his profession he has made no real progress towards goodness, I shall reprove him for neglecting what is of supreme importance, and giving his attention to trivialities. I shall do this to everyone that I meet, young or old, foreigner or fellow-citizen; but especially to you my fellow-citizens, inasmuch as you are closer to me in kinship. This, I do assure you, is what my God commands; and it is my belief that no greater good has ever befallen you in this city than my service to my God; for I spend all my time going about trying to persuade you, young and old, to make your first and chief concern not for your bodies nor for your possessions, but for the highest welfare of your souls, proclaiming as I go, 'Wealth does not bring goodness, but goodness brings wealth and every other blessing, both to the individual and to the State.' Now if I corrupt the young by this message, the message would seem to be harmful; but if anyone says that my message is different from this, he is talking nonsense. And so, gentlemen, I would say, 'You can please yourselves whether you listen to Anytus or not, and whether you acquit me or not; you know that I am not going to alter my conduct, not even if I have to die a hundred deaths.'

Order, please, gentlemen! Remember my request to give me a hearing without interruption; besides, I believe that it will be to your advantage to listen. I am going to tell you something else, which may provoke a storm of protest; but please restrain yourselves. I assure you that if I am what I claim to be, and you put me to death, you will harm yourselves more than me. Neither Meletus nor Anytus can do me any harm at all; they would not have the power, because I do not believe that the law of God permits a better man to be harmed by a worse. No doubt my accuser might put me to death or have me banished or deprived of civic rights; but even if he thinks, as he probably does (and others too, I dare say), that these are great calamities, I do not think so; I believe that it is far worse to do what he is doing now, trying to put an innocent man to death. For this reason, gentlemen, so far from pleading on my own behalf, as might be supposed, I am really pleading on yours, to save you from misusing the gift of God by condemning me. If you put me to death, you will not easily find anyone to take my place. It is literally true (even if it sounds rather comical) that God has specially appointed me to this city, as though it were a large thorough-bred horse which because of its great size is inclined to be lazy and needs the stimulation of some stinging fly. It seems to me that God has attached me to this city to perform the office of such a fly; and all day long I never cease to settle here, there, and everywhere, rousing, persuading, reproving every one of you. You will not easily find another like me, gentlemen, and if you take my advice you will spare my life. I suspect, however, that before long you will awake from your drowsing, and in your annoyance you will take Anytus' advice and finish me off with a single slap; and then you will go on sleeping till the end of your days, unless God in his care for you sends someone to take my place.

If you doubt whether I am really the sort of person who would have been sent to this city as a gift from God, you can convince yourselves by looking at it in this way. Does it seem natural that I should have neglected my own affairs and endured the humiliation of allowing my family to be neglected for all these years, while I busied myself all the time on your behalf, going like a father or an elder brother to see each one of you privately, and urging you to set your thoughts on goodness? If I had got any enjoyment from it, or if I had been paid for my good advice, there would have been some explanation for my conduct; but as it is you can see for yourselves that although my accusers unblushingly charge me with all sorts of other crimes, there is one thing that they have not had the impudence to pretend on any testimony, and that is that I have ever exacted or asked a fee from anyone.

The witness that I can offer to prove the truth of my statement is, I think, a convincing one—my poverty.

It may seem curious that I should go round giving advice like this and busying myself in people's private affairs, and yet never venture publicly to address you as a whole and advise on matters of state. The reason for this is what you have often heard me say before on many other occasions: that I am subject to a divine or supernatural experience, which Meletus saw fit to travesty in his indictment. It began in my early childhood—a sort of voice which comes to me; and when it comes it always dissuades me from what I am proposing to do, and never urges me on. It is this that debars me from entering public life, and a very good thing too, in my opinion; because you may be quite sure, gentlemen, that if I had tried long ago to engage in politics, I should long ago have lost my life, without doing any good either to you or to myself. Please do not be offended if I tell you the truth. No man on earth who conscientiously opposes either you or any other organized democracy, and flatly prevents a great many wrongs and illegalities from taking place in the state to which he belongs, can possibly escape with his life. The true champion of justice, if he intends to survive even for a short time, must necessarily confine himself to private life and leave politics alone.

I will offer you substantial proofs of what I have said; not theories, but what you can appreciate better, facts. Listen while I describe my actual experiences, so that you may know that I would never submit wrongly to any authority through fear of death, but would refuse even at the cost of my life. It will be a commonplace story, such as you often hear in the courts; but it is true.

The only office which I have ever held in our city, gentlemen, was when I was elected to the Council. It so happened that our group was acting as the executive when you decided that the ten commanders who had failed to rescue the men who were lost in the naval engagement should be tried *en bloc;* which was illegal, as you all recognized later. On this occasion I was the only member of the executive who insisted that you should not act unconstitutionally, and voted against the proposal; and although your leaders were all ready to denounce and arrest me, and you were all urging them on at the top of your voices, I thought that it was my duty to face it out on the side of law and justice rather than support you, through fear of prison or death, in your wrong decision.

This happened while we were still under a democracy. When the oligarchy came into power, the Thirty Commissioners in their turn summoned me and four others to the Round Chamber and instructed us to go and fetch Leon of Salamis from his home for execution. This was of course only one of many instances in which they issued such instructions, their object being to implicate as many people as possible in their wickedness. On this occasion, however, I again made it clear not by my words but by my actions that death did not matter to me at all (if that is not too strong an expression); but that it mattered all the world to me that I should do nothing wrong or wicked. Powerful as it was, that government did not terrify me into doing a wrong action; when we came out of the Round Chamber the other four went off to Salamis and arrested Leon, and I went home. I should probably have been put to death for this, if the government had not fallen soon afterwards. There are plenty of people who will testify to these statements.

Do you suppose that I should have lived as long as I have if I had moved in the sphere of public life, and conducting myself in that sphere like an honourable man, had always upheld the cause of right, and conscientiously set this end above all other things? Not by a very long way, gentlemen; neither would any other man. You will find that throughout my life I have been consistent in any public duties that I have performed, and the same also in my personal dealings: I have never countenanced any action that was incompatible with justice on the part of any person, including those whom some people maliciously call my pupils. I have never set up as any man's teacher; but if anyone, young or old, is eager to hear me conversing and carrying out my private mission, I never grudge him the opportunity; nor do I charge a fee for talking to him, and refuse to talk without one; I am ready to answer questions for rich and poor alike, and I am equally ready if anyone prefers to listen to me and answer my questions. If any given one of these people becomes a good citizen or a bad one, I cannot fairly be held responsible, since I have never promised or imparted any teaching to anybody; and if anyone asserts that he has ever learned or heard from me privately anything which was not open to everyone else, you may be quite sure that he is not telling the truth.

But how is it that some people enjoy spending a great deal of time in my company? You have heard the reason, gentlemen; I told you quite frankly. It is because they enjoy hearing me examine those who think that they are wise when they are not; an experience which has its amusing side. This duty I have accepted, as I said, in obedience to God's commands given in oracles and dreams and in every other way that any other divine dispensation has ever impressed a duty upon man.

This is a true statement, gentlemen, and easy to verify. If it is a fact that I am in process of corrupting some of the young, and have succeeded already in corrupting others; and if it were a fact that some of the latter, being now grown up, had discovered that I had ever given them bad advice when they were young, surely they ought now to be coming forward to denounce and punish me; and if they did not like to do it themselves, you would expect some of their families—their fathers and brothers and other near relations—to remember it now, if their own flesh and blood had suffered any harm from me. Certainly a great many of them have found their way into this court, as I can see for myself: first Crito over there, my contemporary and near neighbour, the father of this young man Critobulus; and then Lysanias of Sphettus, the father of Aeschines here; and next Antiphon of Cephisia, over there, the father of Epigenes. Then besides there are all those whose brothers have been members of our circle: Nicostratus the son of Theozotides, the brother of Theodotus—but Theodotus is dead, so he cannot appeal to his brother—and Paralius here, the son of Demodocus; his brother was Theages. And here is Adimantus the son of Ariston, whose brother Plato is over there; and Aeantodorus, whose brother Apollodorus is here on this side. I can name many more besides, some of whom Meletus most certainly ought to have produced as witness in the course of his speech. If he forgot to do so then, let him do it now—I am willing to make way for him; let him state whether he has any such evidence to offer. On the contrary, gentlemen, you will find that they are all prepared to help me—the corrupter and evil genius of their nearest and dearest relatives, as Meletus and Anytus say. The actual victims of my corrupting influence might perhaps be excused for helping me; but as for the uncorrupted, their relations of mature age, what other reason can they have for helping me except the right and proper one, that they know Meletus is lying and I am telling the truth?

There, gentlemen: that, and perhaps a little more to the same effect, is the substance of what I can say in my defence. It may be that some one of you, remembering his own case, will be annoyed that whereas he, in standing his trial upon a less serious charge than this, made pitiful appeals to the jury with floods of tears, and had his infant children produced in court to excite the maximum of sympathy, and many of his relatives and friends as well, I on the contrary intend to do nothing of the sort, and that although I am facing (as it might appear) the utmost danger. It may be that one of you, reflecting on these facts, will be prejudiced against me, and being irritated by his reflections, will give his vote in anger. If one of you is so disposed—I do not expect it, but there is the possibility—I think that I should be quite justified in saying to him, 'My dear sir, of course I have some relatives. To quote the very words of Homer, even I am not sprung "from an oak or from a rock," but from human parents, and consequently I have relatives; yes, and sons too, gentlemen, three of them, one almost grown up and the other two only children; but all the same I am not going to produce them here and beseech you to acquit me.'

Why do I not intend to do anything of this kind? Not out of perversity, gentlemen, nor out of contempt for you; whether I am brave or not in the face of death has nothing to do with it; the point is that for my own credit and yours and for the credit of the state as a whole, I do not think that it is right for me to use any of these methods at my age and with my reputation—which may be true or it may be false, but at any rate the view is held that Socrates is different from the common run of mankind. Now if those of you who are supposed to be distinguished for wisdom or courage or any other virtue are to behave in this way, it would be a disgrace. I have often noticed that some people of this type, for all their high standing, go to extraordinary lengths when they come up for trial, which shows that they think it will be a dreadful thing to lose their lives; as though they would be immortal if you did not put them to death! In my opinion these people bring disgrace upon our city. Any of our visitors might be excused for thinking that the finest specimens of Athenian manhood, whom their fellow-citizens select on their merits to rule over them and hold other high positions, are no better than women. If you have even the smallest reputation, gentlemen, you ought not to descend to these methods; and if we do so, you must not give us licence. On the contrary, you must make it clear that anyone who stages these pathetic scenes and so brings ridicule upon our city is far more likely to be condemned than if he kept perfectly quiet.

But apart from all question of appearances, gentlemen, I do not think that it is right for a man to appeal to the jury or to get himself acquitted by doing so; he ought to inform them of the facts and convince them by argument. The jury does not sit to dispense justice as a favour, but to decide where justice lies; and the oath which they have sworn is not to show favour at their own discretion, but to return a just and lawful verdict. It follows that we must not develop in you, nor you allow to grow in yourselves, the habit of perjury; that would be sinful for us both. Therefore you must not expect me, gentlemen, to behave towards you in a way which I consider neither reputable nor moral nor consistent with my religious duty; and above all you must not expect it when I stand charged with impiety by Meletus here. Surely it is obvious that if I tried to persuade you and prevail upon you by my entreaties to go against your solemn oath, I should be teaching you contempt for religion; and by my very defence I should be accusing myself of having no religious belief. But that is very far from the truth. I have a more sincere belief, gentlemen, than any of my accusers; and I leave it to you and to God to judge me as it shall be best for me and for yourselves.

(The verdict is 'Guilty,' and Meletus proposes the penalty of death)

There are a great many reasons, gentlemen, why I am not distressed by this result—I mean your condemnation of me—but the chief reason is that the result was not unexpected. What does surprise me is the number of votes cast on the two sides. I should never have believed that it would be such a close thing; but now it seems that if a mere thirty votes had gone the other way, I should have been acquitted. Even as it is, I feel that so far as Meletus' part is concerned I have been acquitted; and not only that, but anyone can see that if Anytus and Lycon had not come forward to accuse me, Meletus would actually have lost a thousand drachmae for not having obtained one-fifth of the votes.

However, we must face the fact that he demands the death-penalty. Very good. What alternative penalty shall I propose to you, gentlemen? Obviously it must be adequate. Well, what penalty do I deserve to pay or suffer, in view of what I have done?

I have never lived an ordinary quiet life. I did not care for the things that most people care about: making money, having a comfortable home, high military or civil rank, and all the other activities—political appointments, secret societies, party organizations—which go on in our city; I thought that I was really too strict in my principles to survive if I went in for this sort of thing. So instead of taking a course which would have done no good either to you or to me, I set myself to do you individually in private what I hold to be the greatest possible service: I tried to persuade each one of you not to think more of practical advantages than of his mental and moral well-being, or in general to think more of advantage than of well-being in the case of the state or of anything else. What do I deserve for behaving in this way? Some reward, gentlemen, if I am bound to suggest what I really deserve; and what is more, a reward which would be appropriate for myself. Well, what is appropriate for a poor man who is a public benefactor and who requires leisure for giving you moral encouragement? Nothing could be more appropriate for such a person than free maintenance at the State's expense. He deserves it much more than any victor in the races at Olympia, whether he wins with a single horse or a pair or a team of four. These people give you the semblance of success, but I give you the reality; they do not need maintenance, but I do. So if I am to suggest an appropriate penalty which is strictly in accordance with justice, I suggest free maintenance by the State.

Perhaps when I say this I may give you the impression, as I did in my remarks about exciting sympathy and making passionate appeals, that I am showing a deliberate perversity. That is not so, gentlemen; the real position is this. I am convinced that I never wrong anyone intentionally, but I cannot convince you of this, because we have had so little time for discussion. If it was your practice, as it is with other nations, to give not one day but several to the hearing of capital trials, I believe that you might have been convinced; but under present conditions it is not easy to dispose of grave allegations in a short space of time. So being convinced that I do no wrong to anybody, I can hardly be expected to wrong myself by asserting that I deserve something bad, or by proposing a corresponding penalty. Why should I? For fear of suffering this penalty proposed by Meletus, when, as I said, I do not know whether it is a good thing or a bad? Do you expect me to choose something which I know very well is bad by making my counterproposal? Imprisonment? Why should I spend my days in prison, in subjection to the periodically appointed officers of the law? A fine, with imprisonment until it is paid? In my case the effect would be just the same, because I have no money to pay a fine. Or shall I suggest banishment? You would very likely accept the suggestion.

I should have to be desperately in love with life to do that, gentlemen. I am not so blind that I cannot see that you, my fellow-citizens, have come to the end of your patience with my discussions and conversations; you have found them too irksome and irritating, and now you are trying to get rid of them. Will any other people find them easy to put up with? That is most unlikely, gentlemen. A fine life I should have if I left this country at my age and spent the rest of my days trying one city after another and being turned out every time! I know very well that wherever I go the young people will listen to my conversation just as they do here; and if I try to keep them off, they will make their elders drive me out, while if I do not, the fathers and other relatives will drive me out of their own accord for the sake of the young.

Perhaps someone may say, 'But surely, Socrates, after you have left us you can spend the rest of your life in quietly minding your own business.' This is the hardest thing of all to make some of you understand. If I say that this would be disobedience to God, and that is why I cannot 'mind my own business', you will not believe that I am serious. If on the other hand I tell you that to let no day pass without discussing goodness and all the other subjects about which you hear me talking and examining both myself and others is really the very best thing that a man can do, and that life without this sort of examination is not worth living, you will be even less inclined to believe me. Nevertheless that is how it is, gentlemen, as I maintain; though it is not easy to convince you of it. Besides, I am not accustomed to think of myself as deserving punishment. If I had money, I would have suggested a fine that I could afford, because that would not have done me any harm. As it is, I cannot, because I have none; unless of course you like to fix the penalty at what I could pay. I suppose I could probably afford a hundred drachmae. I suggest a fine of that amount.

One moment, gentlemen. Plato here, and Crito and Critobulus and Apollodorus, want me to propose three thousand drachmae on their security. Very well, I agree to this sum, and you can rely upon these gentlemen for its payment.

(The jury decides for the death-penalty)

Well, gentlemen, for the sake of a very small gain in time you are going to earn the reputation—and the blame from those who wish to disparage our city—of having put Socrates to death, 'that wise man'— because they will say I am wise even if I am not, these people who want to find fault with you. If you had waited just a little while, you would have had your way in the course of nature. You can see that I am well on in life and near to death. I am saying this not to all of you but to those who voted for my execution, and I have something else to say to them as well.

No doubt you think, gentlemen, that I have been condemned for lack of the arguments which I could have used if I had thought it right to leave nothing unsaid or undone to secure my acquittal. But that is very far from the truth. It is not a lack of arguments that has caused my condemnation, but a lack of effrontery and impudence, and the fact that I have refused to address you in the way which would give you most pleasure. You would have liked to hear me weep and wail, doing and saying all sorts of things which I regard as unworthy of myself, but which you are used to hearing from other people. But I did not think then that I ought to stoop to servility because I was in danger, and I do not regret now the way in which I pleaded my case; I would much rather die as the result of this defence than live as the result of the other sort. In a court of law, just as in warfare, neither I nor any other ought to use his wits to escape death by any means. In battle it is often obvious that you could escape being killed by giving up your arms and throwing yourself upon the mercy of your pursuers; and in every kind of danger there are plenty of devices for avoiding death if you are unscrupulous enough to stick at nothing. But I suggest, gentlemen, that the difficulty is not so much to escape death; the real difficulty is to escape from doing wrong, which is far more fleet of foot. In this present instance I, the slow old man, have been overtaken by the slower of the two, but my accusers, who are clever and quick, have been overtaken by the faster: by iniquity. When I leave this court I shall go away condemned by you to death, but they will go away convicted by Truth herself of depravity and wickedness. And they accept their sentence even as I accept mine. No doubt it was bound to be so, and I think that the result is fair enough.

Having said so much, I feel moved to prophesy to you who have given your vote against me; for I am now at that point where the gift of prophecy comes most readily to men: at the point of death. I tell you, my executioners, that as soon as I am dead, vengeance shall fall upon you with a punishment far more painful than your killing of me. You have brought about my death in the belief that through it you will be delivered from submitting your conduct to criticism; but I say that the result will be just the opposite. You will have more critics, whom up till now I have restrained without your knowing it; and being younger they will be harsher to you and will cause you more annoyance. If you expect to stop denunciation of your wrong way of life by putting people to death, there is something amiss with your reasoning. This way of escape is neither possible nor creditable; the best and easiest way is not to stop the mouths of others, but to make yourselves as good men as you can. This is my last message to you who voted for my condemnation.

As for you who voted for my acquittal, I should very much like to say a few words to reconcile you to the result, while the officials are busy and I am not yet on my way to the place where I must die. I ask you, gentlemen, to spare me these few moments; there is no reason why we should not exchange fancies while the law permits. I look upon you as my friends, and I want you to understand the right way of regarding my present position.

Gentlemen of the jury—for *you* deserve to be so called—I have had a remarkable experience. In the past the prophetic voice to which I have become accustomed has always been my constant companion, opposing me even in quite trivial things if I was going to take the wrong course. Now something has happened to me, as you can see, which might be thought and is commonly considered to be a supreme calamity; yet neither when I left home this morning, nor when I was taking my place here in the court, nor at any point in any part of my speech did the divine sign oppose me. In other discussions it has often checked me in the middle of a sentence; but this time it has never opposed me in any part of this business in anything that I have said or done. What do I suppose to be the explanation? I will tell you. I suspect that this thing that has happened to me is a blessing, and we are quite mistaken in supposing death to be an evil. I have good grounds for thinking this, because my accustomed sign could not have failed to oppose me if what I was doing had not been sure to bring some good result.

We should reflect that there is much reason to hope for two things. Either it is annihilation, and the dead have no consciousness of anything; or, as we are told, it is really a change: a migration of the soul from this place to another. Now if there is no consciousness but only a dreamless sleep, death must be a marvellous gain. I suppose that if anyone were told to pick out the night on which he slept so soundly as not even to dream, and then to compare it with all the other nights and days of his life, and then were told to say, after due consideration, how many better and happier days and nights than this he had spent in the course of his life—well, I think that the Great King himself, to say nothing of any private person, would find these days and nights easy to count in comparison with the rest. If death is like this, then, I call it gain; because the whole of time, if you look at it in this way, can be regarded as no more than one single night. If on the other hand death is a removal from here to some other place, and if what we are told is true, that all the dead are there, what greater blessing could there be than this, gentlemen? If on arrival in the other world, beyond the reach of our so-called justice, one will find there the true judges who are said to preside in those courts, Minos and Rhadamanthys and Aeacus and Triptolemus and all those other half-divinities who were upright in their earthly life, would that be an unrewarding journey? Put it in this way: how much would one of you give to meet Orpheus and Musaeus, Hesiod and Homer? I am willing to die ten times over if this account is true. It would be a specially interesting experience for me to join them there, to meet Palamedes and Ajax the son of Telamon and any other heroes of the old days who met their death through an unfair trial, and to compare my fortunes with theirs—it would be rather amusing, I think—; and above all I should like to spend my time there, as here, in examining and searching people's minds, to find out who is really wise among them, and who only thinks that he is. What would one not give, gentlemen, to be able to question the leader of that great host against Troy, or Odysseus, or Sisyphus, or the thousands of other men and women whom one could mention, to talk and mix and argue with whom would be unimaginable happiness? At any rate I presume that they do not put one to death there for such conduct; because apart from the other happiness in which their world surpasses ours, they are now immortal for the rest of time, if what we are told is true.

You too, gentlemen of the jury, must look forward to death with confidence, and fix your minds on this one belief, which is certain: that nothing can harm a good man either in life or after death, and his fortunes are not a matter of indifference to the gods. This present experience of mine has not come about mechanically; I am quite clear that the time had come when it was better for me to die and be released from my distractions. That is why my sign never turned me back. For my own part I bear no grudge at all against those who condemned me and accused me, although it was not with this kind intention that they did so, but because they thought that they were hurting me; and that is culpable of them. However, I ask them to grant me one favour. When my sons grow up, gentlemen, if you think that they are putting money or anything else before goodness, take your revenge by plaguing them as I plagued you; and if they fancy themselves for no reason, you must scold them just as I scolded you, for neglecting the important things and thinking that they are good for something when they are good for nothing. If you do this, I shall have had justice at your hands, both I myself and my children.

Now it is time that we were going, I to die and you to live; but which of us has the happier prospect is unknown to anyone but God.

Socrates' Decision to Die

Plato

When Socrates was condemned to death, everyone in Athens expected him to flee to another city. But he did not. He stayed in his cell, drank the poisonous hemlock, lay down on his back and died. The fact that Socrates followed his arguments to the end—to his *own* end—has inspired humanity for over 2400 years. In this selection, Socrates explains to his friend Crito why he won't run away.

Socrates (c. 470–399 B.C.) left us no written work. We know about him primarily through his pupil Plato (427–347 B.C.), who in turn was the teacher of Aristotle (384–322 B.C.). Of the twenty-seven or so dialogues that Plato wrote, scholars believe that this was one of the first.

SOCRATES: Why have you come so early, Crito? Or is it not still early?
CRITO: It certainly is.
SOCRATES: How early?
CRITO: Early dawn.
SOCRATES: I am surprised that the warder was willing to listen to you.
CRITO: He is quite friendly to me by now, Socrates. I have been here often and I have given him something.
SOCRATES: Have you just come, or have you been here for some time?

Source: Excerpt from *Plato, Five Dialogues (Crito),* translated by G. M. A. Grube (Indianapolis, IN: Hackett, 2002). Reprinted by permission of Hackett Publishing Company, Inc. All rights reserved.

CRITO: A fair time.

SOCRATES: Then why did you not wake me right away but sit there in silence?

CRITO: By Zeus no, Socrates. I would not myself want to be in distress and awake so long. I have been surprised to see you so peacefully asleep. It was on purpose that I did not wake you, so that you should spend your time most agreeably. Often in the past throughout my life, I have considered the way you live happy, and especially so now that you bear your present misfortune so easily and lightly.

SOCRATES: It would not be fitting at my age to resent the fact that I must die now.

CRITO: Other men of your age are caught in such misfortunes, but their age does not prevent them resenting their fate.

SOCRATES: That is so. Why have you come so early?

CRITO: I bring bad news, Socrates, not for you, apparently, but for me and all your friends the news is bad and hard to bear. Indeed, I would count it among the hardest.

SOCRATES: What is it? Or has the ship arrived from Delos, at the arrival of which I must die?

CRITO: It has not arrived yet, but it will, I believe, arrive today, according to a message some men brought from Sunium, where they left it. This makes it obvious that it will come today, and that your life must end tomorrow.

SOCRATES: May it be for the best. If it so please the gods, so be it. However, I do not think it will arrive today.

CRITO: What indication have you of this?

SOCRATES: I will tell you. I must die the day after the ship arrives.

CRITO: That is what those in authority say.

SOCRATES: Then I do not think it will arrive on this coming day, but on the next. I take to witness of this a dream I had a little earlier during this night. It looks as if it was the right time for you not to wake me.

CRITO: What was your dream?

SOCRATES: I thought that a beautiful and comely woman dressed in white approached me. She called me and said: "Socrates, may you arrive at fertile Phthia[1] on the third day."

[1] A quotation from *Iliad* ix.363. Achilles has rejected all the presents Agamemnon offered him to get him to return to the battle, and threatens to go home. He says his ships will sail in the morning, and with good weather he might arrive on the third day "in fertile Phthia" (which is his home). The dream means that Socrates' soul, after death, will find its home on the third day (counting, as usual among the Greeks, both the first and the last member of the series).

CRITO: A strange dream, Socrates.

SOCRATES: But it seems clear enough to me, Crito.

CRITO: Too clear it seems, my dear Socrates, but listen to me even now and be saved. If you die, it will not be a single misfortune for me. Not only will I be deprived of a friend, the like of whom I shall never find again, but many people who do not know you or me very well will think that I could have saved you if I were willing to spend money, but that I did not care to do so. Surely there can be no worse reputation than to be thought to value money more highly than one's friends, for the majority will not believe that you yourself were not willing to leave prison while we were eager for you to do so.

SOCRATES: My good Crito, why should we care so much for what the majority think? The most reasonable people, to whom one should pay more attention, will believe that things were done as they were done.

CRITO: You see, Socrates, that one must also pay attention to the opinion of the majority. Your present situation makes clear that the majority can inflict not the least but pretty well the greatest evils if one is slandered among them.

SOCRATES: Would that the majority could inflict the greatest evils, for they would then be capable of the greatest good, and that would be fine, but now they cannot do either. They cannot make a man either wise or foolish, but they inflict things haphazardly.

CRITO: That may be so. But tell me this, Socrates, are you anticipating that I and your other friends would have trouble with the informers if you escape from here, as having stolen you away, and that we should be compelled to lose all our property or pay heavy fines and suffer other punishment besides? If you have any such fear, forget it. We would be justified in running this risk to save you, and worse, if necessary. Do follow my advice, and do not act differently.

SOCRATES: I do have these things in mind, Crito, and also many others.

CRITO: Have no such fear. It is not much money that some people require to save you and get you out of here. Further, do you not see that those informers are cheap, and that not much money would be needed to deal with them? My money is available and is, I think, sufficient. If, because of your affection for me, you feel you should not spend any of mine, there are those strangers here ready to spend money. One of them, Simmias the Theban, has brought enough for this very purpose. Cebes, too, and a good many others. So, as I say, do not let this fear make you hesitate to save yourself, nor let what you said in court trouble you, that you would not know what to do with yourself if you left Athens, for you would be welcomed in many places to which you might go. If you want to go to Thessaly, I have friends there who will greatly appreciate you and keep you safe, so that no one in Thessaly will harm you.

Besides, Socrates, I do not think that what you are doing is just, to give up your life when you can save it, and to hasten your fate as your enemies would hasten it, and indeed have hastened it in their wish to destroy you. Moreover, I think you are betraying your sons by going away and leaving them, when you could bring them up and educate them. You thus show no concern for what their fate may be. They will probably have the usual fate of orphans. Either one should not have children, or one should share with them to the end the toil of upbringing and education. You seem to me to choose the easiest path, whereas one should choose the path a good and courageous man would choose, particularly when one claims throughout one's life to care for virtue.

I feel ashamed on your behalf and on behalf of us, your friends, lest all that has happened to you be thought due to cowardice on our part: the fact that your trial came to court when it need not have done so, the handling of the trial itself, and now this absurd ending which will be thought to have got beyond our control through some cowardice and unmanliness on our part, since we did not save you, or you save yourself, when it was possible and could be done if we had been of the slightest use. Consider, Socrates, whether this is not only evil, but shameful, both for you and for us. Take counsel with yourself, or rather the time for counsel is past and the decision should have been taken, and there is no further opportunity, for this whole business must be ended tonight. If we delay now, then it will no longer be possible, it will be too late. Let me persuade you on every count, Socrates, and do not act otherwise.

SOCRATES: My dear Crito, your eagerness is worth much if it should have some right aim; if not, then the greater your keenness the more difficult it is to deal with. We must therefore examine whether we should act in this way or not, as not only now but at all times I am the kind of man who listens only to the argument that on reflection seems best to me. I cannot, now that this fate has come upon me, discard the arguments I used; they seem to me much the same. I value and respect the same principles as before, and if we have no better arguments to bring up at this moment, be sure that I shall not agree with you, not even if the power of the majority were to frighten us with more bogeys, as if we were children, with threats of incarcerations and executions and confiscation of property. How should we examine this matter most reasonably? Would it be by taking up first your argument about the opinions of men, whether it is sound in every case that one should pay attention to some opinions, but not to others? Or was that well-spoken before the necessity to die came upon me, but now it is clear that this was said in vain for the sake of argument, that it was in truth play and nonsense? I am eager to examine together with you, Crito, whether this argument will appear in any way different to me in my present circumstances, or whether it remains the same, whether we are to abandon it or believe it. It was said on every occasion by those who thought they were speaking sensibly, as I have just now been speaking, that one should greatly value some people's opinions, but not others. Does that seem to you a sound statement?

You, as far as a human being can tell, are exempt from the likelihood of dying tomorrow, so the present misfortune is not likely to lead you astray. Consider then, do you not think it a sound statement that one must not value all the opinions of men, but some and not others, nor the opinions of all men, but those of some and not of others? What do you say? Is this not well said?

CRITO: It is.

SOCRATES: One should value the good opinions, and not the bad ones?

CRITO: Yes.

SOCRATES: The good opinions are those of wise men, the bad ones those of foolish men?

CRITO: Of course.

SOCRATES: Come then, what of statements such as this: Should a man professionally engaged in physical training pay attention to the praise and blame and opinion of any man, or to those of one man only, namely a doctor or trainer?

CRITO: To those of one only.

SOCRATES: He should therefore fear the blame and welcome the praise of that one man, and not those of the many?

CRITO: Obviously.

SOCRATES: He must then act and exercise, eat and drink in the way the one, the trainer and the one who knows, thinks right, not all the others?

CRITO: That is so.

SOCRATES: Very well. And if he disobeys the one, disregards his opinion and his praises while valuing those of the many who have no knowledge, will he not suffer harm?

CRITO: Of course.

SOCRATES: What is that harm, where does it tend, and what part of the man who disobeys does it affect?

CRITO: Obviously the harm is to his body, which it ruins.

SOCRATES: Well said. So with other matters, not to enumerate them all, and certainly with actions just and unjust, shameful and beautiful, good and bad, about which we are now deliberating, should we follow the opinion of the many and fear it, or that of the one, if there is one who has knowledge of these things and before whom we feel fear and shame more than before all the others. If we do not follow his directions, we shall harm and corrupt that part of ourselves that is improved by just actions and destroyed by unjust actions. Or is there nothing in this?

CRITO: I think there certainly is, Socrates.

SOCRATES: Come now, if we ruin that which is improved by health and corrupted by disease by not following the opinions of those who know, is life worth living for us when that is ruined? And that is the body, is it not?

CRITO: Yes.

SOCRATES: And is life worth living with a body that is corrupted and in bad condition?

CRITO: In no way.

SOCRATES: And is life worth living for us with that part of us corrupted that unjust action harms and just action benefits? Or do we think that part of us, whatever it is, that is concerned with justice and injustice, is inferior to the body?

CRITO: Not at all.

SOCRATES: It is more valuable?

CRITO: Much more.

SOCRATES: We should not then think so much of what the majority will say about us, but what he will say who understands justice and injustice, the one, that is, and the truth itself. So that, in the first place, you were wrong to believe that we should care for the opinion of the many about what is just, beautiful, good, and their opposites. "But," someone might say, "the many are able to put us to death."

CRITO: That too is obvious, Socrates, and someone might well say so.

SOCRATES: And, my admirable friend, that argument that we have gone through remains, I think, as before. Examine the following statement in turn as to whether it stays the same or not, that the most important thing is not life, but the good life.

CRITO: It stays the same.

SOCRATES: And that the good life, the beautiful life, and the just life are the same; does that still hold, or not?

CRITO: It does hold.

SOCRATES: As we have agreed so far, we must examine next whether it is just for me to try to get out of here when the Athenians have not acquitted me. If it is seen to be just, we will try to do so; if it is not, we will abandon the idea. As for those questions you raise about money, reputation, the upbringing of children, Crito, those considerations in truth belong to those people who easily put men to death and would bring them to life again if they could, without thinking; I mean the majority of men. For us, however, since our argument leads to this, the only valid consideration, as we were saying just now, is whether we should be acting rightly in giving money and gratitude to those who will lead me out of here, and ourselves helping with the escape, or whether in truth we shall do wrong in doing all this. If it appears that we shall be acting unjustly, then we have no need at all to take into account whether we shall have to die if we stay here and keep quiet, or suffer in another way, rather than do wrong.

CRITO: I think you put that beautifully, Socrates, but see what we should do.

SOCRATES: Let us examine the question together, my dear friend, and if you can make any objection while I am speaking, make it and I will listen to you, but if you have no objection to make, my dear Crito, then stop now from saying the same thing so often, that I must leave here against the will of the Athenians. I think it important to persuade you before I act, and not to act against your wishes. See whether the start of our inquiry is adequately stated, and try to answer what I ask you in the way you think best.

CRITO: I shall try.

SOCRATES: Do we say that one must never in any way do wrong willingly, or must one do wrong in one way and not in another?

Is to do wrong never good or admirable, as we have agreed in the past, or have all these former agreements been washed out during the last few days? Have we at our age failed to notice for some time that in our serious discussions we were no different from children? Above all, is the truth such as we used to say it was, whether the majority agree or not, and whether we must still suffer worse things than we do now, or will be treated more gently, that nonetheless, wrongdoing is in every way harmful and shameful to the wrongdoer? Do we say so or not?

CRITO: We do.

SOCRATES: So one must never do wrong.

CRITO: Certainly not.

SOCRATES: Nor must one, when wronged, inflict wrong in return, as the majority believe, since one must never do wrong.

CRITO: That seems to be the case.

SOCRATES: Come now, should one injure anyone or not, Crito?

CRITO: One must never do so.

SOCRATES: Well then, if one is oneself injured, is it right, as the majority say, to inflict an injury in return, or is it not?

CRITO: It is never right.

SOCRATES: Injuring people is no different from wrongdoing.

CRITO: That is true.

SOCRATES: One should never do wrong in return, nor injure any man, whatever injury one has suffered at his hands. And Crito, see that you do not agree to this, contrary to your belief. For I know that only a few people hold this view or will hold it, and there is no common ground between those who hold this view and those who do not, but they inevitably despise each other's views. So then consider very carefully whether we have this view in common, and whether you agree, and let this be the basis of our deliberation, that neither to do wrong or to return a wrong is ever right, not even to injure in return for an injury received. Or do you disagree and do not share this view as a basis for discussion? I have held it for a long time and still hold it now, but if you think otherwise, tell me now. If, however, you stick to our former opinion, then listen to the next point.

CRITO: I stick to it and agree with you. So say on.

SOCRATES: Then I state the next point, or rather I ask you: when one has come to an agreement that is just with someone, should one fulfill it or cheat on it?

CRITO: One should fulfill it.

SOCRATES: See what follows from this: if we leave here without the city's permission, are we injuring people whom we should least injure? And are we sticking to a just agreement, or not?

CRITO: I cannot answer your question, Socrates. I do not know.

SOCRATES: Look at it this way. If, as we were planning to run away from here, or whatever one should call it, the laws and the state came and confronted us and asked: "Tell me, Socrates, what are you intending to do? Do you not by this action you are attempting intend to destroy us, the laws, and indeed the whole city, as far as you are concerned? Or do you think it possible for a city not to be destroyed if the verdicts of its courts have no force but are nullified and set at naught by private individuals?" What shall we answer to this and other such arguments? For many things could be said, especially by an orator on behalf of this law we are destroying, which orders that the judgments of the courts shall be carried out. Shall we say in answer, "The city wronged me, and its decision was not right." Shall we say that, or what?

CRITO: Yes, by Zeus, Socrates, that is our answer.

SOCRATES: Then what if the laws said: "Was that the agreement between us, Socrates, or was it to respect the judgments that the city came to?" And if we wondered at their words, they would perhaps add: "Socrates, do not wonder at what we say but answer, since you are accustomed to proceed by question and answer. Come now, what accusation do you bring against us and the city, that you should try to destroy us? Did we not, first, bring you to birth, and was it not through us that your father married your mother and begat you? Tell you, do you find anything to criticize in those of us who are concerned with marriage?" And I would say that I do not criticize them. "Or in those of us concerned with the nurture of babies and the education that you too received? Were those assigned to that subject not right to instruct your father to educate you in the arts and in physical culture?" And I would say that they were right. "Very well," they would continue, "and after you were born and nurtured and educated, could you, in the first place, deny that you are our offspring and servant, both you and your forefathers? If that is so, do you think that we are on an equal footing as regards the right, and that whatever we do to you it is right for you to do to us? You were not on an equal footing with your father as regards the right, nor with your master if you had one, so as to retaliate for anything they did to you, to revile them if they reviled you, to beat them if they beat you, and so with many other things. Do you think you have this right to retaliation against your country and its laws? That if we undertake to destroy you and think it right to do so, you can undertake to destroy us, as far as you can, in return? And will you say that you are right to do so, you who truly care for virtue? Is your wisdom such as not to realize that your country is to be honored more than your mother, your father and all your ancestors, that it is more to be revered and more sacred, and that it counts for more among the gods and sensible men, that you must worship it, yield to it and placate its anger more than your father's? You must either persuade it or obey its orders, and endure in silence whatever it instructs you to endure, whether blows or bonds, and if it leads you into war to be wounded or killed, you must obey. To do so is right, and one must not give way or retreat or leave one's post, but both in war and in courts and everywhere else, one must obey the commands of one's city and country, or persuade it as to the nature of justice. It is impious to bring violence to bear against your mother or father, it is much more so to use it against your country." What shall we say in reply, Crito, that the laws speak the truth, or not?

CRITO: I think they do.

SOCRATES: "Reflect now, Socrates," the laws might say, "that if what we say is true, you are not treating us rightly by planning to do what you are planning. We have given you birth, nurtured you, educated you, we have given you and all other citizens a share of all the good things we could. Even so, by giving every Athenian the opportunity, after he has reached manhood and observed the affairs of the city and us the laws, we proclaim that if we do not please him, he can take his possessions and go wherever he pleases. Not one of our laws raises any obstacle or forbids him, if he is not satisfied with us or the city, if one of you wants to go and live in a colony or wants to go anywhere else, and keep his property. We say, however, that whoever of you remains, when he sees how we conduct our trials and manage the city in other ways, has in fact come to an agreement with us to obey our instructions. We say that the one who disobeys does wrong in three ways, first because in us he disobeys his parents, also those who brought him up, and because, in spite of his agreement, he neither obeys us nor, if we do something wrong, does he try to persuade us to do better. Yet we only propose things, we do not issue savage commands to do whatever we order; we give two alternatives, either to persuade us or to do what we say. He does neither. We do say that you too, Socrates, are open to those charges if you do what you have in mind; you would be among, not the least, but the most guilty of the Athenians." And if I should say "Why so?" they might well be right to upbraid me and say that I am among the Athenians who most definitely came to that agreement with them. They might well say: "Socrates, we have convincing proofs that we and the city were congenial to you. You would not have dwelt here most consistently of all the Athenians if the city had not been exceedingly pleasing to you. You have never left the city, even to see a festival, nor for any other reason except military service; you have never gone to stay in any other city, as people do; you have had no desire to know another city or other laws; we and our city satisfied you.

"So decisively did you choose us and agree to be a citizen under us. Also, you have had children in this city, thus showing that it was congenial to you. Then at your trial you could have assessed your penalty at exile if you wished, and you are now attempting to do against the city's wishes what you could then have done with her consent. Then you prided yourself that you did not resent death, but you chose, as you said, death in preference to exile. Now, however, those words do not make you ashamed, and you pay no heed to us, the laws, as you plan to destroy us, and you act like the meanest type of slave by trying to run away, contrary to your commitments and your agreement to live as a citizen under us. First then, answer us on this very point, whether we speak the truth when we say that you agreed, not only in words but by your deeds, to live in accordance with us." What are we to say to that, Crito? Must we not agree?

CRITO: We must, Socrates.

SOCRATES: "Surely," they might say, "you are breaking the commitments and agreements that you made with us without compulsion or deceit, and under no pressure of time for deliberation. You have had seventy years during which you could have gone away if you did not like us, and if you thought our agreements unjust. You did not choose to go to Sparta or to Crete, which you are always saying are well governed, nor to any other city, Greek or foreign. You have been away from Athens less than the lame or the blind or other handicapped people. It is clear that the city has been outstandingly more congenial to you than to other Athenians, and so have we, the laws, for what city can please without laws? Will you then not now stick to our agreements? You will, Socrates, if we can persuade you, and not make yourself a laughingstock by leaving the city.

"For consider what good you will do yourself or your friends by breaking our agreements and committing such a wrong? It is pretty obvious that your friends will themselves be in danger of exile, disfranchisement and loss of property. As for yourself, if you go to one of the nearby cities—Thebes or Megara, both are well governed—you will arrive as an enemy to their government; all who care for their city will look on you with suspicion, as a destroyer of the laws. You will also strengthen the conviction of the jury that they passed the right sentence on you, for anyone who destroys the laws could easily be thought to corrupt the young and the ignorant. Or will you avoid cities that are well governed and men who are civilized? If you do this, will your life be worth living? Will you have social intercourse with them and not be ashamed to talk to them? And what will you say? The same as you did here, that virtue and justice are man's most precious possession, along with lawful behavior and the laws? Do you not think that Socrates would appear to be an unseemly kind of person? One must think so. Or will you leave those places and go to Crito's friends in Thessaly? There you will find the greatest license and disorder, and they may enjoy hearing from you how absurdly you escaped from prison in some disguise, in a leather jerkin or some other things in which escapees wrap themselves, thus altering your appearance. Will there be no one to say that you, likely to live but a short time more, were so greedy for life that you transgressed the most important laws? Possibly, Socrates, if you do not annoy anyone, but if you do, many disgraceful things will be said about you.

"You will spend your time ingratiating yourself with all men, and be at their beck and call. What will you do in Thessaly but feast, as if you had gone to a banquet in Thessaly? As for those conversations of yours about justice and the rest of virtue, where will they be? You say you want to live for the sake of your children, that you may bring them up and educate them. How so? Will you bring them up and educate them by taking them to Thessaly and making strangers of them, that they may enjoy that too? Or not so, but they will be better brought up and educated here, while you are alive, though absent? Yes, your friends will look after them. Will they look after them if you go and live in Thessaly, but not if you go away to the underworld? If those who profess themselves your friends are any good at all, one must assume that they will.

"Be persuaded by us who have brought you up, Socrates. Do not value either your children or your life or anything else more than goodness, in order that when you arrive in Hades you may have all this as your defense before the rulers there. If you do this deed, you will not think it better or more just or more pious here, nor will any one of your friends, nor will it be better for you when you arrive yonder. As it is, you depart, if you depart, after being wronged not by us, the laws, but by men; but if you depart after shamefully returning wrong for wrong and injury for injury, after breaking your agreements and commitments with us, after injuring those you should injure least—yourself, your friends, your country and us—we shall be angry with you while you are still alive, and our brothers, the laws of the underworld, will not receive you kindly, knowing that you tried to destroy us as far as you could. Do not let Crito persuade you, rather than us, to do what he says."

Crito, my dear friend, be assured that these are the words I seem to hear, as the Corybants seem to hear the music of their flutes, and the echo of these words resounds in me, and makes it impossible for me to hear anything else. As far as my present beliefs go, if you speak in opposition to them, you will speak in vain. However, if you think you can accomplish anything, speak.

CRITO: I have nothing to say, Socrates.

SOCRATES: Let it be then, Crito, and let us act in this way, since this is the way the god is leading us.

CHAPTER 4

Socrates' Question about Justice

Plato

The Oracle at Delphi said that Socrates was the wisest of men. If that is so, Socrates thought, *it can only be because I alone realize how ignorant people are.* In the following passages from Book I of the *Republic,* we find Socrates asking his companions about the nature of justice and then demonstrating that none of them really understands it. The passage ends with Thrasymachus proclaiming that justice is the advantage of the stronger.

I went down to the Piraeus yesterday with Glaucon, the son of Ariston. I wanted to say a prayer to the goddess, and I was also curious to see how they would manage the festival, since they were holding it for the first time. I thought the procession of the local residents was a fine one and that the one conducted by the Thracians was no less outstanding. After we had said our prayer and seen the procession, we started back towards Athens. Polemarchus saw us from a distance as we were setting off for home and told his slave to run and ask us to wait for him. The slave caught hold of my cloak from behind: Polemarchus wants you to wait, he said. I turned around and asked

Source: These selections are from Plato, *The Republic,* trans. G. M. A. Grube, 2nd edition, revised by C. D. C. Reeve (Indianapolis: Hackett Publishing Company, 1997).

where Polemarchus was. He's coming up behind you, he said, please wait for him. And Glaucon replied: All right, we will. . . .

. . . What's the greatest good you've [Cephalus] received from being very wealthy?

What I have to say probably wouldn't persuade most people. But you know, Socrates, that when someone thinks his end is near, he becomes frightened and concerned about things he didn't fear before. It's then that the stories we're told about Hades, about how people who've been unjust here must pay the penalty there—stories he used to make fun of—twist his soul this way and that for fear they're true. And whether because of the weakness of old age or because he is now closer to what happens in Hades and has a clearer view of it, or whatever it is, he is filled with foreboding and fear, and he examines himself to see whether he has been unjust to anyone. If he finds many injustices in his life, he awakes from sleep in terror, as children do, and lives in anticipation of bad things to come. But someone who knows that he hasn't been unjust has sweet good hope as his constant companion—a nurse to his old age, as Pindar says, for he puts it charmingly, Socrates, when he says that when someone lives a just and pious life

> *Sweet hope is in his heart,*
> *Nurse and companion to his age.*
> *Hope, captain of the ever-twisting*
> *Minds of mortal men.*

How wonderfully well he puts that. It's in this connection that wealth is most valuable, I'd say, not for every man but for a decent and orderly one. Wealth can do a lot to save us from having to cheat or deceive someone against our will and from having to depart for that other place in fear because we owe sacrifice to a god or money to a person. It has many other uses, but, benefit for benefit, I'd say that this is how it is most useful to a man of any understanding.

A fine sentiment, Cephalus, but, speaking of this very thing itself, namely, justice, are we to say unconditionally that it is speaking the truth and paying whatever debts one has incurred? Or is doing these things sometimes just, sometimes unjust? I mean this sort of thing, for example: Everyone would surely agree that if a sane man lends weapons to a friend and then asks for them back when he is out of his mind, the friend shouldn't return them, and wouldn't be acting justly if he did. Nor should anyone be willing to tell the whole truth to someone who is out of his mind.

That's true.

Then the definition of justice isn't speaking the truth and repaying what one has borrowed.

It certainly is, Socrates, said Polemarchus, interrupting, if indeed we're to trust Simonides at all.

Well, then, Cephalus said, I'll hand over the argument to you, as I have to look after the sacrifice.

So, Polemarchus said, am I then to be your heir in everything? You certainly are, Cephalus said, laughing, and off he went to the sacrifice.

Then tell us, heir to the argument, I said, just what Simonides stated about justice that you consider correct.

He stated that it is just to give to each what is owed to him. And it's a fine saying, in my view.

Well, now, it isn't easy to doubt Simonides, for he's a wise and godlike man. But what exactly does he mean? Perhaps you know, Polemarchus, but I don't understand him. Clearly, he doesn't mean what we said a moment ago, that it is just to give back whatever a person has lent to you, even if he's out of his mind when he asks for it. And yet what he has lent to you is surely something that's owed to him, isn't it?

Yes.

But it is absolutely not to be given to him when he's out of his mind?

That's true.

Then it seems that Simonides must have meant something different when he says that to return what is owed is just.

Something different indeed, by god. He means that friends owe it to their friends to do good for them, never harm.

I follow you. Someone doesn't give a lender back what he's owed by giving him gold, if doing so would be harmful, and both he and the lender are friends. Isn't that what you think Simonides meant?

It is.

But what about this? Should one also give one's enemies whatever is owed to them?

By all means, one should give them what is owed to them. And in my view what enemies owe to each other is appropriately and precisely—something bad.

It seems then that Simonides was speaking in riddles—just like a poet!—when he said what justice is, for he thought it just to give to each what is appropriate to him, and this is what he called giving him what is owed to him. . . .

. . . But surely people often make mistakes about this, believing many people to be good and useful when they aren't, and making the opposite mistake about enemies?

They do indeed.

And then good people are their enemies and bad ones their friends?

That's right.

And so it's just to benefit bad people and harm good ones?

Apparently.

But good people are just and able to do no wrong?

True.

Then, according to your account, it's just to do bad things to those who do no injustice.

No, that's not just at all, Socrates; my account must be a bad one.

It's just, then, is it, to harm unjust people and benefit just ones?

That's obviously a more attractive view than the other one, anyway.

Then, it follows, Polemarchus, that it is just for the many, who are mistaken in their judgment, to harm their friends, who are bad, and benefit their enemies, who are good. And so we arrive at a conclusion opposite to what we said Simonides meant.

That certainly follows. But let's change our definition, for it seems that we didn't define friends and enemies correctly.

How did we define them, Polemarchus?

We said that a friend is someone who is believed to be useful.

And how are we to change that now?

Someone who is both believed to be useful and is useful is a friend; someone who is believed to be useful but isn't, is believed to be a friend but isn't. And the same for the enemy.

According to this account, then, a good person will be a friend and a bad one an enemy.

Yes.

So you want us to add something to what we said before about justice, when we said that it is just to treat friends well and enemies badly. You want us to add to this that it is just to treat well a friend who is good and to harm an enemy who is bad?

Right. That seems fine to me.

Is it, then, the role of a just man to harm anyone?

Certainly, he must harm those who are both bad and enemies.

Do horses become better or worse when they are harmed?

Worse.

With respect to the virtue that makes dogs good or the one that makes horses good?

The one that makes horses good.

And when dogs are harmed, they become worse in the virtue that makes dogs good, not horses?

Necessarily.

Then won't we say the same about human beings, too, that when they are harmed they become worse in human virtue?

Indeed.

But isn't justice human virtue?

Yes, certainly.

Then people who are harmed must become more unjust?

So it seems.

Can musicians make people unmusical through music?

They cannot.

Or horsemen make people unhorsemanlike through horsemanship?

No.

Well, then, can those who are just make people unjust through justice? In a word, can those who are good make people bad through virtue?

They cannot.

It isn't the function of heat to cool things but of its opposite?

Yes.

Nor the function of dryness to make things wet but of its opposite?

Indeed.

Nor the function of goodness to harm but of its opposite?

Apparently.

And a just person is good?

Indeed.

Then, Polemarchus, it isn't the function of a just person to harm a friend or anyone else, rather it is the function of his opposite, an unjust person?

In my view that's completely true, Socrates.

If anyone tells us, then, that it is just to give to each what he's owed and understands by this that a just man should harm his enemies and benefit his friends, he isn't wise to say it, since what he says isn't true, for it has become clear to us that it is never just to harm anyone?

I agree.

You and I shall fight as partners, then, against anyone who tells us that Simonides, Bias, Pittacus, or any of our other wise and blessedly happy men said this.

I, at any rate, am willing to be your partner in the battle.

Do you know to whom I think the saying belongs that it is just to benefit friends and harm enemies?

Who?

I think it belongs to Periander, or Perdiccas, or Xerxes, or Ismenias of Corinth, or some other wealthy man who believed himself to have great power.

That's absolutely true.

All right, since it has become apparent that justice and the just aren't what such people say they are, what else could they be?

While we were speaking, Thrasymachus had tried many times to take over the discussion but was restrained by those sitting near him, who wanted to hear our argument to the end. When we paused after what I'd just said, however, he couldn't keep quiet any longer. He coiled himself up like a wild beast about to spring, and he hurled himself at us as if to tear us to pieces.

Polemarchus and I were frightened and flustered as he roared into our midst: What nonsense have you two been talking, Socrates? Why do you act like idiots by giving way to one another? If you truly want to know what justice is, don't just ask questions and then refute the answers simply to satisfy your competitiveness or love of honor. You know very well that it is easier to ask questions than answer them. Give an answer yourself, and tell us what you say the just is. And don't tell me that it's the right, the beneficial, the profitable, the gainful, or the advantageous, but tell me clearly and exactly what you mean; for I won't accept such nonsense from you.

His words startled me, and, looking at him, I was afraid. And I think that if I hadn't seen him before he stared at me, I'd have been dumbstruck. But as it was, I happened to look at him just as our discussion began to exasperate him, so I was able to answer, and, trembling a little, I said: Don't be too hard on us, Thrasymachus, for if Polemarchus and I made an error in our investigation, you should know that we did so unwillingly. If we were searching for gold, we'd never willingly give way to each other, if by doing so we'd destroy our chance of finding it. So don't think that in searching for justice, a thing more valuable than even a large quantity of gold, we'd mindlessly give way to one another or be less than completely serious about finding it. You surely mustn't think that, but rather—as I do—that we're incapable of finding it. Hence it's surely far more appropriate for us to be pitied by you clever people than to be given rough treatment.

When he heard that, he gave a loud, sarcastic laugh. By Heracles, he said, that's just Socrates' usual irony. I knew, and I said so to these people earlier, that you'd be unwilling to answer and that, if someone questioned *you*, you'd be ironical and do anything rather than give an answer.

That's because you're a clever fellow, Thrasymachus. You knew very well that if you ask someone how much twelve is, and, as you ask, you warn him by saying "Don't tell me, man, that twelve is twice six, or three times four, or six times two, or four times three, for I won't accept such nonsense," then you'll see clearly, I think, that no one could answer a question framed like that. And if he said to you: "What are you saying, Thrasymachus, am I not to give any of the answers you mention, not even if twelve happens to be one of those things? I'm amazed. Do you want me to say something other than the truth? Or do you mean something else?" What answer would you give him?

Well, so you think the two cases are alike?

Why shouldn't they be alike? But even if they aren't alike, yet seem so to the person you asked, do you think him any less likely to give the answer that seems right to him, whether we forbid him to or not?

Is that what you're going to do, give one of the forbidden answers?

I wouldn't be surprised—provided that it's the one that seems right to me after I've investigated the matter.

What if I show you a different answer about justice than all these—and a better one? What would you deserve then?

What else than the appropriate penalty for one who doesn't know, namely, to learn from the one who does know? Therefore, that's what I deserve.

You amuse me, but in addition to learning, you must pay a fine.

I will as soon as I have some money.

He has some already, said Glaucon. If it's a matter of money, speak, Thrasymachus, for we'll all contribute for Socrates.

I know, he said, so that Socrates can carry on as usual. He gives no answer himself, and then, when someone else does give one, he takes up the argument and refutes it.

How can someone give an answer, I said, when he doesn't know it and doesn't claim to know it, and when an eminent man forbids him to express the opinion he has? It's much more appropriate for you to answer, since you say you know and can tell us. So do it as a favor to me, and don't begrudge your teaching to Glaucon and the others.

While I was saying this, Glaucon and the others begged him to speak. It was obvious that Thrasymachus thought he had a fine answer and that he wanted to earn their admiration by giving it, but he pretended that he wanted to indulge his love of victory by forcing me to answer. However, he agreed in the end, and then said: There you have Socrates' wisdom; he himself isn't willing to teach, but he goes around learning from others and isn't even grateful to them.

When you say that I learn from others you are right, Thrasymachus, but when you say that I'm not grateful, that isn't true. I show what gratitude I can, but since I have no money, I can give only praise. But just how enthusiastically I give it when someone seems to me to speak well, you'll know as soon as you've answered, for I think that you will speak well.

Listen, then. I say that justice is nothing other than the advantage of the stronger. Well, why don't you praise me? But then you'd do anything to avoid having to do that.

I must first understand you, for I don't yet know what you mean. The advantage of the stronger, you say, is just. What do you mean, Thrasymachus? Surely you don't mean something like this: Polydamus, the athlete, is stronger than we are; it is to his advantage to eat beef to build up his physical strength; therefore, this food is also advantageous and just for us who are weaker than he is?

You disgust me, Socrates. Your trick is to take hold of the argument at the point where you can do it the most harm.

Not at all, but tell us more clearly what you mean.

Don't you know that some cities are ruled by a tyranny, some by a democracy, and some by an aristocracy?

Of course.

And in each city this element is stronger, namely, the ruler?

Certainly.

And each makes laws to its own advantage. Democracy makes democratic laws, tyranny makes tyrannical laws, and so on with the others. And they declare what they have made—what is to their own advantage—to be just for their subjects, and they punish anyone who goes against this as lawless and unjust. This, then, is what I say justice is, the same in all cities, the advantage of the established rule. Since the established rule is surely stronger, anyone who reasons correctly will conclude that the just is the same everywhere, namely, the advantage of the stronger.

*G*od

Five Ways to Prove That God Exists

St. Thomas Aquinas

St. Thomas Aquinas (1225–1274), a leading figure in the history of Western thought, believed that some things are known by reason and some are revealed through Church authorities. But where the most important truths are concerned, God has left nothing to chance—we can know them in both ways. Consider, for example, the existence of God. Of course the Church confirms it. But God's existence can also be known by reason.

Here Aquinas argues that God's existence is self-evident, though not self-evident to us (in the First Article); that God's existence can be demonstrated (in the Second Article); and that God does indeed exist—in fact, his existence can be proved in five ways (in the Third Article). In defending these claims, Aquinas first states objections; then he gives his own position; then he replies to the objections, one by one. Aquinas always treats Aristotle with the greatest respect, referring to him only as "The Philosopher."

Source: This selection is reprinted from *Basic Writings of Saint Thomas Aquinas,* Vol. 1, ed. Anton C. Pegis (New York: Random House, 1945), pp. 18–24. Copyright © 1945 by Random House, Inc. Copyright renewed 1973 by Random House, Inc. First Hackett Publishing Company edition 1997. Reprinted by permission of Hackett Publishing Company, Inc. All rights reserved.

Concerning [whether God exists], there are three points of inquiry:—
(1) Whether the proposition *God exists* is self-evident? (2) Whether it is
demonstrable? (3) Whether God exists?

First Article

Whether the Existence of God Is Self-Evident? *We proceed thus to the First Article:—*

Objection 1. It seems that the existence of God is self-evident. For
those things are said to be self-evident to us the knowledge of which
exists naturally in us, as we can see in regard to first principles. But as
Damascene says, *the knowledge of God is naturally implanted in all.* Therefore the existence of God is self-evident.

Obj. 2. Further, those things are said to be self-evident which
are known as soon as the terms are known, which the Philosopher
says is true of the first principles of demonstration. Thus, when the
nature of a whole and of a part is known, it is at once recognized
that every whole is greater than its part. But as soon as the signification of the name *God* is understood, it is at once seen that God
exists. For by this name is signified that thing than which nothing
greater can be conceived. But that which exists actually and mentally is greater than that which exists only mentally. Therefore, since
as soon as the name *God* is understood it exists mentally, it also follows that it exists actually. Therefore the proposition *God exists* is
self-evident.

Obj. 3. Further, the existence of truth is self-evident. For whoever denies the existence of truth grants that truth does not exist:
and, if truth does not exist, then the proposition *Truth does not exist* is
true: and if there is anything true, there must be truth. But God is
truth itself: *I am the way, the truth, and the life* (*Jo.* xiv. 6). Therefore *God
exists* is self-evident.

On the contrary, No one can mentally admit the opposite of what
is self-evident, as the Philosopher states concerning the first principles
of demonstration. But the opposite of the proposition *God is* can be
mentally admitted: *The fool said in his heart, There is no God* (*Ps.* lii. 1).
Therefore, that God exists is not self-evident.

I answer that, A thing can be self-evident in either of two ways: on
the one hand, self-evident in itself, though not to us; on the other,
self-evident in itself, and to us. A proposition is self-evident because
the predicate is included in the essence of the subject: *e.g., Man is an*

animal, for animal is contained in the essence of man. If, therefore, the essence of the predicate and subject be known to all, the proposition will be self-evident to all; as is clear with regard to the first principles of demonstration, the terms of which are certain common notions that no one is ignorant of, such as being and non-being, whole and part, and the like. If, however, there are some to whom the essence of the predicate and subject is unknown, the proposition will be self-evident in itself, but not to those who do not know the meaning of the predicate and subject of the proposition. Therefore, it happens, as Boethius says, that there are some notions of the mind which are common and self-evident only to the learned, as that incorporeal [nonmaterial] substances are not in space. Therefore I say that this proposition, *God exists,* of itself is self-evident, for the predicate is the same as the subject, because God is His own existence as will be hereafter shown. Now because we do not know the essence of God, the proposition is not self-evident to us, but needs to be demonstrated by things that are more known to us, though less known in their nature—namely, by His effects.

Reply Obj. 1. To know that God exists in a general and confused way is implanted in us by nature, inasmuch as God is man's beatitude. For man naturally desires happiness, and what is naturally desired by man is naturally known by him. This, however, is not to know absolutely that God exists; just as to know that someone is approaching is not the same as to know that Peter is approaching, even though it is Peter who is approaching; for there are many who imagine that man's perfect good, which is happiness, consists in riches, and others in pleasures, and others in something else.

Reply Obj. 2. Perhaps not everyone who hears this name *God* understands it to signify something than which nothing greater can be thought, seeing that some have believed God to be a body. Yet, granted that everyone understands that by this name *God* is signified something than which nothing greater can be thought, nevertheless, it does not therefore follow that he understands that what the name signifies exists actually, but only that it exists mentally. Nor can it be argued that it actually exists, unless it be admitted that there actually exists something than which nothing greater can be thought; and this precisely is not admitted by those who hold that God does not exist.

Reply Obj. 3. The existence of truth in general is self-evident, but the existence of a Primal Truth is not self-evident to us.

Second Article

Whether It Can Be Demonstrated That God Exists? *We proceed thus to the Second Article:*—

Objection 1. It seems that the existence of God cannot be demonstrated. For it is an article of faith that God exists. But what is of faith cannot be demonstrated, because a demonstration produces scientific knowledge, whereas faith is of the unseen, as is clear from the Apostle (*Heb.* xi. 1). Therefore it cannot be demonstrated that God exists.

Obj. 2. Further, essence is the middle term of demonstration. But we cannot know in what God's essence consists, but solely in what it does not consist, as Damascene says. Therefore we cannot demonstrate that God exists.

Obj. 3. Further, if the existence of God were demonstrated, this could only be from His effects. But His effects are not proportioned to Him, since He is infinite and His effects are finite, and between the finite and infinite there is no proportion. Therefore, since a cause cannot be demonstrated by an effect not proportioned to it, it seems that the existence of God cannot be demonstrated.

On the contrary, The Apostle says: *The invisible things of Him are clearly seen, being understood by the things that are made* (*Rom.* i. 20). But this would not be unless the existence of God could be demonstrated through the things that are made; for the first thing we must know of anything is, whether it exists.

I answer that, Demonstration can be made in two ways: One is through the cause, and is called *propter quid,* and this is to argue from what is prior absolutely. The other is through the effect, and is called a demonstration *quia;* this is to argue from what is prior relatively only to us. When an effect is better known to us than its cause, from the effect we proceed to the knowledge of the cause. And from every effect the existence of its proper cause can be demonstrated, so long as its effects are better known to us; because, since every effect depends upon its cause, if the effect exists, the cause must preexist. Hence the existence of God, in so far as it is not self-evident to us, can be demonstrated from those of His effects which are known to us.

Reply Obj. 1. The existence of God and other like truths about God, which can be known by natural reason, are not articles of faith, but are preambles to the articles; for faith presupposes natural knowledge, even as grace presupposes nature and perfection the perfectible.

Nevertheless, there is nothing to prevent a man, who cannot grasp a proof, from accepting, as a matter of faith, something which in itself is capable of being scientifically known and demonstrated.

Reply Obj. 2. When the existence of a cause is demonstrated from an effect, this effect takes the place of the definition of the cause in proving the cause's existence. This is especially the case in regard to God, because, in order to prove the existence of anything, it is necessary to accept as a middle term the meaning of the name, and not its essence, for the question of its essence follows on the question of its existence. Now the names given to God are derived from His effects, as will be later shown. Consequently, in demonstrating the existence of God from His effects, we may take for the middle term the meaning of the name *God.*

Reply Obj. 3. From effects not proportioned to the cause no perfect knowledge of that cause can be obtained. Yet from every effect the existence of the cause can be clearly demonstrated, and so we can demonstrate the existence of God from His effects; though from them we cannot know God perfectly as He is in His essence.

Third Article

Whether God Exists? *We proceed thus to the Third Article:—*

Objection 1. It seems that God does not exist; because if one of two contraries be infinite, the other would be altogether destroyed. But the name *God* means that He is infinite goodness. If, therefore, God existed, there would be no evil discoverable; but there is evil in the world. Therefore God does not exist.

Obj. 2. Further, it is superfluous to suppose that what can be accounted for by a few principles has been produced by many. But it seems that everything we see in the world can be accounted for by other principles, supposing God did not exist. For all natural things can be reduced to one principle, which is nature; and all voluntary things can be reduced to one principle, which is human reason, or will. Therefore there is no need to suppose God's existence.

On the contrary, It is said in the person of God: *I am Who am* (*Exod.* iii. 14).

I answer that, The existence of God can be proved in five ways. The first and most manifest way is the argument from motion. It is certain, and evident to our senses, that in the world some things are in motion. Now whatever is moved is moved by another, for nothing can be moved except it is in potentiality to that towards which it is moved; whereas a thing moves inasmuch as it is in actuality. For motion is nothing else than the reduction of something from potentiality to actuality. But nothing can be reduced from potentiality to actuality, except by something in a state of actuality. Thus that which is actually hot, as fire, makes wood, which is potentially hot, to be actually hot, and thereby moves and changes it. Now it is not possible that the same thing should be at once in actuality and potentiality in the same respect, but only in different respects. For what is actually hot cannot simultaneously be potentially hot; but it is simultaneously potentially cold. It is therefore impossible that in the same respect and in the same way a thing should be both mover and moved, *i.e.*, that it should move itself. Therefore, whatever is moved must be moved by another. If that by which it is moved be itself moved, then this also must needs be moved by another, and that by another again. But this cannot go on to infinity, because then there would be no first mover, and, consequently, no other mover, seeing that subsequent movers move only inasmuch as they are moved by the first mover; as the staff moves only because it is moved by the hand. Therefore it is necessary to arrive at a first mover, moved by no other; and this everyone understands to be God.

The second way is from the nature of efficient cause. In the world of sensible things we find there is an order of efficient causes. There is no case known (neither is it, indeed, possible) in which a thing is found to be the efficient cause of itself; for so it would be prior to itself, which is impossible. Now in efficient causes it is not possible to go on to infinity, because in all efficient causes following in order, the first is the cause of the intermediate cause, and the intermediate is the cause of the ultimate cause, whether the intermediate cause be several, or one only. Now to take away the cause is to take away the effect. Therefore, if there be no first cause among efficient causes, there will be no ultimate, nor any intermediate, cause. But if in efficient causes it is possible to go on to infinity, there will be no first efficient cause, neither will there be an ultimate effect, nor any intermediate efficient causes; all of which is plainly false. Therefore it is necessary to admit a first efficient cause, to which everyone gives the name of God.

The third way is taken from possibility and necessity, and runs thus. We find in nature things that are possible to be and not to be, since they are found to be generated, and to be corrupted, and consequently, it is possible for them to be and not to be. But it is impossible for these always to exist, for that which can not-be at some time is not. Therefore, if everything can not-be, then at one time there was nothing in existence. Now if this were true, even now there would be nothing in existence, because that which does not exist begins to exist only through something already existing. Therefore, if at one time nothing was in existence, it would have been impossible for anything to have begun to exist; and thus even now nothing would be in existence—which is absurd. Therefore, not all beings are merely possible, but there must exist something the existence of which is necessary. But every necessary thing either has its necessity caused by another, or not. Now it is impossible to go on to infinity in necessary things which have their necessity caused by another, as has been already proved in regard to efficient causes. Therefore we cannot but admit the existence of some being having of itself its own necessity, and not receiving it from another, but rather causing in others their necessity. This all men speak of as God.

The fourth way is taken from the gradation to be found in things. Among beings there are some more and some less good, true, noble, and the like. But *more* and *less* are predicated of different things according as they resemble in their different ways something which is the maximum, as a thing is said to be hotter according as it more nearly resembles that which is hottest; so that there is something which is truest, something best, something noblest, and, consequently, something which is most being, for those things that are greatest in truth are greatest in being, as it is written in *Metaph.* ii. Now the maximum in any genus is the cause of all in that genus, as fire, which is the maximum of heat, is the cause of all hot things, as is said in the same book. Therefore there must also be something which is to all beings the cause of their being, goodness, and every other perfection; and this we call God.

The fifth way is taken from the governance of the world. We see that things which lack knowledge, such as natural bodies, act for an end, and this is evident from their acting always, or nearly always, in the same way, so as to obtain the best result. Hence it is plain that they achieve their end not fortuitously, but designedly. Now whatever lacks knowledge cannot move towards an end, unless it be directed by some being endowed with knowledge and intelligence; as the arrow is directed by the archer. Therefore some intelligent being exists by whom all natural things are directed to their end; and this being we call God.

Reply Obj. 1. As Augustine says: *Since God is the highest good, He would not allow any evil to exist in His works, unless His omnipotence and goodness were such as to bring good even out of evil.* This is part of the infinite goodness of God, that He should allow evil to exist, and out of it produce good.

Reply Obj. 2. Since nature works for a determinate end under the direction of a higher agent, whatever is done by nature must be traced back to God as to its first cause. So likewise whatever is done voluntarily must be traced back to some higher cause other than human reason and will, since these can change and fail; for all things that are changeable and capable of defect must be traced back to an immovable and self-necessary first principle, as has been shown.

CHAPTER 6

The Watch and the Watch-Maker

William Paley

William Paley (1743–1805) was the foremost advocate of the Design Argument. The wonders of nature, he thought, can be best explained as the product of intelligent design.

Paley's books include *The Moral and Political Philosophy* (1786), *A View of the Evidences of Christianity* (1794), and *Natural Theology* (1802), from which this selection is taken.

In crossing a heath, suppose I pitched my foot against a *stone,* and were asked how the stone came to be there; I might possibly answer, that, for any thing I knew to the contrary, it had lain there for ever: nor would it perhaps be very easy to show the absurdity of this answer. But suppose I had found a *watch* upon the ground, and it should be inquired how the watch happened to be in that place; I should hardly think of the answer which I had before given, that, for any thing I knew, the watch might have always been there. Yet why should not this answer serve for the watch as well as for the stone? Why is it not as admissible in the second case, as in the first? For this reason, and for no other, namely that, when we come to inspect the watch, we perceive (what we could not discover in the stone) that its several parts

---

Source: This selection is from chapter 1 of Paley's *Natural Theology* (1802). I have updated the language in a few places.

are framed and put together for a purpose—that they are so formed and adjusted as to produce motion, and that motion so regulated as to point out the hour of the day; that, if the different parts had been differently shaped from what they are, of a different size from what they are, or placed after any other manner, or in any other order, than that in which they are placed, either no motion at all would have been carried on in the machine, or none which would have answered the use that is now served by it. To consider a few of the plainest of these parts, and of their workings, all tending to one result—we see a cylindrical box containing a coiled elastic spring, which, by its endeavour to relax itself, turns round the box. We next observe a flexible chain (artificially wrought for the sake of flexure), communicating the action of the spring from the box to the fusee. We then find a series of wheels, the teeth of which catch in, and apply to, each other, conducting the motion from the fusee to the balance, and from the balance to the pointer; and at the same time, by the size and shape of those wheels, so regulating that motion, as to terminate in causing an index, by an equable and measured progression, to pass over a given space in a given time. We take notice that the wheels are made of brass in order to keep them from rust; the springs of steel, no other metal being so elastic; that over the face of the watch there is placed a glass, a material employed in no other part of the work, but in the room of which, if there had been any other than a transparent substance, the hour could not be seen without opening the case. This mechanism being observed (it requires indeed an examination of the instrument, and perhaps some previous knowledge of the subject, to perceive and understand it; but being once, as we have said, observed and understood), the inference, we think, is inevitable, that the watch must have had a maker: that there must have existed, at some time, and at some place or other, an artificer or artificers who formed it for the purpose which we find it actually to answer; who comprehended its construction, and designed its use.

I. Nor would it, I apprehend, weaken the conclusion, that we had never seen a watch made; that we had never known an artist capable of making one; that we were altogether incapable of executing such a piece of workmanship ourselves, or of understanding in what manner it was performed; all this being no more than what is true of some exquisite remains of ancient art, of some lost arts, and, to the generality of mankind, of the more curious productions of modern manufacture. Does one man in a million know how oval frames are turned? Ignorance of this kind exalts our opinion of the unseen and unknown artist's skill, if he be unseen and unknown, but raises no doubt in our minds of the existence and agency of such an artist, at some former time, and in some place or other. Nor can I perceive that it varies at all the inference, whether the question arise concerning a human agent, or concerning an agent of a different species, or an agent possessing, in some respects, a different nature.

II. Neither, secondly, would it invalidate our conclusion, that the watch sometimes went wrong, or that it seldom went exactly right. The purpose of the machinery, the design, and the designer, might be evident, and in the case supposed would be evident, in whatever way we accounted for the irregularity of the movement, or whether we could account for it or not. It is not necessary that a machine be perfect, in order to show with what design it was made: still less necessary, where the only question is, whether it were made with any design at all.

III. Nor, thirdly, would it bring any uncertainty into the argument, if there were a few parts of the watch, concerning which we could not discover, or had not yet discovered, in what manner they conduced to the general effect; or even some parts, concerning which we could not ascertain, whether they conduced to that effect in any manner whatever. For, as to the first branch of the case; if by the loss, or disorder, or decay of the parts in question, the movement of the watch were found in fact to be stopped, or disturbed, or retarded, no doubt would remain in our minds as to the utility or intention of these parts, although we should be unable to investigate the manner according to which, or the connexion by which, the ultimate effect depended upon their action or assistance; and the more complex is the machine, the more likely is this obscurity to arise. Then, as to the second thing supposed, namely, that there were parts which might be spared, without prejudice to the movement of the watch, and that we had proved this by experiment—these superfluous parts, even if we were completely assured that they were such, would not vacate the reasoning which we had instituted concerning other parts. The indication of contrivance remained, with respect to them, nearly as it was before.

IV. Nor, fourthly, would any man in his senses think the existence of the watch, with its various machinery, accounted for, by being told that it was one out of possible combinations of material forms; that whatever he had found in the place where he found the watch, must have contained some internal configuration or other; and that this configuration might be the structure now exhibited, namely, of the works of a watch, as well as a different structure.

V. Nor, fifthly, would it yield his inquiry more satisfaction to be answered, that there existed in things a principle of order, which had disposed the parts of the watch into their present form and situation. He never knew a watch made by the principle of order; nor can he even form to himself an idea of what is meant by a principle of order, distinct from the intelligence of the watch-maker.

VI. Sixthly, he would be surprised to hear that the mechanism of the watch was no proof of contrivance, only a motive to induce the mind to think so:

VII. And not less surprised to be informed, that the watch in his hand was nothing more than the result of the laws of *metallic* nature. It is a perversion of language to assign any law, as the efficient, operative cause of any thing. A law presupposes an agent; for it is only the mode, according to which an agent proceeds: it implies a power; for it is the order, according to which that power acts. Without this agent, without this power, which are both distinct from itself, the *law* does nothing; is nothing. The expression, the law of metallic nature, may sound strange and harsh to a philosophic ear; but it seems quite as justifiable as some others which are more familiar to him, such as the law of vegetable nature, the law of animal nature, or indeed as the law of nature in general, when assigned as the cause of phænomena, in exclusion of agency and power; or when it is substituted into the place of these.

VIII. Neither, lastly, would our observer be driven out of his conclusion, or from his confidence in its truth, by being told that he knew nothing at all about the matter. He knows enough for his argument: he knows the utility of the end: he knows the subserviency and adaptation of the means to the end. These points being known, his ignorance of other points, his doubts concerning other points, affect not the certainty of his reasoning. The consciousness of knowing little, need not beget a distrust of that which he does know. . . .

. . . Every indication of contrivance, every manifestation of design, which existed in the watch, exists in the works of nature; with the difference, on the side of nature, of being greater and more, and that in a degree which exceeds all computation. I mean that the contrivances of nature surpass the contrivances of art, in the complexity, subtlety, and curiosity of the mechanism; and still more, if possible, do they go beyond them in number and variety; yet, in a multitude of cases, are not less evidently mechanical, not less evidently contrivances, not less evidently accommodated to their end, or suited to their office, than are the most perfect productions of human ingenuity.

I know no better method of introducing so large a subject, than that of comparing a single thing with a single thing; an eye, for example, with a telescope. As far as the examination of the instrument goes, there is precisely the same proof that the eye was made for vision, as there is that the telescope was made for assisting it. They are made upon the same principles; both being adjusted to the laws by which the transmission and refraction of rays of light are regulated. I speak not of the origin of the laws themselves; but such laws being fixed, the construction, in both cases, is adapted to them. For instance; these laws require, in order to produce the same effect, that the rays of light, in passing from water into the eye, should be refracted by a more convex surface, than when it passes out of air into the eye. Accordingly we find that the eye of a fish, in that part of it called the crystalline lens, is much rounder than the eye of terrestrial animals. What plainer manifestation of design can there be than this difference? What could a mathematical-instrument-maker have done more, to show his knowledge of his principle, his application of that knowledge, his suiting of his means to his end; I will not say to display the compass or excellence of his skill and art, for in these all comparison is indecorous, but to testify counsel, choice, consideration, purpose?

CHAPTER 7

The Fine-Tuning Argument

Peter van Inwagen

The Design Argument looks at the beauty and order in the world and concludes that a creator exists. In this selection, Peter van Inwagen (1942–) presents this argument in its most challenging form. Life as we know it originated from millions of years of evolution, fueled by energy from the sun. Scientists tell us that, had the laws of physics governing that process been ever so slightly different, life could never have evolved, and rational creatures like us would never have existed. Thus, it appears as if the laws of physics were "fine-tuned" to make life possible—and a fine-tuner is an intelligent creator.

Peter van Inwagen is John Cardinal O'Hara Professor of Philosophy at the University of Notre Dame. He has written several books, including *God, Knowledge and Mystery* (1995) and *The Problem of Evil* (2006).

Our present picture of the cosmos has two main components: our picture of the nature of the elementary particles that make up the cosmos and the forces by which they interact (supplied by physics) and our picture of the large-scale structure and the history of the cosmos, from the Big Bang to the present (supplied by cosmology). These two components form a very tightly integrated whole. Each of these components involves a lot of numbers. The description of the particles and the forces, for example, involves a number called the fine-structure

Source: Peter van Inwagen, *Metaphysics* (Boulder, CO: Westview Press, 1993), pp. 129–136, 138–145. Notes have been omitted. Copyright © 2008 Peter van Inwagen. Reprinted by permission of Westview Press, a member of the Perseus Books Group.

constant, which relates to the way in which electrically charged particles interact with the electromagnetic field. Other constants have to do with other kinds of interaction, such as gravity and special interactions that take place at very short range between some kinds of elementary particles. The description of the large-scale structure of the cosmos involves numbers like the number of elementary particles that belong to each "family" of particles allowed by theory. Lots of the numbers that are needed to describe the cosmos cannot be predicted theoretically. They are numbers that, as the physicists say, "have to be filled in by hand." That is, their values have to be established by the laborious process of measurement and experiment. There seems to be no necessity in the values that these numbers actually have. Therefore, it looks as if there are perfectly possible cosmoi (the plural of 'cosmos') in which these numbers are different, and we can ask what those possible cosmoi would be like. And, because our present picture of the world is so precise and unified, we can often answer such questions. There is quite a lot that can be said in answer to a question like, What features would the cosmos have if the fine-structure constant had twice its actual value?

The interesting thing about the answers to these questions is that it appears that if the cosmos were much different at all, there would be no life (and therefore no rational animals). Small changes in various of these numbers would result in a cosmos that lasted only a few seconds or in which there were no atoms or in which there were only hydrogen and helium atoms or in which all matter was violently radioactive or in which there were no stars. In no cosmos of these sorts could there be life, and, as a consequence, in no cosmos of these sorts could there be human beings or any other rational animals. (And there are many, many other ways in which small changes in certain of the numbers that describe the features of the cosmos would produce a cosmos that was inimical to life.)

Suppose we fancifully think for a moment of the cosmos as the product of a machine designed to produce cosmoi. The machine has a largish number of dials on it, perhaps twenty or thirty, and the overall features of the cosmos are the result of the ways the dials were set when the cosmos was produced. If they had been set in other positions, a different type of cosmos would have emerged from the machine. It seems to be the lesson of modern physics and cosmology that *many* statements like the following ones will be true: 'The pointer on dial 18 is set at .0089578346198711. If it had not been set at some value between .0089578346198709 and .0089578346198712, there would be no carbon atoms and hence no life'; 'The pointer on dial 23 is set at 5.113446 and the pointer on dial 5 is set at 5.113449; if the values of the two readings had been exactly equal, there would have been no matter, but only radiation; if the two readings had differed by more than .000006, all stars would be of a type that would burn out before multicellular organisms could evolve on their planets.

The suggestive metaphor of a cosmos-producing machine with lots of dials on it that must be very precisely set if the machine is to produce a cosmos that could contain life (notice, by the way, that we say 'could contain' and not 'will necessarily produce') has led some writers to say that the cosmos is "fine-tuned" in such a way as to enable it to contain life. Only a vanishingly small proportion of the totality of possible cosmoi are suitable abodes for life, and yet the actual cosmos is one of these very few (in fact, not only is it a suitable abode for life, but it actually contains life; in fact, not only does it actually contain life, but it contains life that is rational; these features make it an even rarer specimen among the total of possible cosmoi than a mere "life-permitting" cosmos; how *much* rarer is hard to say, but our present presuppositions about the emergence of life and the mechanisms of evolution say, in effect, "Not all that much rarer"). Why is the cosmos one of the few possible cosmoi that permit life? Why does the cosmos appear to have been fine-tuned by someone who had life in mind? Why are the numbers right for life?

One answer to these questions is provided by the so-called teleological argument. Late in the thirteenth century, Saint Thomas Aquinas presented the following argument for the existence of God:

> We observe that things that have no knowledge—objects that we find in the natural world, for example—sometimes act for an end. (That this is so is proved by the fact that they always, or nearly always, behave in the same way, and this way is the way that will lead to the best result. It is evident from this that their behaving in these ways is due not to chance but to design.) But a thing that has no knowledge cannot act for an end unless it is directed by a being that has knowledge and intelligence, as an arrow is directed by an archer. There is, therefore, some intelligent being who directs all of those things in the natural world that act for an end, and we call this being God.

This argument has been variously called the teleological argument (from the Greek *telos,* meaning an end or goal), the argument from design ("due not to chance but to design"), and the analogical argument (because it proceeds by drawing an analogy between the apparently goal-directed behavior of things in the natural world—birds flying south for the winter or the leaves of a phototropic plant turning toward the sun—and the behavior of things designed or controlled by human begins: "as an arrow is directed by an archer").

It is commonly held that the teleological argument has been refuted by the Darwinian account of evolution—indeed by the very existence of the Darwinian account, whether or not we know it to be true. And this may very well be so if we take the scope of the argument to be limited to living organisms (that is, to those objects in the natural world whose features the Darwinian theory gives an account of). But what of the cosmos as a whole? If the cosmos is a very special cosmos among all possible cosmoi, and if it has every appearance of being a cosmos that has been designed to be an abode for life, might not the most obvious explanation of this appearance be that the appearance is reality? Might not the most obvious explanation of the fine-tuning of the cosmos be that it has *been* fine-tuned? That its large-scale features (if no others) have been carefully chosen and put into place by a conscious, purposive being who wanted to make an abode for living things? And if a conscious, purposive being designed the cosmos to be an abode for living things, and if, as we know it does, the cosmos also contains rational beings like ourselves—rational animals—is it not reasonable to infer further that the existence of those rational beings is a part of the purposes of the Designer (who is, after all, also a rational being and may therefore be presumed to take a special interest in rational beings)?

If the existence of rational animals was intended by the Designer of the cosmos, the rational animals have a purpose. Their purpose is to be found in the intentions of the Designer, and to discover the purpose of rational animals one need only discover what the Designer's intentions were in bringing them into existence. It is important to realize that if this argument shows that rational animals exist for a purpose, it gives us no clue whatever as to what that purpose is. It is plain enough that we may know that something has a purpose without having any idea what that purpose might be. Many artifacts dug up by archaeologists obviously have a purpose, but what their purpose *is* is often a subject of interminable debate. . . .

It is consistent with the conclusion of the teleological argument that the Designer's purposes be analogous to a scientist's (we are part of a vast experiment) or a dramatist's ("All the world's a stage," in a sense that is uncomfortably close to the literal). Neither of these purposes would be possible for God: He does not need to conduct experiments, since, being omniscient, He knows how they would turn out without having to conduct them; being loving and good, He would not employ self-aware, flesh-and-blood beings for purely aesthetic purposes—all the more so because He would see all possible dramas laid out simultaneously and in their entirety in the infinite theater of His mind and could therefore have no reason for wanting to watch the actual performance of any play.

The teleological argument, therefore, does not claim to prove the existence of a being that is all-powerful or all-knowing or recognizes any moral obligations toward the rational beings whose existence it is responsible for. A moment's reflection will show that it cannot claim to prove the existence of a being that is infinite or necessarily existent or eternal. (As to eternity, it may be, for all the teleological argument can claim to show, that the Designer has been outlasted by its cosmos, just as the pharaohs have been outlasted by their pyramids.) It is consistent with the conclusion of the teleological argument that the creation of the cosmos was a cooperative endeavor involving the labors of many beings, like the construction of a ship by human beings. For all the teleological argument can claim to show, it may not only be that the cosmos is the work of many beings but also that these beings have to learn to build cosmoi by trial and error; it may be that somewhere outside our ken there are lying about a lot of "botched and bungled" cosmoi that represent their earlier and less successful attempts at a working cosmos; it may be that *our* cosmos is an "early draft" and that various of its more unfortunate features like disease and parasitism and natural disasters are due to their not yet having fully mastered the craft of cosmos building.

Let all this be granted, however, and it still seems to be true that the teleological argument does show that we should think of rational animals in a way somewhat like the way in which we should think of a cache of mysterious artifacts unearthed by an archaeologist: We may not know what their purpose is, but it is clear that they do have a purpose; they exist because some designers—known to us only through their productions—made them to fulfill that unknown purpose. . . .

The conclusion of the teleological argument seems to imply that we serve some purpose and that our existence therefore has a meaning. But does the teleological argument prove its conclusion—that the cosmos is the product of design and not of chance or necessity— or does it at least make that conclusion more reasonable to believe than not? How might those who deny that the cosmos is a product of design reply to the teleological argument?

There are several replies that are of little or no value and one that seems to me to be decisive.

Some philosophers have argued that there is nothing in the fact that the universe is fine-tuned that should be the occasion for any surprise. After all (the objection runs), if a machine has dials, the dials have to be set *some* way, and any particular setting is as unlikely as any other. Since any setting of the dials is as unlikely as any other, there can be nothing more surprising about the actual setting of the dials, whatever it may be, than there would be about any possible setting of the dials if that possible setting were the actual setting. (Here is a parallel argument. If you toss a coin and it comes up "heads" twenty times in a row, you shouldn't be surprised. After all, you wouldn't be surprised if the sequence HHTTHTHTTTHTHHTTHTHT occurred, and that sequence and the sequence HHHHHHHHHHHHHHHHHHHH both have exactly the same probability of occurring: 1 in 1,048,576, or about .000000954.) This reasoning is sometimes combined with the point that if "our" numbers hadn't been set into the cosmic dials, the equally improbable setting that did occur would have differed from the actual setting mainly in that there would have been no one there to wonder at its improbability.

This must be one of the most annoyingly obtuse arguments in the history of philosophy. Let us press the "parallel" argument a bit. Suppose that you are in a situation in which you must draw a straw from a bundle of 1,048,576 straws of different length and in which it has been decreed that if you don't draw the shortest straw in the bundle you will be instantly and painlessly killed: you will be killed so fast that you won't have time to realize that you didn't draw the shortest straw. Reluctantly—but you have no alternative—you draw a straw and are astonished to find yourself alive and holding the shortest straw. What should you conclude?

In the absence of further information, only one conclusion is reasonable. Contrary to appearances, you did *not* draw the straw at random; the whole situation in which you find yourself is some kind of "set-up"; the bundle was somehow rigged to ensure that the straw that you drew was the shortest one. The following argument to the contrary is simply silly. "Look, you had to draw some straw or other. Drawing the shortest was no more unlikely than drawing the 256,057th-shortest: the probability in either case was .000000954. But your drawing the 256,057th-shortest straw isn't an outcome that would suggest a 'set-up' or would suggest the need for any sort of explanation, and, therefore, drawing the shortest shouldn't suggest the need for an explanation either. The only real difference between the two cases is that you wouldn't have been around to remark on the unlikelihood of drawing the 256,057th-shortest straw."

It is one thing, however, to note that an argument is silly and another thing to say why it is silly. But an explanation is not hard to come by. The argument is silly because it violates the following principle:

> Suppose that there is a certain fact that has no known explanation; suppose that one can think of a possible explanation of that fact, an explanation that (if only it were true) would be a very *good* explanation; then it is wrong to say that that event stands in no more need of an explanation than an otherwise similar event for which no such explanation is available.

My drawing the shortest straw out of a bundle of over a million straws in a situation in which my life depends on my drawing just that straw certainly suggests a possible explanation. If an audience were to observe my drawing the shortest straw, they would very justifiably conclude that I had somehow "cheated": they would conclude that I had had some way of knowing which straw was the shortest and that (to save my life) I had deliberately drawn it. (If I know that I *didn't* know which straw was the shortest—if I am just as astounded as anyone in the audience at my drawing the shortest straw—then the situation will not suggest *to me* that particular explanation of my drawing the shortest straw, but it will suggest the one that I have already mentioned, namely that some unknown benefactor has rigged the drawing in my favor.) But if an audience were to observe my drawing the 256,057th-shortest straw (and my consequent immediate demise), this would not suggest *any* explanation to them: no one would suppose—nor would it be reasonable for anyone to suppose—that I knew which straw was the 256,057th-shortest and that I deliberately drew it; nor would anyone suppose that someone had rigged the drawing to ensure my getting the 256,057th-shortest straw; nor would any other possible explanation come to anyone's mind.

We have seen that the setting of the cosmic dials does suggest an explanation: the dials were so set by a rational being who wanted the cosmos to be a suitable abode for other rational beings. Therefore, those critics of the teleological argument who say that one setting of the cosmic dials is no more remarkable than any other possible setting are certainly mistaken. We should note that our principle does not say that if one can think of a really good explanation for some fact, one should automatically assume that that explanation is correct; the principle says only that in such cases it would be a mistake simply to assume that that fact required no explanation. . . .

Another possible reply to the teleological argument is to protest that even if the universe has been purposely fine-tuned, it does not follow that it was fine-tuned in order that creatures like ourselves should exist. Perhaps the Designer who carefully adjusted the value of the fine-structure constant and the relative strengths of gravity and the strong nuclear force and many other parameters to astonishingly exact values had *something* in mind for its carefully designed cosmos, but the fact that the cosmos is a suitable abode for rational beings was entirely irrelevant to its purposes. Perhaps we are, so to speak, the mice in the walls of the cosmos. If the mice that lived in the walls of a house were capable of contemplating such matters, they might, after a careful examination of the whole structure of the house, conclude—correctly, of course—that the house was designed for a purpose by a rational being. And they might naturally, but incorrectly, proceed to conclude that it had been designed to be an abode for *them.* (The spaces between the walls are just right for mice, there is lots of food lying about that is nourishing for mice, the house is comfortable for mice even in the dead of winter, and so on. But no doubt the theologians among them would be profoundly troubled by the Problem of the Cat.)

Now this objection is not, properly speaking, an objection to the teleological argument as such (the conclusion of which is that the cosmos was designed by a rational being or beings), but to the secondary conclusion that we drew from the existence of a Designer: that among the Designer's purposes in making the cosmos was to provide an abode for rational beings like ourselves. This secondary conclusion, however, seems to me to be very reasonable, given that the cosmos is a product of intelligent design. The analogy of "the mice within the walls" is defective in several important respects. The properties of mice were "settled" by evolution long before there were houses, and houses just happen to be suitable for infestation by creatures having those properties. There are so many species that it would be surprising if there were not a few that were suited for living within the walls of houses. House mice exist independently of the houses they inhabit, and they infest houses because it happens that houses are suited for them. Houses are not infested by sheep (except in one episode of "Monty Python's Flying Circus") or even by rabbits because the interiors of houses are not suited for occupation by sheep and rabbits. (It is no wonder that the spaces between the walls of a house are just right for mice: the mice would not have moved in if they were not.) If mice had evolved inside houses, and if the slightest change in the design of a house would have the consequence of rendering it uninhabitable by living things, and if houses had been designed by enormous rational mice, the analogy between the two cases would be much closer. But, it seems to me, if we knew all of these things to be true, it would be at least very reasonable for us to conclude that the enormous mice *had* designed houses as abodes for common-or-pantry-variety mice.

I will now turn to a reply to the teleological argument that I believe to be decisive. I said earlier that the common belief that the teleological argument had been refuted by the Darwinian account of evolution (or even by the *possible* truth of this account) was mistaken. It was mistaken because evolution is a phenomenon that occurs only within the realm of living things (or at least of self-reproducing things) and the version of the teleological argument we have been examining applies to the cosmos as a whole. And the cosmos is not a living thing or a self-reproducing thing: it is not the product of the operation of natural selection on ancestral cosmoi that reproduced themselves with variations in an environment that contained limited amounts of the resources needed for cosmic survival and reproduction. Nevertheless, the Darwinian account of evolution does have a feature that can be adapted to the needs of the present discussion. Darwin showed how it was possible, in certain circumstances, for chance to produce results that one might be initially inclined to ascribe to the purposive action of rational beings; some of the ideas on which this demonstration rests are so simple and general that they can be lifted out of the biological context in which Darwin applied them and applied to the apparent design exhibited by the cosmos.

An example will illustrate these ideas. Suppose that each of the citizens of Wormsley Glen has a job; and suppose that each of them has an alarm clock; and suppose that each alarm clock goes off at just the right time each day to enable its owner to get up and get to work on time. For example, Alice's clock goes off at 5:36 each morning, and if it went off even a few minutes later she would frequently be late for work; as it is, she breezes into the office just under the wire every day. And Tim's clock goes off at 6:07, which is just right for letting him sleep as late as possible and still get to work on time. (And so on and so on, for every citizen of Wormsley Glen. They all have clocks that enable them to arise at the optimum time, given the time they are expected at work, the amount of time they need to deal with their morning domestic chores, the amount of time they need to travel to work, and whatever other factors in their lives may be relevant to the times at which they have to get up in the morning.)

Here, we might suppose, is an obvious case of purposive design: on the back of each of the alarm clocks there is a little knob or something that regulates the time at which the alarm rings, and all of the citizens have calculated the times at which they have to get up and have set their individual alarms accordingly. But this is not so. The real explanation is different and rather unpleasant. Not so long ago there were hundreds of times as many people in Wormsley Glen as there are today. Each of them was issued an alarm clock that was unchangeably set to go off at some particular time each day, and no returns or trading allowed. The alarm settings were in every case entirely random, and this had just the consequence you would expect: almost every alarm was set wrong (that is, was set for a time that was not the time at which its owner needed to get up), and these wrong settings, owing to the laissez-faire economic system that prevailed in Wormsley Glen, had disastrous consequences for their owners. Sally's was set for 11:23 A.M., and she was, as a consequence, consistently late for work and lost her job and starved to death. Frank's was set for 4:11 A.M., and, once it had gone off, he could either go back to sleep and be late for work or stay up and try to deal with the demands of his job (he was a brain surgeon) without having had a good night's sleep. He chose the latter course, but his being chronically short of sleep led him to make a few serious mistakes, and he had to be let go; shortly thereafter, he starved to death.

And that is what happened to everyone in Wormsley Glen who was issued a "bad" alarm clock. (Even those whose clocks were set just slightly wrong lost their competitive edge and were forced out of their jobs by more punctual and better-rested rivals.) Wormsley Glen is no welfare state, and they're all dead of starvation now. Knowing this to be the case we can see that there is no conscious purpose behind the setting of Alice's or Tim's alarms. Each of them received an alarm clock that *just happened* to be set at the "right" time, and each of them therefore survived. And this is what happened with all of the other citizens of Wormsley Glen. It was statistically likely that a certain percentage of the original inhabitants would, simply by the luck of the draw, receive clocks that were set at the time that was right for them. And that is what happened: a certain not-at-all-surprising proportion of the original inhabitants got clocks that were set at the right time, and the unforgiving social arrangements of Wormsley Glen removed everyone else from the picture. . . .

In our story of Wormsley Glen, chance produced a large number of actual "alarm-clock situations," and the grim necessities of

Wormsley Glen then proceeded to eliminate from actuality all of them but a few that closely resembled the alarm-clock situations that a rational being would have chosen from among possible alarm-clock situations to be actual. As rationality decides which possibilities are to be actual, so a non-rational cosmos or nature may decide which actualities . . . are to remain actual.

According to Darwin, chance and nature have combined in just this way—but there are a few factors peculiar to the evolutionary process that are not represented in the schema laid out in the preceding paragraph—to produce the appearance of conscious design in living organisms. Chance produces random inheritable variations among the offspring of an organism, and nature (which, like Wormsley Glen, is no welfare state) tends to favor the preservation of those variations that contribute to an organism's ability to have descendants. The appearance of design in organisms is due to the accumulation of such useful (useful for having descendants) variations. Organisms are adapted to their environments—to the extent that they *are* adapted to their environments; adaptation is often imperfect—owing to the fact that the better adapted an organism is to its environment, the more likely it is to have descendants. It will be noted that our "alarm clock" story includes only some of the features of the Darwinian account of apparent design in living things: those that do not involve reproduction and inheritability. . . .

It is the possibility of an interplay of chance and an observational selection effect that is the undoing of the teleological argument in the form in which we are considering it. In our initial statement of the teleological argument, we asked the following question: "Might not the most obvious explanation of the fine-tuning of the cosmos be that it has *been* fine-tuned?" If the answer to this question is No, then the teleological argument fails. And the answer to this question is No if there is even one other explanation of the fine-tuning of the cosmos that is at least as good as the explanation that it has been fine-tuned. And another explanation, one at least as good, is available: an explanation that appeals to the interplay of chance and an observational selection effect.

The alternative explanation goes like this. First, the cosmos is only one among a vast number of *actual* cosmoi. (If there are people who insist on using 'the cosmos' as a name for the whole of physical reality, we could accommodate them by saying instead that what appears to us to be the whole of the cosmos is in reality a very small *part* of the cosmos. The difference between the two statements seems to me to be merely verbal. I shall continue to talk of a multitude of cosmoi, and anyone who does not like my way of talking can easily translate it into talk of a multitude of parts of the one cosmos.)

These cosmoi exhibit a vast number of "cosmos-designs." To see what is intended by this statement, think of our cosmos-designing machine as containing a randomizing device. The randomizing device sets the dials on the machine at random. The machine turns out a cosmos. Then the randomizing device resets the dials and the machine turns out another cosmos, and so on through a very large number of resettings. Alternatively, we could suppose that there were an enormous number of cosmos-producing machines on each of which the dials were set at random and that each machine turned out one cosmos. (Compare the alarm clocks issued to the citizens of Wormsley Glen.) Since the dial settings are random, and since the existence of life is allowed by hardly any of the possible combinations of settings, only a very small proportion of these cosmoi will be suitable abodes for life. Most of them will last only a few seconds or will contain no protons or will contain no atoms or will contain only hydrogen and helium atoms or will be composed entirely of violently radioactive matter or will be devoid of stars or will contain only stars of a kind that would burn out before evolution could get started on their planets.

We suppose, however, that there are so *many* actual cosmoi that it is statistically unsurprising that there are a few of them that are possible abodes for life and in fact that it is statistically unsurprising that there are a few that actually contain life. The total number of cosmoi needed to render unsurprising the existence of even a few cosmoi that were suitable abodes for life would be enormous: perhaps comparable to the number of elementary particles in "our" cosmos, perhaps vastly greater than that. (It is hard to think of a reason to suppose that the number of actual cosmoi would have to be finite. If the number of cosmoi were infinite, it would certainly not be surprising that some of them were suitable abodes for life.)

There are various conceivable mechanisms that are more realistic than our imaginary cosmos-producing machine that might generate an appropriate variety of cosmoi. In [an earlier chapter], we considered the possibility that the cosmos might have arisen as a fluctuation in some pre-cosmic analogue of the quantum field. Let us, following Milton, refer to this analogue as Chaos and Old Night—Chaos for short. Chaos is a sort of arena in which random fluctuations occur. A very few among these fluctuations are impressive enough to be called cosmoi. We suppose that the cosmoi that arise in Chaos do not resemble one another as closely as the bubbles in a pot of boiling porridge resemble one another. The differences among them—which, we must remember, are the products of chance—are, or can be, of the radical kind that we should describe as differences in the laws of physics and large-scale cosmic structure: different values of the fine-structure constant, different ratios of the strength of the strong nuclear force to the strength of gravity, different numbers of electrons, and so on. And, finally, a very few of the cosmoi have just the right properties to be possible abodes for life.

One might raise the question where Chaos came from or why it is "there" at all, but that is a question that relates to the cosmological rather than to the teleological argument. One might also raise the question why Chaos has properties that fit it for being a generator of random cosmoi. . . . This is a question that is relevant to the teleological argument. If there were a large number of "possible chaoses" and only a very few of them had the right properties to be random cosmos generators, then we should have made no progress in appealing to Chaos in our attempt to deal with the teleological argument.

Since we know next to nothing that is relevant to this question, let us simply stipulate that the properties of Chaos are determined by "the laws of hyperphysics" and that there is only one possible set of laws of hyperphysics. (In one sense, the laws of hyperphysics would be the real laws of physics. What we normally think of as the laws of physics would not really be laws, since they would not apply to the whole of physical reality. They would be mere descriptions of local regularities.) It is important to remember in this connection that we are not attempting to construct an explanation for the apparent design of the cosmos that is known to be correct, but only an explanation that is at least as good as the hypothesis that the cosmos was designed by a rational being. And an explanation will be at least as good as that explanation if it contains no element that is known on independent grounds to be false or improbable—for that (together with the fact that it does explain the observed phenomenon of the fine-tuning of the cosmos) is really all that can be said in favor of the hypothesis of rational design.

The final part of our alternative explanation of apparent cosmic design takes the form of an appeal to an observational selection effect: we cannot observe the cosmoi that are unsuitable for life. We cannot observe them because something restricts the scope of our observations to our own cosmos—the space-time curvature of our cosmos, or the simple fact that everything that is not a part of our cosmos is just too far away for us to see, or some other factor. And any rational beings that there may be anywhere in the macrocosm (so to call the aggregate of all the cosmoi) will be in the same position as we. The members of every rational species anywhere in the macrocosm will be able to observe only the "insides" of their own cosmos. It will look to them as if they inhabited a cosmos that was both carefully designed to be an abode for life (it will have to be suitable for life, since they are in it) and unique (since they can't see any of the others). But this will be appearance rather than reality. It will be the result of the interplay between chance and an observational selection effect.

We can gain some insight into the way this reply to the teleological argument works if we look again at the case in which you would have been killed if you had not drawn the shortest straw from a bundle of 1,048,576 straws. You were (you remember) astonished to find that, lo and behold, you had drawn the shortest straw and were still there to be astonished. I said that the most reasonable thing for you to conclude would be that some unknown benefactor had rigged the drawing in your favor. And this is true provided that you know that your situation is unique. But suppose that you knew that your situation was not unique. Suppose that you knew that you were only one among many millions of people who had been placed in a situation in which they had to draw the shortest straw from a bundle of 1,048,576 or else be instantly killed. In that case the most reasonable hypothesis would not be that an unknown benefactor had rigged the drawing in your favor. The most reasonable hypothesis would be that you were just lucky.

If someone tosses a coin exactly twenty times, and if there is no other occasion on which someone tosses a coin twenty or more times, it is most improbable that anyone will *ever* toss a coin "heads" twenty times in a row: the chances are 1 in 1,048,576. If millions of people toss a coin twenty times, it is likely that someone will toss "heads" twenty times in a row. If millions of millions of people toss a coin twenty times, it is a virtual certainty that someone will toss "heads" twenty times in a row. The odds are, of course, the same with respect to drawing the shortest straw from a bundle of 1,048,576 straws. If you draw the shortest straw from a bundle of that size, and if you know that millions of millions of other people have been drawing straws from a bundle of that size, you should reason as follows: "It was all but inevitable that a fair number of people would draw the shortest straw. Luckily for me, I happened to be one of that number." But if you draw the shortest straw and know that you were the only one engaged in such a drawing, you cannot reason this way, for you will know that it was *not* all but inevitable that a fair number of people would draw the shortest straw; on the contrary, you will know that it was all but inevitable that *no one* would draw the shortest straw. It is for that reason that you will have to turn to the alternative hypothesis that someone has rigged the drawing in your favor.

Now given our everyday knowledge of the world, it would never be reasonable for one to believe that millions of millions of other people were in circumstances that almost exactly duplicated one's own, and this would be true with a vengeance if one's circumstances were as bizarre as those laid out in the "straw-drawing" story. But suppose that the conditions of human life were very different from what they actually are. Suppose that you were in the circumstances of the hero of the straw-drawing story and that *for all you knew* there were millions of millions of people in the same circumstances. Suppose that, as far as your knowledge went, the following two hypotheses were about equally probable:

- This is the only drawing, and someone has rigged it in my favor.
- This is only one among millions of millions of such drawings, in some of which the short straw is drawn.

What could you say then? Only this: that you didn't know whether you had an unobserved benefactor or whether you were "surrounded" by millions of millions of such drawings.

This, I believe, is exactly analogous to our situation with respect to the fine-tuning of the cosmos. As far as our present knowledge goes (aside from any divine revelation that certain individuals or groups may be privy to) we have to regard the following two hypotheses as equally probable:

- This is the only cosmos, and some rational being has (or rational beings have) fine-tuned it in such a way that it is a suitable abode for life.
- This is only one among a vast number of cosmoi, some few of which are suitable abodes for life.

We do not know whether the apparently purposive fine-tuning of the cosmos is reality or mere appearance, a product of chance and an observational selection effect. The fine-tuning of the cosmos that has been pretty well established by modern physics and cosmology does, however, make one thing clear: the cosmos does not exist on its own. There is something that accounts for the fact that we observe a cosmos that has very specific features (those required for the existence of life) and, presumably, accounts for the existence of that cosmos as well. . . .

CHAPTER 8

*W*hy Doesn't God Intervene?

B. C. Johnson

Why does God allow so much suffering? One possibility is that God doesn't exist. This is the line taken in the argument from evil, a long-standing thorn in the side of religious belief. In this chapter from *The Atheist Debater's Handbook*, B. C. Johnson presents a version of the argument from evil. He asks why God won't do what we expect any good fire department to do—namely, to save children from burning to death.

We don't know who wrote this essay; "B. C. Johnson" is a pen name.

Here is a common situation: a house catches on fire and a six-month-old baby is painfully burned to death. Could we possibly describe as "good" any person who had the power to save this child and yet refused to do so? God undoubtedly has this power and yet in many cases of this sort he has refused to help. Can we call God "good"? Are there adequate excuses for his behavior?

First, it will not do to claim that the baby will go to heaven. It was either necessary for the baby to suffer or it was not. If it was not, then it was wrong to allow it. The child's ascent to heaven does not change this fact. If it was necessary, the fact that the baby will go to heaven does not explain why it was necessary, and we are still left without an excuse for God's inaction.

Source: Chapter XII, "God and the Problem of Evil," B. C. Johnson, *The Atheist Debater's Handbook* (Amherst, NY: Prometheus Books, 1983), pp. 99–108. Copyright © 1981 by B. C. Johnson. All rights reserved. Reprinted with permission of the publisher.

It is not enough to say that the baby's painful death would in the long run have good results and therefore should have happened, otherwise God would not have permitted it. For if we know this to be true, then we know—just as God knows—that every action successfully performed must in the end be good and therefore the right thing to do, otherwise God would not have allowed it to happen. We could deliberately set houses ablaze to kill innocent people and if successful we would then know we had a duty to do it. A defense of God's goodness which takes as its foundation duties known only after the fact would result in a morality unworthy of the name. Furthermore, this argument does not explain why God allowed the child to burn to death. It merely claims that there is some reason discoverable in the long run. But the belief that such a reason is within our grasp must rest upon the additional belief that God is good. This is just to counter evidence against such a belief by assuming the belief to be true. It is not unlike a lawyer defending his client by claiming that the client is innocent and therefore the evidence against him must be misleading—that proof vindicating the defendant will be found in the long run. No jury of reasonable men and women would accept such a defense and the theist cannot expect a more favorable outcome.

The theist often claims that man has been given free will so that if he accidentally or purposefully causes fires, killing small children, it is his fault alone. Consider a bystander who had nothing to do with starting the fire but who refused to help even though he could have saved the child with no harm to himself. Could such a bystander be called good? Certainly not. If we would not consider a mortal human being good under these circumstances, what grounds could we possibly have for continuing to assert the goodness of an all-powerful God?

The suggestion is sometimes made that it is best for us to face disasters without assistance, otherwise we would become dependent on an outside power for aid. Should we then abolish modern medical care or do away with efficient fire departments? Are we not dependent on their help? Is it not the case that their presence transforms us into soft, dependent creatures? The vast majority are not physicians or firemen. These people help in their capacity as professional outside sources of aid in much the same way that we would expect God to be helpful. Theists refer to aid from firemen and physicians as cases of man helping himself. In reality, it is a tiny minority of men helping a great many. We can become just as dependent on them as we can on God. Now the existence of this kind of outside help is either wrong or right. If it is right, then God should assist those areas of the world which do not have this kind of help. In fact, throughout history, such help has not been available. If aid ought to have been provided, then God should have provided it. On the other hand, if it is wrong to provide this kind of assistance, then we should abolish the aid altogether. But we obviously do not believe it is wrong.

Similar considerations apply to the claim that if God interferes in disasters, he would destroy a considerable amount of moral urgency to make things right. Once again, note that such institutions as modern medicine and fire departments are relatively recent. They function irrespective of whether we as individuals feel any moral urgency to support them. To the extent that they help others, opportunities to feel moral urgency are destroyed because they reduce the number of cases which appeal to us for help. Since we have not always had such institutions, there must have been a time when there was greater moral urgency than there is now. If such a situation is morally desirable, then we should abolish modern medical care and fire departments. If the situation is not morally desirable, then God should have remedied it.

Besides this point, we should note that God is represented as one who tolerates disasters, such as infants burning to death, in order to create moral urgency. It follows that God approves of these disasters as a means to encourage the creation of moral urgency. Furthermore, if there were no such disasters occurring, God would have to see to it that they occur. If it so happened that we lived in a world in which babies never perished in burning houses, God would be morally obliged to take an active hand in setting fire to houses with infants in them. In fact, if the frequency of infant mortality due to fire should happen to fall below a level necessary for the creation of maximum moral urgency in our real world, God would be justified in setting a few fires of his own. This may well be happening right now, for there is no guarantee that the maximum number of infant deaths necessary for moral urgency are occurring.

All of this is of course absurd. If I see an opportunity to create otherwise nonexistent opportunities for moral urgency by burning an infant or two, then I should *not* do so. But if it is good to maximize moral urgency, then I *should* do so. Therefore, it is not good to maximize moral urgency. Plainly we do not in general believe that it is a good thing to maximize moral urgency. The fact that we approve of modern medical care and applaud medical advances is proof enough of this.

The theist may point out that in a world without suffering there would be no occasion for the production of such virtues as courage, sympathy, and the like. This may be true, but the atheist need not demand a world without suffering. He need only claim that there is suffering which is in excess of that needed for the production of various virtues. For example, God's active attempts to save six-month-old infants from fires would not in itself create a world without suffering. But no one could sincerely doubt that it would improve the world.

The two arguments against the previous theistic excuse apply here also. "Moral urgency" and "building virtue" are susceptible to the same criticisms. It is worthwhile to emphasize, however, that we encourage efforts to eliminate evils; we approve of efforts to promote peace, prevent famine, and wipe out disease. In other words, we do value a world with fewer or (if possible) no opportunities for the development of virtue (when "virtue" is understood to mean the reduction of suffering). If we produce such a world for succeeding generations, how will they develop virtues? Without war, disease, and famine, they will not be virtuous. Should we then cease our attempts to wipe out war, disease, and famine? If we do not believe that it is right to cease attempts at improving the world, then by implication we admit that virtue-building is not an excuse for God to permit disasters. For we admit that the development of virtue is no excuse for permitting disasters.

It might be said that God allows innocent people to suffer in order to deflate man's ego so that the latter will not be proud of his apparently deserved good fortune. But this excuse succumbs to the arguments used against the preceding excuses and we need discuss them no further.

Theists may claim that evil is a necessary by-product of the laws of nature and therefore it is irrational for God to interfere every time a disaster happens. Such a state of affairs would alter the whole causal order and we would then find it impossible to predict anything. But the death of a child caused by an electrical fire could have been prevented by a miracle and no one would ever have known. Only a minor alteration in electrical equipment would have been necessary. A very large disaster could have been avoided simply by producing in Hitler a miraculous heart attack—and no one would have known it was a miracle. To argue that continued miraculous intervention by God would be wrong is like insisting that one should never use salt because ingesting five pounds of it would be fatal. No one is requesting that God interfere all of the time. He should, however, intervene to prevent especially horrible disasters. Of course, the question arises: where does one draw the line? Well, certainly the line should be drawn somewhere this side of infants burning to death. To argue that we do not know where the line should be drawn is no excuse for failing to interfere in those instances that would be called clear cases of evil.

It will not do to claim that evil exists as a necessary contrast to good so that we might know what good is. A very small amount of evil, such as a toothache, would allow that. It is not necessary to destroy innocent human beings.

The claim could be made that God has a "higher morality" by which his actions are to be judged. But it is a strange "higher morality" which claims that what we call "bad" is good and what we call "good" is bad. Such a morality can have no meaning to us. It would be like calling black "white" and white "black." In reply the theist may say that God is the wise Father and we are ignorant children. How can we judge God any more than a child is able to judge his parent? It is true that a child may be puzzled by his parents' conduct, but his basis for deciding that their conduct is nevertheless good would be the many instances of good behavior he has observed. Even so, this could be misleading. Hitler, by all accounts, loved animals and children of the proper race; but if Hitler had had a child, this offspring would hardly have been justified in arguing that his father was a good man. At any rate, God's "higher morality," being the opposite of ours, cannot offer any grounds for deciding that he is somehow good.

Perhaps the main problem with the solutions to the problem of evil we have thus far considered is that no matter how convincing they may be in the abstract, they are implausible in certain particular cases. Picture an infant dying in a burning house and then imagine God simply observing from afar. Perhaps God is reciting excuses in his own behalf. As the child succumbs to the smoke and flames, God may be pictured as saying: "Sorry, but if I helped you I would have considerable trouble deflating the ego of your parents. And don't forget I have to keep those laws of nature consistent. And anyway if you weren't dying in that fire, a lot of moral urgency would just go down the drain. Besides, I didn't start this fire, so you can't blame *me*."

It does no good to assert that God may not be all-powerful and thus not able to prevent evil. He can create a universe and yet is conveniently unable to do what the fire department can do—rescue a baby from a burning building. God should at least be as powerful as a man. A man, if he had been at the right place and time, could have killed Hitler. Was this beyond God's abilities? If God knew in 1910 how to produce polio vaccine and if he was able to communicate with somebody, he should have communicated this knowledge. He must be incredibly limited if he could not have managed this modest accomplishment. Such a God if not dead, is the next thing to it. And a person who believes in such a ghost of a God is practically an atheist. To call such a thing a god would be to strain the meaning of the word.

The theist, as usual, may retreat to faith. He may say that he has faith in God's goodness and therefore the Christian Deity's existence has not been disproved. "Faith" is here understood as being much like confidence in a friend's innocence despite the evidence against him. Now in order to have confidence in a friend one must know him well enough to justify faith in his goodness. We cannot have justifiable faith in the supreme goodness of strangers. Moreover, such confidence must come not just from a speaking acquaintance. The friend may continually assure us with his words that he is good but if he does not act like a good person, we would have no reason to trust him. A person who says he has faith in God's goodness is speaking as if he had known God for a long time and during that time had never seen Him do any serious evil. But we know that throughout history God has allowed numerous atrocities to occur. No one can have justifiable faith in the goodness of such a God. This faith would have to be based on a close friendship wherein God was never found to do anything wrong. But a person would have to be blind and deaf to have had such a relationship with God. Suppose a friend of yours had always claimed to be good yet refused to help people when he was in a position to render aid. Could you have justifiable faith in his goodness?

You can of course say that you trust God anyway—that no arguments can undermine your faith. But this is just a statement describing how stubborn you are; it has no bearing whatsoever on the question of God's goodness.

The various excuses theists offer for why God has allowed evil to exist have been demonstrated to be inadequate. However, the conclusive objection to these excuses does not depend on their inadequacy.

First, we should note that every possible excuse making the actual world consistent with the existence of a good God could be used in reverse to make that same world consistent with an evil God. For example, we could say that God is evil and that he allows free will so that we can freely do evil things, which would make us more truly evil than we would be if forced to perform evil acts. Or we could say that natural disasters occur in order to make people more selfish and bitter, for most people tend to have a "me-first" attitude in a disaster (note, for example, stampedes to leave burning buildings). Even though some people achieve virtue from disasters, this outcome is necessary if persons are to react freely to disaster—necessary if the development of moral degeneracy is to continue freely. But, enough; the point is made. Every excuse we could provide to make the world consistent with a good God can be paralleled by an excuse to make the world consistent with an evil God. This is so because the world is a mixture of both good and bad.

Now there are only three possibilities concerning God's moral character. Considering the world as it actually is, we may believe: (*a*) that God is more likely to be all evil than he is to be all good; (*b*) that God is less likely to be all evil than he is to be all good; or (*c*) that God is equally as likely to be all evil as he is to be all good. In case (*a*) it would be admitted that God is unlikely to be all good. Case (*b*) cannot be true at all, since—as we have seen—the belief that God is all evil can be justified to precisely the same extent as the belief that God is all good. Case (*c*) leaves us with no reasonable excuses for a good God to permit evil. The reason is as follows: if an excuse is to be a reasonable excuse, the circumstances it identifies as excusing conditions must be actual. For example, if I run over a pedestrian and my excuse is that the brakes failed because someone tampered with them, then the facts had better bear this out. Otherwise the excuse will not hold. Now if case (*c*) is correct and, given the facts of the actual world, God is as likely to be all evil as he is to be all good, then these facts do not support the excuses which could be made for a good God permitting evil. Consider an analogous example. If my excuse for running over the pedestrian is that my brakes were tampered with, and if the actual facts lead us to believe that it is no more likely that they were tampered with than that they were not, the excuse is no longer reasonable. To make good my excuse, I must show that it is a fact or at least highly probable that my brakes were tampered with—not that it is just a possibility. The same point holds for God. His excuse must not be a possible excuse, but an actual one. But case (*c*), in maintaining that it is just as likely that God is all evil as that he is all good, rules this out. For if case (*c*) is true, then the facts of the actual world do not make it any more likely that God is all good than that he is all evil. Therefore, they do not make it any more likely that his excuses are good than that they are not. But, as we have seen, good excuses have a higher probability of being true.

Cases (*a*) and (*c*) conclude that it is unlikely that God is all good, and case (*b*) cannot be true. Since these are the only possible cases, there is no escape from the conclusion that it is unlikely that God is all good. Thus the problem of evil triumphs over traditional theism.

CHAPTER 9

The Problem of Evil

Peter van Inwagen

The greatest problem for traditional religious belief has always been the existence of evil. Why would God allow it? In this selection, Peter van Inwagen (1942–) does not claim to know why God permits evil—he does not offer a "theodicy"—but he does defend belief in God. As the selection begins, the "Atheist" is advancing the Global Argument from Evil, which appeals to the vast amount of horrendous suffering in the world.

God, if he exists, is omniscient, or at the very least, knows as much as we human beings do. He therefore knows at least about the evils of the world we know about, and we know that the world contains a vast amount of evil. Now consider those evils God knows about. Since he's morally perfect, he must desire that these evils not exist—their non-existence must be what he *wants*. And an omnipotent being can achieve or bring about whatever he wants—or at least whatever he wants that is intrinsically possible. And the non-existence of evil, of bad things, is obviously intrinsically possible. So if there were an omnipotent, morally perfect being who knew about the evils we know about—well, they wouldn't have arisen in the first place, for he'd have prevented their occurrence. Or if, for some reason, he didn't do that, he'd certainly remove them the instant they began to exist. But

Source: Peter van Inwagen, *The Problem of Evil* (Oxford University Press, 2006), pp. 64–66, 70–72, 83–90, 95–106, 111. Notes have been omitted. Copyright © 2006 by Peter van Inwagen.

we observe evils, and very long-lasting ones. So we must conclude that God does not exist.

What shall Theist—who grants that the world contains vast amounts of truly horrible evil—say in reply? I think that he should begin with an obvious point about the relations between what one wants, what one can do, and what one will, in the event, do:

I grant that, in some sense of the word, the non-existence of evil must be what a perfectly good being *wants*. But we often don't bring about states of affairs we can bring about and want to bring about. Suppose, for example, that Alice's mother is dying in great pain and that Alice yearns desperately for her mother to die—today and not next week or next month. And suppose it would be easy for Alice to arrange this—she is perhaps a doctor or a nurse and has easy access to pharmaceutical resources that would enable her to achieve this end. Does it follow that she will act on this ability that she has? It is obvious that it does not, for Alice might have *reasons* for not doing what she can do. Two obvious candidates for such reasons are: she thinks it would be morally wrong; she is afraid that her act would be discovered, and that she would be prosecuted for murder. And either of these reasons might be sufficient, in her mind, to outweigh her desire for an immediate end to her mother's sufferings. So it may be that someone has a very strong desire for something and is able to obtain this thing. The conclusion that evil does not exist does not, therefore, follow *logically* from the premise that the non-existence of evil is what God wants and that he is able to bring about the object of his desire—since, for all logic can tell us, God might have reasons for allowing evil to exist that, in his mind, outweigh the desirability of the non-existence of evil.

Theist begins his reply with these words. But he must say a great deal more than this. . . . Before I allow him to do this, however, I will remind you of some terminology. . . .

Suppose I believe both in God and in the real existence of evil. Suppose I think I know what God's reasons for allowing evil to exist are, and that I tell them to you. Then I have presented you with a *theodicy*. If I could present a theodicy, and if the audience to whom I presented it found it convincing, I'd have an effective reply to the argument from evil, at least as regards that particular audience. But suppose that, although I believe in both God and evil, I *don't* claim to know what God's reasons for allowing evil are. Is there any way for someone in my position to reply to the argument from evil? There is. Consider this analogy.

Your friend Clarissa, a single mother, left her two very young children alone in her flat for several hours very late last night. Your Aunt Harriet, a maiden lady of strong moral principles, learns of this and declares that Clarissa is unfit to raise children. You spring to your friend's defense:

"Now, Aunt Harriet, don't go jumping to conclusions. There's probably a perfectly good explanation. Maybe Billy or Annie was ill, and she decided to go over to the clinic for help. You know she hasn't got a phone or a car and no one in that neighborhood of hers would come to the door at two o'clock in the morning." If you tell your Aunt Harriet a story like this, you don't claim to know what Clarissa's reasons for leaving her children alone really were. And you're not claiming to have said anything that shows that Clarissa really is a good mother. You're claiming only to show that the fact Aunt Harriet has adduced doesn't prove that she isn't one; what you're trying to establish is that for all you or Aunt Harriet know, she had some good reason for what she did. And you're not trying to establish only that there is some remote possibility that she had a good reason. No counsel for the defense would try to raise doubts in the minds of the members of a jury by pointing out to them that for all they knew the defendant had an identical twin, of whom all record had been lost, and who was the person who had actually committed the crime the defendant was charged with. That may be a possibility—I suppose it *is* a possibility—but it is too remote a possibility to raise real doubts in anyone's mind. What you're trying to convince Aunt Harriet of is that there is, as we say, *a very real possibility* that Clarissa had a good reason for leaving her children alone; and your attempt to convince her of this consists in your presenting her with an example of what such a reason *might* be.

Critical responses to the argument from evil—at least responses by philosophers—usually take just this form. A philosopher who responds to the argument from evil typically does so by telling a story, a story in which God allows evil to exist. This story will, of course, represent God as having reasons for allowing the existence of evil, reasons that, if the rest of the story were true, would be good ones. Such a story philosophers call a *defense*. If I offer a story about God and evil as a defense, I hope for the following reaction from my audience: "Given that God exists, the rest of the story might well be true. I can't see any reason to rule it out." . . .

There seems to me to be only one defense that has any hope of succeeding, and that is the so-called free-will defense. In saying this, I place myself in a long tradition that goes back at least to St. Augustine, although I do not propose, like many in that tradition, to offer a theodicy. I do not claim to know that free will plays any central part in God's reasons for allowing the existence of evil. I employ the free-will defense as just precisely a defense, a story that includes both God and evil and, given that there is a God, is true for all anyone knows. . . .

I am going to imagine Theist putting forward a very simple form of the free-will defense; I will go on to ask what Atheist might say in response:

God made the world and it was very good. An indispensable part of the goodness he chose was the existence of rational beings: self-aware beings capable of abstract thought and love and having the power of free choice between contemplated alternative courses of action. This last feature of rational beings, free choice or free will, is a good. But even an omnipotent being is unable to control the exercise of the power of free choice, for a choice that was controlled would *ipso facto* not be free. In other words, if I have a free choice between x and y, even God cannot ensure that I choose x. To ask God to give me a free choice between x and y and to see to it that I choose x instead of y is to ask God to bring about the intrinsically impossible; it is like asking him to create a round square, a material body that has no shape, or an invisible object that casts a shadow. Having this power of free choice, some or all human beings misused it and produced a certain amount of evil. But free will is a sufficiently great good that its existence outweighs the evils that have resulted and will result from its abuse; and God foresaw this. . . .

Let us return to Atheist. What shall she say in response to the free-will defense?

. . . I will concede that the free-will defense shows that the mere existence of *some evil or other* cannot be used to prove that there is no God. If we lived in a world in which everyone, or most people, suffered in certain relatively minor ways, and if each instance of suffering could be traced to the wrong or foolish acts of human beings, you would be making a good point. . . . But the evils of the world as it is are not at all like that. First, the sheer *amount* of evil in the world is overwhelming. The existence of free will may be worth some evil, but it certainly isn't worth the amount we actually observe. Secondly, there are lots of evils that aren't productions of the human will, be it free or unfree. Earthquakes and tornados and genetic defects and . . . well, one hardly knows where to stop. The free-will defense, therefore, is quite unable to deal either with the amount of evil that actually exists or with one of the kinds of evil that actually exists: evil that is not a consequence of human acts.

How is Theist to reply to this argument? I am going to put a very long speech into his mouth:

The free-will defense, in the simple form in which I first stated it suggests—though it does not entail—that God created human beings with free will, and then just left them to their own devices. It suggests that the evils of the world are the more or less unrelated consequences of countless millions of largely unrelated abuses of free will by human beings. Let me now propose a sort of plot to be added to the bare and abstract free-will defense that I stated above. Consider the story of creation and rebellion and expulsion from paradise that is told in the first three chapters of Genesis. Could this story be true—I mean literally true, true in every detail? Well, no. It contradicts what science has discovered about human evolution and the history of the physical universe. And that is hardly surprising, for it long antedates these discoveries. The story is a reworking—with much original material—by Hebrew authors (or, as *my* author, Mr van Inwagen, believes, *a* Hebrew author) of elements found in many ancient Middle Eastern mythologies. Like the *Aeneid,* it is a literary refashioning of materials drawn from myth and legend, and it retains a strong flavor of myth. It is possible, nevertheless, that the first three chapters of Genesis are a mythico-literary representation of actual events of human pre-history. The following story is consistent with what we know of human pre-history. Our current knowledge of human evolution, in fact, presents us with no particular reason to believe that this story is false:

For millions of years, perhaps for thousands of millions of years, God guided the course of evolution so as eventually to produce certain very clever primates, the immediate predecessors of *Homo sapiens.* At some time in the last few hundred thousand years, the whole population of our pre-human ancestors formed a small breeding community—a few thousand or a few hundred or even a few score. That is to say, there was a time when every ancestor of modern human beings who was then alive was a member of this tiny, geographically tightly knit group of primates. In the fullness of time, God took the members of this breeding group and miraculously raised them to rationality. That is, he gave them the gifts of language, abstract thought, and disinterested love—and, of course, the gift of free will. Perhaps we cannot understand *all* his reasons for giving human beings free will, but here is one very important one we *can* understand: He gave them the gift of free will because free will is necessary for love. Love, and not only erotic love, implies free will. . . .

God not only raised these primates to rationality—not only made of them what we call human beings—but also took them into a kind of mystical union with himself, the sort of union that Christians hope for in Heaven and call the Beatific Vision. Being in union with God, these new human beings, these primates who had become human beings at a certain point in their lives, lived together in the harmony of perfect love and also possessed what theologians used to call preternatural powers— something like what people who believe in them today call "paranormal abilities." Because they lived in the harmony of perfect love, none of them did any harm to the others. Because of their preternatural powers, they were able somehow to protect themselves from wild beasts (which they were able to tame with a look), from disease (which they were able to cure with a touch), and from random, destructive natural events (like earthquakes), which they knew about in advance and were able to escape. There was thus no evil in their world. And it was God's intention that they should never become decrepit with age or die, as their primate forebears had. But, somehow, in some way that must be mysterious to us, they were not content with this paradisal state. They abused the gift of free will and separated themselves from their union with God.

The result was horrific: not only did they no longer enjoy the Beatific Vision, but they now faced destruction by the random forces of nature, and were subject to old age and natural death. Nevertheless, they were too proud to end their rebellion. As the generations passed, they drifted further and further from God—into the worship of false gods (a worship that sometimes involved human sacrifice), intertribal warfare (complete with the gleeful torture of prisoners of war), private murder, slavery, and rape. On one level, they realized, or some of them realized, that something was horribly wrong, but they were unable to do anything about it. After they had separated themselves from God, they were, as an engineer might say, "not operating under design conditions." A certain frame of mind had become dominant among them, a frame of mind latent in the genes they had inherited from a million or more generations of ancestors. I mean the frame of mind that places one's own desires and perceived welfare above everything else, and which accords to the welfare of one's immediate relatives a subordinate privileged status, and assigns no status at all to the welfare of anyone else. And this frame of mind was now married to rationality, to the power of abstract thought; the progeny of this marriage were continuing resentment against those whose actions interfere with the fulfillment of one's desires, hatreds cherished in the heart, and the desire for revenge. The inherited genes that produced these baleful effects had been harmless as long as human beings had still had constantly before their minds a representation of perfect love in the Beatific Vision. In the state of separation from God, and conjoined with rationality, they formed the genetic substrate of what is called original or birth sin: an inborn tendency to do evil against which all human efforts are vain. We, or most of us, have some sort of perception of the distinction between good and evil, but, however we struggle, in the end we give in and do evil. In all cultures there are moral codes (more similar than some would have us believe), and the members of every tribe and nation stand condemned not only by alien moral codes but by their own. The only human beings who consistently do right in their own eyes, whose consciences are always clear, are those who, like the Nazis, have given themselves over entirely to evil, those who say, in some twisted and self-deceptive way, what Milton has his Satan say explicitly and clearly: "Evil, be thou my Good."

When human beings had become like this, God looked out over a ruined world. ("And God saw that the wickedness of man was great in the earth, and that every imagination of the thoughts of his heart was only evil continually" [Gen. 6.5].) It would have been just of him to leave human beings in the ruin they had made of themselves and their world. But God is more than a God of justice. He is, indeed, more than a God of mercy—a God who was merely merciful might simply have brought the story of humanity to an end at that point, like a man who shoots a horse with a broken leg. But God is more than a God of mercy: he is a God of love. He therefore neither left our species to its own devices nor mercifully destroyed it. Rather, he set in motion a rescue operation. He put into operation a plan designed to restore separated humanity to union with himself. This defense will not specify the nature of this plan of atonement. The three Abrahamic religions, Judaism, Christianity, and Islam, tell three different stories about the nature of this plan, and I do not propose to favor one of them over another in telling a story that, after all, I do not maintain is true. This much must be said, however: the plan has the following feature, and any plan with the object of restoring separated humanity to union with God would have to have this feature: its object is to bring it about that human beings once more love God. And, since love essentially involves free will, love is not something that can be imposed from the outside, by an act of sheer power. Human beings must choose freely to be reunited with God and to love him, and this is something they are unable to do by their own efforts. They must therefore cooperate with God. As is the case with many rescue operations, the rescuer and those whom he is rescuing must cooperate. For human beings to cooperate with God in this rescue operation, they must know that they need to be rescued. They must know what it means to be separated from him. And what it means to be separated from God is to live in a world of horrors. If God simply "canceled" all the horrors of this world by an endless series of miracles, he would thereby frustrate his own plan of reconciliation. If he did that, we should be content with our lot and should see no reason to cooperate with him.

Here is an analogy. Suppose Dorothy suffers from angina, and that what she needs to do is to stop smoking and lose weight. Suppose her doctor knows of a drug that will stop the pain but will do nothing to cure the condition. Should the doctor prescribe the drug for her, in the full knowledge that if the pain is alleviated, there is no chance that she will stop smoking and lose weight? Well, perhaps the answer is Yes—if that's what Dorothy insists on. The doctor is Dorothy's fellow adult and fellow citizen, after all. Perhaps it would be insufferably paternalistic to refuse to alleviate Dorothy's pain in order to provide her with a motivation to do what is to her own advantage. If one were of an especially libertarian cast of mind, one might even say that someone who did that was "playing God." It is far from clear, however, whether there is anything wrong with God's behaving as if he were God. It is at least very plausible to suppose that it is morally permissible for God to allow human beings to suffer if the inevitable result of suppressing the suffering would be to deprive them of a very great good, one that far outweighs the suffering. But God does shield us from much evil, from a great proportion of the sufferings that would be a natural consequence of our rebellion. If he did not, all human history would be at least this bad: every human society would be on the moral level of Nazi Germany. But, however much evil God shields us from, he must leave in place a vast amount of evil if he is not to deceive us about what separation from him means. The amount he has left us with is so vast and so horrible that we cannot really comprehend it, especially if we are middle-class Europeans or Americans. Nevertheless, it could have been much worse. The inhabitants of a world in which human beings had separated themselves from God and he had then simply left them to their own devices would regard our world as a comparative paradise. All this evil, however, will come to an end. At some point, for all eternity, there will be no more unmerited suffering: this present darkness, "the age of evil," will eventually be remembered as a brief flicker at the beginning of human history. Every evil done by the wicked to the innocent will have been avenged, and every tear will have been wiped away. If there is still suffering, it will be merited: the suffering of those who refuse to cooperate with God's great rescue operation and are allowed by him to exist forever in a state of elected ruin—those who, in a word, are in Hell. . . .

According to the story I have told, there is generally no explanation of why *this* evil happened to *that* person. What there is, is an explanation of why evils happen to people without any reason. If a much-loved child dies of leukemia, there may well be no explanation of why that happened—although there is an explanation of why events of that *sort* happen. And the explanation is: that is part of what being separated from God means; it means being the playthings of chance. It means living in a world in which innocent children die horribly, and it means something worse than that: it means living in a world in which innocent children die horribly *for no reason at all.* It means living in a world in which the wicked, through sheer luck, often prosper. Anyone who does not want to live in such a world, a world in which we are the playthings of chance, had better accept God's offer of a way out of that world.

Here ends the very long story I—it is still Theist who is speaking—said was consistent with what we know of human prehistory. I will call this story the *expanded* free-will defense. I mean it to include the "simple" free-will defense as a part. Thus, it is a feature of the expanded free-will defense that even an omnipotent being, having raised our remote ancestors to rationality and having given them the gift of free will, which included a free choice between remaining united with him in bonds of love and turning away from him to follow the devices and desires of their own hearts, was not able to *ensure* that they have done the former—although we may be sure that he did everything omnipotence could do to raise the probability of their doing so. But the omniscient God knew that, however much evil might result from the elected separation from himself, and consequent self-ruin, of his creatures—if it should occur—the gift of free will would be, so to speak, worth it. For the existence of an eternity of love depends on this gift, and that eternity outweighs the horrors of the very long but, in the most literal sense, temporary period of divine-human estrangement. And he has done what he can to keep the horrors of estrangement to a minimum—if there is a minimum. At any rate, he has made them vastly less horrible than they might have been.

I contend that the expanded free-will defense is a possible story (internally consistent, at least as far as we can see). I contend that, given that the central character of the story, God, exists, the rest of the story might well be true. I contend that, in the present state of human knowledge, we could have no reason for thinking that the story was false unless we had some reason—a reason other than the existence of evil—for thinking that there was no God. . . .

[Atheist's] best response to the expanded free-will defense, I think, would proceed along these lines:

You, Theist, may have told a story that accounts for the enormous amount of evil in the world, and for the fact that much evil is not caused by human beings. But there is a challenge to theism that is based on the evils we find in the world, and not simply on what might be called the general fact of evil. There is an argument that is based on the obvious gratuitousness of many particular evils. I will present such an argument, and I will try to convince these estimable agnostics that even if you have effectively answered what our creator, Mr van Inwagen, has called the global argument from evil, your response to this argument does not touch what he has called local arguments from evil.

Let us consider certain particular very bad events—"horrors" I will call them. Here are some examples of what I call horrors: a school bus full of children is crushed by a landslide; a good woman's life is gradually destroyed by the progress of Huntington's Chorea; a baby is born without limbs. Some horrors are consequences of human choices, and some are not. But whether a particular horror is connected with human choices or not, it is evident, at least in many cases, that God could have prevented the horror without sacrificing any great good or allowing some even greater horror.

Now a moment ago, I mentioned the enormous amount of evil in the world, and it is certainly true that there is an enormous amount of evil in the world. The phrase "the amount of evil" suggests—perhaps it even implies—that evil is quantifiable, like distance or weight. That may be false or unintelligible, but if it is true, even in a rough-and-ready sort of way, it shows that horrors raise a problem for the theist that is distinct from the problem raised by the enormous amount of evil. If evil can be, even roughly, quantified, as talk about amounts seems to imply, it might be that there was *more* evil in a world in which there were thousands of millions of relatively minor episodes of suffering (broken ribs, for example) than in a world in which there were a few horrors. But an omnipotent and omniscient creator could be called to moral account for creating a world in which there was even *one* horror. And the reason is obvious: that horror could have been "left out" of creation without the sacrifice of any great good or the permitting of some even greater horror. And leaving it out is just what a morally perfect being would do; such good things as might depend causally on the horror could—given the being's omnipotence and omniscience—be secured by (if the word is not morally offensive in this context) more "economical" means. Thus, the sheer amount of evil (which might be distributed in a fairly uniform way) is not the only fact about evil that Theist needs to take into account. He must also take into account what we might call (again with some risk of using morally offensive language) *high local concentrations* of evil—that is, horrors. And it is hard to see how the free-will defense, however elaborated, could provide any resources for dealing with horrors. . . .

There are many horrors, vastly many, from which no discernible good results—and certainly no good, discernible or not, that an omnipotent being couldn't have achieved without the horror; in fact, without any suffering at all. Here is a true story. A man came upon a young woman in an isolated place. He overpowered her, chopped off her arms at the elbows with an axe, raped her, and left her to die. Somehow she managed to drag herself on the stumps of her arms to the side of a road, where she was discovered. She lived, but she experienced indescribable suffering, and although she is alive, she must live the rest of her life without arms and with the memory of what she had been forced to endure. No discernible good came of this, and it is wholly unreasonable to believe that any good could have come of it that an omnipotent being couldn't have achieved without employing the raped and mutilated woman's horrible suffering as a means to it. . . . I will now draw on these reflections to construct a version of the argument from evil, a version that, unlike the version I presented earlier, refers not to all the evils of the world, but just to this one event. I will refer to the events in the story I have told collectively as "the Mutilation." I argue:

(1) If the Mutilation had not occurred, if it had been, so to speak, simply *left out* of the world, the world would be no worse than it is. (It would seem, in fact, that the world would be significantly *better* if the Mutilation had been left out of it, but my argument doesn't require that premise.)

(2) The Mutilation in fact occurred (and was a horror).

(3) If a morally perfect creator could have left a certain horror out of the world he created, and if the world he created would have been no worse if that horror had been left out of it than it would have been if it had included that horror, then the morally perfect creator would have left the horror out of the world he created—or at any rate he would have left it out if he had been able to.

(4) If an omnipotent being created the world, he was able to leave the Mutilation out of the world (and was able to do so in a way that would have left the world otherwise much as it is).

There is, therefore, no omnipotent and morally perfect creator.

So speaks Atheist. How might Theist reply? Atheist has said that her argument is modeled on an argument of William Rowe's. If Theist models his reply on the replies made by most of the theists who have written on Rowe's argument, he will attack the first premise. He will try to show that, for all anyone knows, the world (considered under the aspect of eternity) is a better place for containing the Mutilation. He will defend the thesis that, for all anyone knows, God has brought, or will at some future time bring, some great good out of the Mutilation, a good that outweighs it, or else has employed the Mutilation as a means to the prevention of some even greater evil; and he will contend that, for all anyone knows, the great good achieved or the great evil prevented could not have been, respectively, achieved or prevented, even by an omnipotent being, in any other way than by some means that involved the Mutilation or some other horror at least as bad as the Mutilation.

I am not going to have Theist reply to Atheist's argument in this way. . . .

I am going to represent Theist as employing another line of attack on Atheist's response to his expanded free-will defense. I am going to represent him as denying premise (3) or, more precisely, as trying to show that the expanded free-will defense casts considerable doubt on premise (3). In order to enable you the better to follow what Theist says, I will attempt to fix the essential content of premise (3) in your minds by restating it in terms of a rather fanciful metaphor. Consider a morally perfect creator who is taking a final look at the four-dimensional blueprint of the world he is about to create. His eye falls on a patch in the blueprint that represents a horror. He reflects a moment and sees that if he simply erases that patch, replaces it with something innocuous, and does a little smoothing around the spatiotemporal edges to render the lines of causation in the revised blueprint continuous (or nearly so), a world made according to the revised blueprint will contain at least as favorable a balance of good and evil as a world made according to the unrevised blueprint. He therefore perceives a moral obligation to revise the blueprint in the way he has thought of and to incorporate the revision into his creation, and, being morally perfect, necessarily revises and creates accordingly. Premise (3) simply says that this is what *must* happen when a morally perfect creator perceives in his plan for the world a horror that can be "edited out" without significantly altering the balance of good and evil represented in that plan.

Now that we have, I hope, got the content of premise (3) into our minds in an intuitive and memorable form, we are ready to hear Theist's reply to Atheist's rejoinder to the expanded free-will defense:

> Why should we accept this premise? . . . I believe there is really just one moral principle that it would be plausible to appeal to in defense of premise (3). It might be stated like this:
>
>> If one is in a position to prevent some evil, one should not allow that evil to occur—not unless allowing it to occur would result in some good that would outweigh it or preventing it would result in some other evil at least as bad.
>
> Now: Is the moral principle correct? I think not. Consider this case. Suppose you are an official who has the power to release anyone from prison at any time. Blodgett has been sentenced to ten years in prison for felonious assault. His sentence is nearing its end, and he petitions you to release him from prison a day early. Should you? Well, the principle says so. A day spent in prison is an evil—if you don't think so, I invite you to spend a day in prison. (Or consider the probable reaction of a prisoner who is, by bureaucratic foot-dragging, kept in prison one day longer than the term of his sentence.) Let's suppose that the only good that results from someone's being in prison is the deterrence of crime. (This assumption is made to simplify the argument I am going to present. That it is false introduces no real defect into the argument.) Obviously, 9 years and 364 days spent in prison is not going to have a significantly different power to deter felonious assault from 10 years spent in prison. So: no good will be secured by visiting on Blodgett that last day in prison, and that last day spent in prison is an evil. The principle tells you, the official, to let

him out a day early. This much, I think, is enough to show that the principle is wrong, for you have no such obligation. But the principle is in more trouble than this simple criticism suggests.

It would seem that if a threatened punishment of n days in prison has a certain power to deter felonious assault, $n - 1$ days spent in prison will have a power to deter felonious assault that is not significantly less. Consider the power to deter felonious assault that belongs to a threatened punishment of 1,023 days in prison. Consider the power to deter felonious assault that belongs to a threatened punishment of 1,022 days in prison. There is, surely, no significant difference? Consider the power to deter felonious assault that belongs to a threatened punishment of 98 days in prison. Consider the power to deter felonious assault that belongs to a threatened punishment of 97 days in prison. There is, surely, no significant difference? Consider the power to deter felonious assault that belongs to a threatened punishment of one day in prison. Consider the power to deter felonious assault that belongs to a threatened punishment of no time in prison at all. There is, surely, no significant difference?

A moment's reflection shows that if this is true, as it seems to be, then the moral principle entails that Blodgett ought to spend no time in prison at all. For suppose that Blodgett had lodged his appeal to have his sentence reduced by a day not shortly before he was to be released but before he had entered prison at all. He lodges this appeal with you, the official who accepts the moral principle. For the reason I have set out, you must grant his appeal. Now suppose that when it has been granted, clever Blodgett lodges a second appeal: that his sentence be reduced to 10 years less *two* days. This second appeal you will also be obliged to grant, for there is no difference between 10 years less a day and 10 years less two days as regards the power to deter felonious assault. I am sure you can see where this is going. Provided only that Blodgett has the time and the energy to lodge 3,648 successive appeals for a one-day reduction of his sentence, he will escape prison altogether.

This result is, I take it, a *reductio ad absurdum* of the moral principle. As the practical wisdom has it (but this is no compromise between practical considerations and strict morality; this *is* strict morality), "You have to draw a line somewhere." And this means an *arbitrary* line. The principle fails precisely *because* it forbids the drawing of morally arbitrary lines. There is nothing wrong, or nothing that can be determined a priori to be wrong, with a legislature's setting 10 years in prison as the minimum punishment for felonious assault—and this despite the fact that 10 years in prison, considered as a *precise span of days,* is an arbitrary punishment. . . .

So: the moral principle is false. What are the consequences of its falsity, of its failure to be an acceptable moral principle, for the local argument from evil? Let us return to the expanded free-will defense. This story accounts for the existence of horrors—that is, that there are horrors is a part of the story. . . .

A general account of the existence of horrors does not constitute a reply to the argument from horrors, because it does not tell us which premise of the argument to deny. . . .

But we are now in a position to imagine how one might reply to Atheist's invitation to Theist to say which of the premises of the argument to ask the agnostics to declare "not proven."

God removes many horrors from the world, and he does more than this; he makes specific local changes in the world in such a way that what would have happened doesn't, and the threatened horror is prevented. But he cannot remove *all* the horrors from the world, for that would frustrate his plan for reuniting human beings with himself. And if he prevents only some horrors, how shall he decide which ones to prevent? Where shall he draw the line?—the line between threatened horrors that are prevented and threatened horrors that are allowed to occur? I suggest that wherever he draws the line, it will be an arbitrary line. That this must be so is easily seen by thinking about the Mutilation. If God had added that particular horror to his list of horrors to be prevented, and that one alone, the world, considered as a whole, would not have been a significantly less horrible place, and the general realization of human beings that they live in a world of horrors would not have been significantly different from what it is. Therefore, preventing the Mutilation would in no way have interfered with his plan for the restoration of our species' original perfection. If the expanded free-will defense is a true story, God has made a choice about where to draw the line, the line between the actual horrors of history, the horrors that are *real,* and the horrors that are mere averted possibilities, might-have-beens. And the Mutilation falls on the "actual horrors of history" side of the line. And this fact shows that the line is an arbitrary one; for if he had drawn it so as to exclude the Mutilation from reality (and had excluded no other horror from reality), he would have lost no good thereby and he would have allowed no greater evil. He had no reason for drawing the line where he did. And what justifies him in doing this? What justifies him in allowing the Mutilation to occur in reality when he could have excluded it from reality without losing any good thereby? Has the victim of the Mutilation not got a moral case against him? He could have saved her, and he did not; and he does not even *claim* to have achieved some good by not saving her. It would seem that God is, in C. S. Lewis's words, in the dock; if he is, then I, Theist, am playing the part of his barrister, and you, the agnostics, are the jury. I offer the following obvious defense. There was no non-arbitrary line to be drawn. Wherever he drew the line, there would have been countless horrors left in the world—his plan requires the actual existence of countless horrors—and the victim or victims of any of those horrors could bring the same charge against him that we have imagined the victim of the Mutilation bringing against him.

But I see Atheist stirring in protest; she is planning to tell you that, given the terms of the expanded free-will defense, God should have allowed the *minimum* number of horrors consistent with his project of reconciliation, and that it is obvious he has not done this. She is going to tell you that there *is* a non-arbitrary line for God to draw, and that it is the line that has the minimum number of horrors on the "actuality" side. But there is no such line to be drawn. There is no minimum number of horrors consistent with God's plan of reconciliation, for the prevention of any one particular horror could not possibly have any effect on God's plan. For any n, if the existence of at most n horrors is consistent with God's plan, the existence of at most $n - 1$ horrors will be equally consistent with God's plan. To ask what the minimum number of horrors consistent with God's plan is, is like asking, What is the minimum number of raindrops that could have fallen on France in the twentieth century that is consistent with France's having been a fertile country in the twentieth century? . . .

It seems clear, therefore, that there can be cases in which it is morally permissible for an agent to permit an evil that agent could have prevented, despite the fact that no good is achieved by doing so. But then, it would seem, if the expanded free-will defense is a true story, this is exactly the moral structure of the situation in which God finds himself when he contemplates the world of horrors that is the consequence of humanity's separation from him. The local argument from evil, the argument from horrors, therefore, fails.

CHAPTER 10

Why I Am Not a Christian

Bertrand Russell

Bertrand Russell (1872–1970), a pioneer in logic and philosophy of mathematics, wrote on virtually every subject in philosophy. Many consider him to have been the greatest philosophical thinker of the twentieth century. During his lifetime, Lord Russell's atheism and defense of "free love" were regarded as scandalous.

Russell's major works include *Principia Mathematica* (three volumes, 1910, 1912, and 1913, with Alfred North Whitehead), *Our Knowledge of the External World* (1914), *Political Ideals* (1917), *The Analysis of Matter* (1927), *Marriage and Morals* (1929), *An Inquiry into Meaning and Truth* (1940), *Human Knowledge: Its Scope and Limits* (1948), and *Human Society in Ethics and Politics* (1954).

This lecture was delivered on March 6, 1927, at Battersea Town Hall under the auspices of the South London Branch of the National Secular Society.

As your Chairman has told you, the subject about which I am going to speak to you tonight is "Why I Am Not a Christian." Perhaps it would be as well, first of all, to try to make out what one means by the word *Christian*. It is used these days in a very loose sense by a great many

Source: Bertrand Russell, *Why I Am Not a Christian.* Reprinted with the permission of Simon & Schuster Adult Publishing Group, Taylor & Francis Books Ltd., and the Bertrand Russell Peace Foundation. Copyright © 1957, 1985 by George Allen & Unwin Ltd.

people. Some people mean no more by it than a person who attempts to live a good life. In that sense I suppose there would be Christians in all sects and creeds; but I do not think that that is the proper sense of the word, if only because it would imply that all the people who are not Christians—all the Buddhists, Confucians, Mohammedans, and so on—are not trying to live a good life. I do not mean by a Christian any person who tries to live decently according to his lights. I think that you must have a certain amount of definite belief before you have a right to call yourself a Christian. The word does not have quite such a full-blooded meaning now as it had in the times of St. Augustine and St. Thomas Aquinas. In those days, if a man said that he was a Christian it was known what he meant. You accepted a whole collection of creeds which were set out with great precision, and every single syllable of those creeds you believed with the whole strength of your convictions.

What Is a Christian?

Nowadays it is not quite that. We have to be a little more vague in our meaning of Christianity. I think, however, that there are two different items which are quite essential to anybody calling himself a Christian. The first is one of a dogmatic nature—namely, that you must believe in God and immortality. If you do not believe in those two things, I do not think that you can properly call yourself a Christian. Then, further than that, as the name implies, you must have some kind of belief about Christ. The Mohammedans, for instance, also believe in God and in immortality, and yet they would not call themselves Christians. I think you must have at the very lowest the belief that Christ was, if not divine, at least the best and wisest of men. If you are not going to believe that much about Christ, I do not think you have any right to call yourself a Christian. Of course, there is another sense, which you find in *Whitaker's Almanack* and in geography books, where the population of the world is said to be divided into Christians, Mohammedans, Buddhists, fetish worshipers, and so on; and in that sense we are all Christians. The geography books count us all in, but that is a purely geographical sense, which I suppose we can ignore. Therefore I take it that when I tell you why I am not a Christian I have to tell you two different things: first, why I do not believe in God and in immortality; and, secondly, why I do not think that Christ was the best and wisest of men, although I grant him a very high degree of moral goodness.

But for the successful efforts of unbelievers in the past, I could not take so elastic a definition of Christianity as that. As I said before, in olden days it had a much more full-blooded sense. For instance, it included the belief in hell. Belief in eternal hell-fire was an essential item of Christian belief until pretty recent times. In this country, as you know, it ceased to be an essential item because of a decision of the Privy Council, and from that decision the Archbishop of Canterbury and the Archbishop of York dissented; but in this country our religion is settled by Act of Parliament, and therefore the Privy Council was able to override their Graces and hell was no longer necessary to a Christian. Consequently I shall not insist that a Christian must believe in hell.

The Existence of God

To come to this question of the existence of God: it is a large and serious question, and if I were to attempt to deal with it in any adequate manner I should have to keep you here until Kingdom Come, so that you will have to excuse me if I deal with it in a somewhat summary fashion. You know, of course, that the Catholic Church has laid it down as a dogma that the existence of God can be proved by the unaided reason. That is a somewhat curious dogma, but it is one of their dogmas. They had to introduce it because at one time the freethinkers adopted the habit of saying that there were such and such arguments which mere reason might urge against the existence of God, but of course they knew as a matter of faith that God did exist. The arguments and the reasons were set out at great length, and the Catholic Church felt that they must stop it. Therefore they laid it down that the existence of God can be proved by the unaided reason and they had to set up what they considered were arguments to prove it. There are, of course, a number of them, but I shall take only a few.

The First Cause Argument

Perhaps the simplest and easiest to understand is the argument of the First Cause. (It is maintained that everything we see in this world has a cause, and as you go back in the chain of causes further and further you must come to a First Cause, and to that First Cause you give the name of God.) That argument, I suppose, does not carry very much weight nowadays, because, in the first place, cause is not quite what it used to be. The philosophers and the men of science have got going on cause, and it has not anything like the vitality it used to have; but, apart from that, you can see that the argument that there must be a First Cause is one that cannot have any validity. I may say that when I was a young man and was debating these questions very seriously in my mind, I for a long time accepted the argument of the First Cause, until one day, at the age of eighteen, I read John Stuart Mill's *Autobiography*, and I there found this sentence: "My father taught me that the question 'Who made me?' cannot be answered, since it immediately suggests the further question 'Who made God?'" That very simple sentence showed me, as I still think, the fallacy in the argument of the First Cause. If everything must have a cause, then God must have a cause. If there can be anything without a cause, it may just as well be the world as God, so that there cannot be any validity in that argument. It is exactly of the same nature as the Hindu's view, that the world rested upon an elephant and the elephant rested upon a tortoise; and when they said, "How about the tortoise?" the Indian said, "Suppose we change the subject." The argument is really no better than that. There is no reason why the world could not have come into being without a cause; nor, on the other hand, is there any reason why it should not have always existed. There is no reason to suppose that the world had a beginning at all. The idea that things must have a beginning is really due to the poverty of our imagination. Therefore, perhaps, I need not waste any more time upon the argument about the First Cause.

The Natural-law Argument

Then there is a very common argument from natural law. That was a favorite argument all through the eighteenth century, especially under the influence of Sir Isaac Newton and his cosmogony. People observed the planets going around the sun according to the law of gravitation, and they thought that God had given a behest to these planets to move in that particular fashion, and that was why they did so. That was, of course, a convenient and simple explanation that saved them the trouble of looking any further for explanations of the law of gravitation. Nowadays we explain the law of gravitation in a somewhat complicated fashion that Einstein has introduced. I do not propose to give you a lecture on the law of gravitation, as interpreted by Einstein, because that again would take some time; at any rate, you no longer have the sort of natural law that you had in the Newtonian system, where, for some reason that nobody could understand, nature behaved in a uniform fashion. We now find that a great many things we thought were natural laws are really human conventions. You know that even in the remotest depths of stellar space there are still three feet to a yard. That is, no doubt, a very remarkable fact, but you would hardly call it a law of nature. And a great many things that have been regarded as laws of nature are of that kind. On the other hand, where you can get down to any knowledge of what atoms actually do, you will find they are much less subject to law than people thought, and that the laws at which you arrive are statistical averages of just the sort that would emerge from chance. There is, as we all know, a law that if you throw dice you will get double sixes only about once in thirty-six times, and we do not regard that as evidence that the fall of the dice is regulated by design; on the contrary, if the double sixes came every time we should think that there was design. The laws of nature are of that sort as regards a great many of them. They are statistical averages such as would emerge from the laws of chance; and that makes this whole business of natural law much less impressive than it formerly was. Quite apart from that, which represents the momentary state of science that may change tomorrow, the whole idea that natural laws imply a lawgiver is due to a confusion between natural and human laws. Human laws are behests commanding you to behave a certain way, in which way you may choose to behave, or you may choose not to behave; but natural laws are a description of how things do in fact behave, and being a mere description of what they in fact do, you cannot argue that there must be somebody who told them to do that, because even supposing that there were, you are then faced with the question "Why did God issue just those natural laws and no others?" If you say that he did it simply from his own good pleasure, and without any reason, you then find that there is something which is not subject to law, and so your train of natural law is interrupted. If you say, as more orthodox theologians do, that in all the laws which God issues he had a reason for giving those laws rather than others—the reason, of course, being to create the best universe, although you would never think it to look at it—if there were a reason for the laws which God gave, then God himself was subject to law, and therefore you do not get any advantage by introducing God as an intermediary. You have really a law outside and anterior to the divine edicts, and God does not serve your purpose, because he is not the ultimate lawgiver. In short, this whole argument about natural law no longer has anything like the strength that it used to have. I am traveling on in time in my review of the arguments. The arguments that are used for the existence of God change their character as time goes on. They were at first hard intellectual arguments embodying certain quite definite fallacies. As we come to modern times they become less respectable intellectually and more and more affected by a kind of moralizing vagueness.

The Argument from Design

The next step in this process brings us to the argument from design. You all know the argument from design: everything in the world is made just so that we can manage to live in the world, and if the world was ever so little different, we could not manage to live in it. That is the argument from design. It sometimes takes a rather curious form; for instance, it is argued that rabbits have white tails in order to be easy to shoot. I do not know how rabbits would view that application. It is an easy argument to parody. You all know Voltaire's remark, that obviously the nose was designed to be such as to fit spectacles. That sort of parody has turned out to be not nearly so wide of the mark as it might have seemed in the eighteenth century, because since the time of Darwin we understand much better why living creatures are adapted to their environment. It is not that their environment was made to be suitable to them but that they grew to be suitable to it, and that is the basis of adaptation. There is no evidence of design about it.

When you come to look into this argument from design, it is a most astonishing thing that people can believe that this world, with all the things that are in it, with all its defects, should be the best that omnipotence and omniscience have been able to produce in millions of years. I really cannot believe it. Do you think that, if you were granted omnipotence and omniscience and millions of years in which to perfect your world, you could produce nothing better than the Ku Klux Klan or the Fascists? Moreover, if you accept the ordinary laws of science, you have to suppose that human life and life in general on this planet will die out in due course: it is a stage in the decay of the solar system; at a certain stage of decay you get the sort of conditions of temperature and so forth which are suitable to protoplasm, and there is life for a short time in the life of the whole solar system. You see in the moon the sort of thing to which the earth is tending—something dead, cold, and lifeless.

I am told that that sort of view is depressing, and people will sometimes tell you that if they believed that, they would not be able to go on living. Do not believe it; it is all nonsense. Nobody really worries much about what is going to happen millions of years hence. Even if they think they are worrying much about that, they are really deceiving themselves. They are worried about something much more mundane, or it may merely be a bad digestion; but nobody is really seriously rendered unhappy by the thought of something that is going to happen to this world millions and millions of years hence. Therefore, although it is of course a gloomy view to suppose that life will die out—at least I suppose we may say so, although sometimes when I contemplate the things that people do with their lives I think it is almost a consolation—it is not such as to render life miserable. It merely makes you turn your attention to other things.

The Moral Arguments for Deity

Now we reach one stage further in what I shall call the intellectual descent that the Theists have made in their argumentations, and we come to what are called the moral arguments for the existence of God. You all know, of course, that there used to be in the old days three intellectual arguments for the existence of God, all of which were disposed of by Immanuel Kant in the *Critique of Pure Reason;* but no sooner had he disposed of those arguments than he invented a new one, a moral argument, and that quite convinced him. He was like many people: in intellectual matters he was skeptical, but in moral matters he believed implicitly in the maxims that he had imbibed at his mother's knee. That illustrates what the psychoanalysts so much emphasize—the immensely stronger hold upon us that our very early associations have than those of later times.

Kant, as I say, invented a new moral argument for the existence of God, and that in varying forms was extremely popular during the nineteenth century. It has all sorts of forms. One form is to say that there would be no right or wrong unless God existed. I am not for the moment concerned with whether there is a difference between right and wrong, or whether there is not: that is another question. The point I am concerned with is that, if you are quite sure there is a difference between right and wrong, you are then in this situation: Is that difference due to God's fiat or is it not? If it is due to God's fiat, then for God himself there is no difference between right and wrong, and it is no longer a significant statement to say that God is good. If you are going to say, as theologians do, that God is good, you must then say that right and wrong have some meaning which is independent of God's fiat, because God's fiats are good and not bad independently of the mere fact that he made them. If you are going to say that, you will then have to say that it is not only through God that right and wrong came into being, but that they are in their essence logically anterior to God. You could, of course, if you liked, say that there was a superior deity who gave orders to the God who made this world, or could take up the line that some of the gnostics took up—a line which I often thought was a very plausible one—that as a matter of fact this world that we know was made by the devil at a moment when God was not looking. There is a good deal to be said for that, and I am not concerned to refute it.

The Argument for the Remedying of Injustice

Then there is another very curious form of moral argument, which is this: they say that the existence of God is required in order to bring justice into the world. In the part of this universe that we know there is great injustice, and often the good suffer, and often the wicked prosper, and one hardly knows which of those is the more annoying; but if you are going to have justice in the universe as a whole you have to suppose a future life to redress the balance of life here on earth. So they say that there must be a God, and there must be heaven and hell in order that in the long run there may be justice. That is a very curious argument. If you looked at the matter from a scientific point of view, you would say, "After all, I know only this world. I do not know about the rest of the universe, but so far as one can argue at all on probabilities one would say that probably this world is a fair sample, and if there is injustice here the odds are that there is injustice elsewhere also." Supposing you got a crate of oranges that you opened, and you found all the top layer of oranges bad, you would not argue, "The underneath ones must be good, so as to redress the balance." You would say, "Probably the whole lot is a bad consignment"; and that is really what a scientific person would argue about the universe. He would say, "Here we find in this world a great deal of injustice, and so far as that goes that is a reason for supposing that justice does not rule in the world; and therefore so far as it goes it affords a moral argument against deity and not in favor of one." Of course I know that the sort of intellectual arguments that I have been talking to you about are not what really moves people. What really moves people to believe in God is not any intellectual argument at all. Most people believe in God because they have been taught from early infancy to do it, and that is the main reason.

Then I think that the next most powerful reason is the wish for safety, a sort of feeling that there is a big brother who will look after you. That plays a very profound part in influencing people's desire for a belief in God.

The Character of Christ

I now want to say a few words upon a topic which I often think is not quite sufficiently dealt with by Rationalists, and that is the question whether Christ was the best and the wisest of men. It is generally taken for granted that we should all agree that that was so. I do not myself. I think that there are a good many points upon which I agree with Christ a great deal more than the professing Christians do. I do not know that I could go with Him all the way, but I could go with Him much further than most professing Christians can. You will remember that He said, "Resist not evil: but whosoever shall smite thee on thy right cheek, turn to him the other also." That is not a new precept or a new principle. It was used by Lao-tse and Buddha some 500 or 600 years before Christ, but it is not a principle which as a matter of fact Christians accept. I have no doubt that the present Prime Minister, for instance, is a most sincere Christian, but I should not advise any of you to go and smite him on one cheek. I think you might find that he thought this text was intended in a figurative sense.

Then there is another point which I consider excellent. You will remember that Christ said, "Judge not lest ye be judged." That principle I do not think you would find was popular in the law courts of Christian countries. I have known in my time quite a number of judges who were very earnest Christians, and none of them felt that they were acting contrary to Christian principles in what they did. Then Christ says, "Give to him that asketh of thee, and from him that would borrow of thee turn not thou away." That is a very good principle. Your Chairman has reminded you that we are not here to talk politics, but I cannot help observing that the last general election was fought on the question of how desirable it was to turn away from him that would borrow of thee, so that one must assume that the Liberals and Conservatives of this country are composed of people who do not agree with the teaching of Christ, because they certainly did very emphatically turn away on that occasion.

Then there is one other maxim of Christ which I think has a great deal in it, but I do not find that it is very popular among some of our Christian friends. He says, "If thou wilt be perfect, go and sell that which thou hast, and give to the poor." That is a very excellent maxim, but, as I say, it is not much practiced. All these, I think, are good maxims, although they are a little difficult to live up to. I do not profess to live up to them myself; but then, after all, it is not quite the same thing as for a Christian.

Defects in Christ's Teaching

Having granted the excellence of these maxims, I come to certain points in which I do not believe that one can grant either the superlative wisdom or the superlative goodness of Christ as depicted in the Gospels; and here I may say that one is not concerned with the historical question. Historically it is quite doubtful whether Christ ever existed at all, and if He did we do not know anything about Him, so that I am not concerned with the historical question, which is a very difficult one. I am concerned with Christ as He appears in the Gospels, taking the Gospel narrative as it stands, and there one does find some things that do not seem to be very wise. For one thing, He certainly thought that His second coming would occur in clouds of glory before the death of all the people who were living at that time. There are a great many texts that prove that. He says, for instance, "Ye shall not have gone over the cities of Israel till the Son of Man be come." Then He says, "There are some standing here which shall not taste death till the Son of Man comes into His kingdom"; and there are a lot of places where it is quite clear that He believed that His second coming would happen during the lifetime of many then living. That was the belief of His earlier followers, and it was the basis of a good deal of His moral teaching. When He said, "Take no thought for the morrow," and things of that sort, it was very largely because He thought that the second coming was going to be very soon, and that all ordinary mundane affairs did not count. I have, as a matter of fact, known some Christians who did believe that the second coming was imminent. I knew a parson who frightened his congregation terribly by telling them that the second coming was very imminent indeed, but they were much consoled when they found that he was planting trees in his garden. The early Christians did really believe it, and they did abstain from such things as planting trees in their gardens, because they did accept from Christ the belief that the second coming was imminent. In that respect, clearly He was not so wise as some other people have been, and He was certainly not superlatively wise.

The Moral Problem

Then you come to moral questions. There is one very serious defect to my mind in Christ's moral character, and that is that He believed in hell. I do not myself feel that any person who is really profoundly humane can believe in everlasting punishment. Christ certainly as depicted in the Gospels did believe in everlasting punishment, and one does find repeatedly a vindictive fury against those people who would not listen to His preaching—an attitude which is not uncommon with preachers, but which does somewhat detract from superlative excellence. You do not, for instance, find that attitude in Socrates. You find him quite bland and urbane toward the people who would not listen to him; and it is, to my mind, far more worthy of a sage to take that line than to take the line of indignation. You probably all remember the sort of things that Socrates was saying when he was dying, and the sort of things that he generally did say to people who did not agree with him.

You will find that in the Gospels Christ said, "Ye serpents, ye generation of vipers, how can ye escape the damnation of hell." That was said to people who did not like His preaching. It is not really to my mind quite the best tone, and there are a great many of these things about hell. There is, of course, the familiar text about the sin against the Holy Ghost: "Whosoever speaketh against the Holy Ghost it shall not be forgiven him neither in this World nor in the world to come." That text has caused an unspeakable amount of misery in the world, for all sorts of people have imagined that they have committed the sin against the Holy Ghost, and thought that it would not be forgiven them either in this world or in the world to come. I really do not think that a person with a proper degree of kindliness in his nature would have put fears and terrors of that sort into the world.

Then Christ says, "The Son of Man shall send forth His angels, and they shall gather out of His kingdom all things that offend, and them which do iniquity, and shall cast them into a furnace of fire; there shall be wailing and gnashing of teeth"; and He goes on about the wailing and gnashing of teeth. It comes in one verse after another, and it is quite manifest to the reader that there is a certain pleasure in contemplating wailing and gnashing of teeth, or else it would not occur so often. Then you all, of course, remember about the sheep and the goats; how at the second coming He is going to divide the sheep from the goats, and He is going to say to the goats, "Depart from me, ye cursed, into everlasting fire." He continues, "And these shall go away into everlasting fire." Then He says again, "If thy hand offend thee, cut it off; it is better for thee to enter into life maimed, than having two hands to go into hell, into the fire that never shall be quenched; where the worm dieth not and the fire is not quenched." He repeats that again and again also. I must say that I think all this doctrine, that hell-fire is a punishment for sin, is a doctrine of cruelty. It is a doctrine that put cruelty into the world and gave the world generations of cruel torture; and the Christ of the Gospels, if you could take Him as His chroniclers represent Him, would certainly have to be considered partly responsible for that.

There are other things of less importance. There is the instance of the Gadarene swine, where it certainly was not very kind to the pigs to put the devils into them and make them rush down the hill to the sea. You must remember that He was omnipotent, and He could have made the devils simply go away; but He chose to send them into the pigs. Then there is the curious story of the fig tree, which always rather puzzled me. You remember what happened about the fig tree. "He was hungry; and seeing a fig tree afar off having leaves, He came if haply He might find anything thereon; and when He came to it He found nothing but leaves, for the time of figs was not yet. And Jesus answered and said unto it: 'No man eat fruit of thee hereafter for ever' . . . and Peter . . . saith unto Him: 'Master, behold the fig tree which thou cursedst is withered away.'" This is a very curious story, because it was not the right time of year for figs, and you really could not blame the tree. I cannot myself feel that either in the matter of wisdom or in the matter of virtue Christ stands quite as high as some other people known to history. I think I should put Buddha and Socrates above Him in those respects.

The Emotional Factor

As I said before, I do not think that the real reason why people accept religion has anything to do with argumentation. They accept religion on emotional grounds. One is often told that it is a very wrong thing to attack religion, because religion makes men virtuous. So I am told; I have not noticed it. You know, of course, the parody of that argument in Samuel Butler's book, *Erewhon Revisited*. You will remember that in *Erewhon* there is a certain Higgs who arrives in a remote country, and after spending some time there he escapes from that country in a balloon. Twenty years later he comes back to that country and finds a new religion in which he is worshiped under the name of the

"Sun Child," and it is said that he ascended into heaven. He finds that the Feast of the Ascension is about to be celebrated, and he hears Professors Hanky and Panky say to each other that they never set eyes on the man Higgs, and they hope they never will; but they are the high priests of the religion of the Sun Child. He is very indignant, and he comes up to them, and he says, "I am going to expose all this humbug and tell the people of Erewhon that it was only I, the man Higgs, and I went up in a balloon." He was told, "You must not do that, because all the morals of this country are bound round this myth, and if they once know that you did not ascend into heaven they will all become wicked"; and so he is persuaded of that and he goes quietly away.

That is the idea—that we should all be wicked if we did not hold to the Christian religion. It seems to me that the people who have held to it have been for the most part extremely wicked. You find this curious fact, that the more intense has been the religion of any period and the more profound has been the dogmatic belief, the greater has been the cruelty and the worse has been the state of affairs. In the so-called ages of faith, when men really did believe the Christian religion in all its completeness, there was the Inquisition, with its tortures; there were millions of unfortunate women burned as witches; and there was every kind of cruelty practiced upon all sorts of people in the name of religion.

You find as you look around the world that every single bit of progress in humane feeling, every improvement in the criminal law, every step toward the diminution of war, every step toward better treatment of the colored races, or every mitigation of slavery, every moral progress that there has been in the world, has been consistently opposed by the organized churches of the world. I say quite deliberately that the Christian religion, as organized in its churches, has been and still is the principal enemy of moral progress in the world.

How the Churches Have Retarded Progress

You may think that I am going too far when I say that that is still so. I do not think that I am. Take one fact. You will bear with me if I mention it. It is not a pleasant fact, but the churches compel one to mention facts that are not pleasant. Supposing that in this world that we live in today an inexperienced girl is married to a syphilitic man; in that case the Catholic Church says, "This is an indissoluble sacrament. You must endure celibacy or stay together. And if you stay together, you must not use birth control to prevent the birth of syphilitic children." Nobody whose natural sympathies have not been warped by dogma, or whose moral nature was not absolutely dead to all sense of suffering, could maintain that it is right and proper that that state of things should continue.

That is only an example. There are a great many ways in which, at the present moment, the church, by its insistence upon what it chooses to call morality, inflicts upon all sorts of people undeserved and unnecessary suffering. And of course, as we know, it is in its major part an opponent still of progress and of improvement in all the ways that diminish suffering in the world, because it has chosen to label as morality a certain narrow set of rules of conduct which have nothing to do with human happiness; and when you say that this or that ought to be done because it would make for human happiness, they think that has nothing to do with the matter at all. "What has human happiness to do with morals? The object of morals is not to make people happy."

Fear, the Foundation of Religion

Religion is based, I think, primarily and mainly upon fear. It is partly the terror of the unknown and partly, as I have said, the wish to feel that you have a kind of elder brother who will stand by you in all your troubles and disputes. Fear is the basis of the whole thing—fear of the mysterious, fear of defeat, fear of death. Fear is the parent of cruelty, and therefore it is no wonder if cruelty and religion have gone hand in hand. It is because fear is at the basis of those two things. In this world we can now begin a little to understand things, and a little to master them by help of science, which has forced its way step by step against the Christian religion, against the churches, and against the opposition of all the old precepts. Science can help us to get over this craven fear in which mankind has lived for so many generations. Science can teach us, and I think our own hearts can teach us, no longer to look around for imaginary supports, no longer to invent allies in the sky, but rather to look to our own efforts here below to make this world a fit place to live in, instead of the sort of place that the churches in all these centuries have made it.

What We Must Do

We want to stand upon our own feet and look fair and square at the world—its good facts, its bad facts, its beauties, and its ugliness; see the world as it is and be not afraid of it. Conquer the world by intelligence and not merely by being slavishly subdued by the terror that comes from it. The whole conception of God is a conception derived from the ancient Oriental despotisms. It is a conception quite unworthy of free men. When you hear people in church debasing themselves and saying that they are miserable sinners, and all the rest of it, it seems contemptible and not worthy of self-respecting human beings. We ought to stand up and look the world frankly in the face. We ought to make the best we can of the world, and if it is not so good as we wish, after all it will still be better than what these others have made of it in all these ages. A good world needs knowledge, kindliness, and courage; it does not need a regretful hankering after the past or a fettering of the free intelligence by the words uttered long ago by ignorant men. It needs a fearless outlook and a free intelligence. It needs hope for the future, not looking back all the time toward a past that is dead, which we trust will be far surpassed by the future that our intelligence can create.

CHAPTER 11

You Bet Your Life: Pascal's Wager Defended

William Lycan and George Schlesinger

Suppose we cannot prove that God exists, nor can we prove that he does not. In this situation, what should we do? The French thinker Blaise Pascal (1623–1662) argued that we should accept Christianity rather than risk missing its rewards. As William Lycan and George Schlesinger show, this reasoning is hard to refute.

Professors Lycan and Schlesinger were colleagues for many years at the University of North Carolina at Chapel Hill. Lycan (1945–) has written over 150 articles and 7 books, including *Consciousness* (1987), *Modality and Meaning* (2001), and *Real Conditionals* (2001). Schlesinger (1925–) has written 10 books, including *The Sweep of Probability* (1991) and *Timely Topics* (1994).

Pascal's famous Wager is often mentioned in introductory philosophy classes and very occasionally addressed in the professional literature, but never favorably on the whole. It is considered an amusing bonbon and an entertaining early (mis)application of decision theory, but it is hardly thought convincing or even intellectually respectable. We maintain, to the contrary, that the Wager is seriously defensible and that the

Source: Reason and Responsibility, 10th ed., ed. Joel Feinberg and Russ Shafer-Landau (Belmont, CA: Wadsworth, 1999), pp. 118–123. Copyright © 1988 by William Lycan and George Schlesinger. Reprinted by permission of William Lycan.

stock objections to it can be answered, even if there are more sophisticated criticisms to be made of Pascal's argument. We are inclined to
think that the Wager is rational, and we propose to defend it here.

1. The Original Argument

We shall concentrate on the standard expected-utility version of the
Wager. Pascal supposed that the relevant alternatives are either that
God exists or that God does not exist, and, at least for the sake of argu-
ment, that both options are equally likely to be true, since

> [r]eason can decide nothing here. There is an infinite chaos
> which separates us. A game is being played at the extremity of
> this infinite distance where heads or tails will turn up. What will
> you wager?[1]

The relevant *choices* are to believe in God and adopt a reverent and
devout lifestyle, or not to believe and to behave however one otherwise would.[2] Since the Christian God, at least, promises eternal joy
and blissful union with Himself to those who do truly believe, and
damnation (on some accounts eternal torment) to those who have
heard but do not believe, the expected payoffs are as follows:

	God exists	God doesn't exist
Believe	∞	-20
Don't	$-\infty$	20

The two nonfinite payoffs represent (respectively) the eternal joy
granted to the believer if God does exist, and the infinite suffering one
will undergo if God exists and one chooses not to believe in Him. "−20"
somewhat arbitrarily represents the inconvenience of living a devout
and continent life when one doesn't have to, and "20" represents the
fun one would have if totally released from religious hangups. (We
assume for the moment that sin is fun; if not, so much the better
for Pascal's argument.) The expected utility (EU) of theism is
thus $.5(\infty) + .5(-20) = \infty$; the EU of agnosticism or atheism is
$.5(-\infty) + .5(20) = -\infty$.[3] According to Pascal, this doesn't even leave room
for discussion; one would have to be demented to pass up such an offer.
Whatever inconveniences may attend the devout and unpolluted life,
they pale beside the hope of eternal joy and the fear of damnation.

Pascal is not, of course, arguing for the existence of God; he affects to think that no such argument can be given and that the balance of evidence favors agnosticism. He is contending that despite the epistemic irrationality of theism, if you like, it is *prudentially* rational—i.e., in one's interest—to believe in God regardless of the balance of evidence.

2. Misguided Objections

Just to get a better feel for the Wager, let us very quickly run through a few preliminary objections, before coming to the two which we consider serious.

(i) "But my beliefs are not under my control; if I don't believe, then I can't believe, any more than I can believe there to be a live swordfish in front of me just because someone offers me $1,000 if I can get myself to believe that." *Reply:* In the long run, most people's beliefs *are* under their control; as Pascal himself emphasized, behavior therapy is remarkably effective even upon intellectuals. Start going to church and observing its rituals; associate with intelligent and congenial religious people; stop reading philosophy and associating with cynics and logical positivists. To quote William James's pungent paraphrase of Pascal,[4] "Go then and take holy water, and have masses said; belief will come and stupefy your scruples." It may be that some people, of an indefatigably analytical and incredulous temperament, simply cannot let themselves neglect the evidence and acquiesce in faith, just as some people simply cannot let themselves be hypnotized. But this is no reflection on the prudential rationality of the Wager; many people are psychologically incapable of doing what is demonstrably in their interest and known by them to be in their interest.[5]

(ii) "The Wager is cynical and mercenary; God wouldn't reward a 'believer' who makes it." *Reply:* Of course He wouldn't, just like that. Pascal's claim is rather that our interest lies in leaving our cynicism behind and eventually *becoming* believers, if we can. There is no particular reason to think that God would punish a truly sincere and devout believer just because of the historical origins of his/her belief. People are reportedly saved as a result of deathbed conversions, even after lives of the most appalling corruption, if their new belief is sincere and authentic.

(iii) "Pascal is wrong in conjecturing that the probability of theism is as high as 50%. It isn't; it's miniscule." *Reply:* That doesn't matter; even if the probability of theism is one in a thousand, the expected payoffs are still infinite. "All right, then, the probability is *zero*. I'm *certain* there is no God." *Reply:* How certain? And on what grounds? We would need to see a very convincing argument that no God of even roughly the traditional sort *could* exist, and it would have to be better than most philosophical arguments. (How many philosophical arguments do we know that confer probability *1* [i.e., absolute certainty] on their conclusions??)

(iv) "But if I bet on theism and in fact there is no God, my life will have been based on a lie." *Reply:* But if one bets on atheism and in fact there is a God, one's life will have been based on a lie. (And one's *after*life will be based on the worm that dieth not and the fire that is not quenched.) "But Pascal is telling us, brazenly, to form a firm belief that is unsupported by evidence and may even go directly against the evidence. That is an epistemic vice, the shirking of an epistemic obligation. As a professional philosopher I couldn't live with myself knowing I had done that." *Reply:* Epistemic obligation is not moral obligation. No one suffers if (in this sort of case) one violates an epistemic norm. No one could possibly care except (a) academic philosophers, (b) self-righteous textbook slaves, and (c) God Himself. As history abundantly shows, the first two of these may safely be ignored; the third is ultimately to be counted on Pascal's side (see the reply to objection [ii]). What does an epistemic peccadillo matter, compared to infinite joy or damnation?

(v) "What do you mean, '–20'? I *love* sin! And we're not talking about just a few Sunday mornings here, but proposing to bet an entire lifestyle." *Reply:* Does anyone *really* love sin so much as to be *rationally and without AKRASIA* [weakness of will] willing to risk eternal damnation for it? That cannot be true of many people. Indeed (to make a slightly different point), a survey would probably show that religious people are on the average happier and more satisfied with their lives than are nonreligious people[6] (whether this happiness is an *opiate* in some objectionable sense is a vexed question, resting on mixed empirical issues and philosophical concerns). How bad could a devout life be, compared to the (possible) alternative?

Actually, we are forced to agree, the devout life *could* be very bad indeed. The strictly correct answer to our rhetorical question leads directly to the first of the two objections to Pascal's argument that we are inclined to take more seriously. (After addressing it, we will turn to the second, namely, the celebrated Many-Gods problem.)

3. The Two Serious Objections

We need not dwell on the potential intolerability of time-consuming weekly devotions and of even more frequent abstinence from sin; for many leading religions, including Christianity and particularly Islam, require potentially far more: specifically, *martyrdom*. If political conditions are inimical, you or I might be faced with the choice of denying our faith or being put very horribly to death. Now, even if we grant that a few Sunday mornings and even a fully reverent Christian lifestyle of the 1980s are an eminently good bet *sub specie aeternitatis*, what if we were suddenly faced with real martyrdom? Would Pascal counsel beheading for anyone in Thomas More's position? Should we be willing, *just in virtue of making the Wager*, to be cast into the Coliseum and wait patiently for the biggest lion?

A first and sensible reply would be that most of us who are reading this paper have excellent (though hardly conclusive) grounds for thinking that we will never in fact be called upon to martyr ourselves; and if so, then the Wager remains reasonable at least *for us* until such time as we are presented with ominous new contrary evidence. But this is too simple. For in order to attain the *genuinely* religious life, as is required for salvation, we must achieve a condition in which we *would* gladly martyr ourselves if called upon to do so, even though we could not rationally want this in our present agnostic state. Could it possibly be reasonable for us, now, in our *present* circumstances and state of mind, to embark on a procedure that we fully intend will brainwash us into accepting a potentially disastrous course of action?—Is this any more rational than (for money) taking a pill that will make us into suicidal depressives or lunatic daredevils?

Yes, of course it is. The expected payoff is still infinite. For death, even horrible and very painful death, is still only finitely disutile [harmful]. There are fates worse than death, as is evidenced by the plain fact that countless human beings *have* willingly and not irrationally chosen death before dishonor, death rather than drastic indignity, death to save a loved one, death in service of a cherished cause, or the like. In that sense one's life is one's own, and is available as a stake among other stakes in a gamble, though such a gamble must be a desperate one.

If this is right, then our instinctive recoil from martyrdom is just that—instinctive recoil. Of course we shrink from violent death, and of course the prospect of immediate rending and shredding would very likely cause us (quickly) to rethink the Wager. But this does nothing *argumentatively* to show that the Wager is not still in fact rational. At best it shows that visceral fear drives out sound argument, and we knew that anyway. . . .

Let us turn at last to the Many-Gods problem. Pascal assumes a very specific sort of god—roughly a Christian god who rewards His own partisans with infinite bliss and who perhaps sentences opponents and even neutrals to damnation of one truly awful sort or another. But logical space contains countless possible gods of very different natures—all infinite, if you like—and if we can know nothing of infinitude then we cannot have reason to prefer any one of these gods to another. Unfortunately, their respective expected payoffs are diverse and conflicting: What if instead of the Christian God there is a Baal, a Moloch, a Wotan, or a Zeus, who prepares a particularly nasty fate for devout Christians? What if there is a very shy and reclusive god who does not want to be believed in and who enforces this desire by damning all believers to eternal torment? Etc., etc. Pascal assumed that *his* God has a 50% probability of existing, but this is grossly presumptuous in the face of all the other gods who cannot be ruled out *a priori*. Either Pascal's Christian God must take His place equiprobably alongside the indefinitely many other possible deities, in which case the probability of His existence is negligible, or Pascal's argument could be reiterated for every other god who offers infinite payoffs, in which case it proves too much and leads directly to contradiction due to incompatibly jealous gods.

4. A First Answer to the Many-Gods Objection

A natural response is to say that for one reason or another all the various possible gods are *not* equiprobable. Intuitively, it is far more likely that the Christian God, the God of the Jews, or Allah exists, than that there is a vindictively shy god or a god who rewards all and only those who do not shave themselves or a god who wears pink bowties that light up. For here, we believe, empirical evidence is relevant to a certain extent. There is *some* empirical reason for thinking that the Christian God or the God of Israel—or even Allah—exists, in the form of partially checkable scriptures, historical reports (made by ostensibly intelligent and impartial observers) of divine manifestations, and the like, even if this evidence is pathetically far from convincing; while there is simply no reason of any sort for thinking that there is a reclusive god or a divine rewarder of non-self-shaving or whatever. (We also think that the ability of a particular religion to attract and sustain millions of adherents over thousands of years is epistemically a mark in its favor, even if a very weak one.) . . .

There is still another powerful objection . . . to this initial response: . . . how are we to choose between the gods of the major religions? Why should we believe in the Christian God rather than Yahweh? (These deities may well be considered identical by theorists, but their worship is not; they respectively require incompatible conduct.) For that matter, why should we believe in either of those rather than in Allah, or in one or more of the Hindu gods? There are probably more Muslims and more Hindus than there are genuinely religious Christians or Jews, so consensus is of no help in the present regard.

Here some fine-tuning is in order, though we cannot pursue the question in any detail. (i) Empirical indications are still germane. If one looks carefully, one may find that history provides more respectable evidence (however imperfect) for one of the major gods than for another. (ii) One must attend to the details of the respective payoffs; other things being equal, one should go for the deity that offers the more attractive afterlife and/or the nastiest form of damnation. (More on this shortly.) (iii) Given the facts taken account of in (i) and (ii), one must try for the lowest common denominator in terms of tolerance: that is, one must keep one's faith as ecumenical as one dares. Some gods are more jealous than others, of course; some deny salvation to any but the adherents of some crackpot sect, while others grant it to anyone who has led the right sort of life and had an appropriately respectful attitude toward something or other. So, overall, one must balance considerations (i), (ii) and (iii) against each other for each particular case and see how the resulting EUs come out. This is a very tricky but not completely unfeasible bit of comparison shopping. Of course, we may get it wrong and back the wrong god. In fact, given the multiplicity of major deities and the narrow tolerances involved in our attempt at judicious ecumenism, we *probably will* get it wrong. But a significant chance of infinite success offset by a greater chance of infinite failure is still better odds than *no* chance of success supplemented by a *still* greater chance of failure. . . .

5. A Second Answer to the Many-Gods Objection

A deeper and more authentic approach would take into account the special nature of the reward on which one is bid to wager. First, we are to realize that what Pascal is urging is for the gambler to set his eyes upon a prize of a sort entirely different from the "poisonous plea-sures" Pascal advises him to abandon. The gratification to be pursued by the religious seeker is not something extrinsic to the devout life, but an organic outgrowth of it. It does not differ in kind from the seek-ing, as if one were to be handed a new IBM color-graphics monitor as a prize for having won the Carrboro Marathon, but is the natural fruit of one's way of life. Theists in every age have anticipated the dissolving of their narrow selves in the ecstasy of a God-centered life here on earth and, more to Pascal's point, their eventual smooth translation into a disembodied existence in holy felicity—an eternal love of the Divine. A human being becomes capable of this kind of love only after he/she has grasped the idea of God. Maimonides puts it as follows:

> What is the proper love of God? It is the love of the Lord with a great and very strong love so that one's soul shall be tied to the love of the Lord, and one should be continually enraptured by it, like a love-sick individual, whose mind is at no time free from his passion for a particular woman, the thought of her filling his heart at all times, when sitting down or rising up, even when he is eating or drinking. Still more intense should be the love of God in the hearts of those who love Him.[7]

According to classical theologians, one who has spent one's life as a passionate servant of the Lord will have developed and perfected one's soul adequately to have acquired the capacity to partake in the transmundane bliss that awaits in the afterlife. The suitably groomed soul, when released from its earthly fetters, will bask in the radiance of the Divine presence and delight in the adoring communion with a loving God (if this is a multiply mixed metaphor, it doesn't matter).

It is appropriate at this point to comment again upon objection (ii) considered in sec. 2 above, the complaint that because of its calcu-lating and mercenary character, the Wager is both morally repugnant and inefficacious, and incompatible with the spirit of any genuine religion. Many people would recoil from a Wagerer just as they would from a hypocrite who went out of his way to brighten the mood of an enfeebled (but wealthy) elderly person for no loftier reason than to increase his chance of being mentioned in that person's will. Such misgivings could not easily be dismissed if Pascal had had in mind a pie-in-the-sky, anthropocentric sort of heaven such as that which Heinrich Heine sardonically claimed to be reserved for the righteous. According to Heine's mouth-watering description, Heaven is a place where roast geese fly around with gravy boats in their bills and there are brooks of bouillon and champagne and everyone revels in eternal feasting and carousing. It would and should be hard to admire anyone who pursued a godly, righteous and sober life mainly in the hope of gaining admission to that kind of paradise. But we are considering the Wager in the context of an infinitely more exalted afterlife. Suppose that we have always had great admiration for Smith because of the noteworthy humanitarian works he has performed, and that lately we have heard of further truly heroic acts of benevolence on his part that make his previous accomplishments pale into insignificance. Then we should hardly be condemned for making efforts to discover more information concerning Smith's further laudable deeds—even if we are fully conscious of the sentiments of Thomas Carlyle, who wrote, "Does not every true man feel that he is himself made higher by doing reverence to what is really above him?"[8] Most people would find our conduct neither ignoble nor stupid, even if our efforts to discover the grounds of Smith's greatly intensified worthiness were done explicitly for the sake of feeling ourselves made higher by doing reverence to a more exalted personage. . . .

It is the crux of our problem that for more than one deity there is an eternal and hence infinite payoff. Still, the very nature of the sublime gratification the believer aspires to ensures that its quality will vary with the character of the deity he/she bets on. When Carlyle spoke of the self-enhancement resulting from doing reverence to what is above oneself, he had in mind an entirely worldly context. But when the object of one's homage is a divine being, the uplift is immeasurably greater. Pascal wagered on the ecstasy to be derived from exalting a supereminent being and basking in its radiance, and naturally, the more glorious and sublime the being, the greater that worshipful ecstasy would be. Thus, Pascal's argument leads us to maximize religious benefit by positing that superbeing which is the very most worthy of worship, namely, the absolutely perfect being, which we take to be the God of Judeo-Christian theism and of some other, non-Western religions as well, minus some of the tendentious if traditional special features ascribed to Him by sectarian practitioners of those religions.

6. Conclusion

If one does not already incline toward theism, or perhaps even if one does so incline, there is still a temptation—a powerful one—to refuse to take the Wager seriously. How, again, can one listen to all this stuff about grooming one's soul, absolute perfection, infinite ecstasy, and the like, if one (as things are) *simply does not* believe in any god and regards theism of any sort as being on an equal epistemic footing with belief in the Easter Bunny?

To this we say: Consider the arguments fairly. We maintain that the *standard* and ubiquitous intuitive rejection of the Wager by philosophers is grounded in a confused conflation of the objections we have already addressed, particularly: the feeling that one could not do anything about one's beliefs even if one tried, the feeling that theism has probability zero, and the feeling that any failure to proportion one's belief to the evidence is a shameful if secret vice. But once these various misgivings have been separated and cast explicitly in the form of objections, they are seen to have little rational force. If one wishes to decline the Wager one will have to think of more subtle criticisms than those which have appeared in the literature to date.

We do not claim that our case is conclusive, or that the Wager is now dictated by reason. We do contend that at the present stage of investigation Pascal's argument is unrefuted and not unreasonable.

Let us pray.

Notes

1. Blaise Pascal, "The Wager."
2. Of course there are degrees of belief in between, including a significant range of agnosticism. The possibility of metaphysical agnosticism accompanied by a selflessly beneficent—even saintly—life is a piquant one, and much debated by some major religions, but we shall neglect it here.
3. Expected utility refers to the likely good or harm one can expect from choosing one option over another. We determine expected utility as follows. First, identify the relevant alternatives. (In the wager, this refers to belief or lack of belief in god's existence.) Then identify and assign a numerical value to all of the outcomes ("payoffs") associated with each alternative. In the wager, the payoffs associated with belief are either infinite happiness or a so-so life of religious propriety. Lycan and Schlesinger value this latter payoff as –20. The payoffs associated with nonbelief are infinite misery or a decent life of secular satisfactions. The authors value this last payoff as 20. Now determine the probability or likelihood that each of the outcomes will occur. Pascal claims that there is a 50% chance of God's existing, so there is a 50% probability that any one of the payoffs will be generated. Now you need to do a little math. Start by focusing on one alternative (say, belief in God). In the wager,

theism is associated with two outcomes or payoffs. Multiply each payoff (infinite happiness, –20) by the probability that it will be realized (50%). Then add the products together. This (infinite happiness) is the expected utility of belief in god. Work through the same steps to figure out the expected utility of nonbelief in god. To decide what best serves one's interests (i.e., what it is *prudent* to do), compare the relevant alternatives (here, belief or nonbelief in god) and opt for the one with the greatest expected utility. If Pascal is right, this is an easy call. [Feinberg and Shafer-Landau]

4. William James, "The Will to Believe."

5. Someone experiences an ominous medical symptom, and does not—cannot—go to the doctor because he is paralyzed with fear. He ends up dead. Someone else does not—cannot—make Pascal's Wager because he is paralyzed with textbook rationality. He ends up dead. Permanently.

6. Actual demographic surveys do show at least that religious people fare better with respect to divorce, suicide, and other indicators of troubled personal lives.

7. Maimonides, *Mishneh Torah,* Hilkhot Teshuvah X.

8. Thomas Carlyle, *On Heroes, Hero-Worship and the Heroic in History* (London: J. Fraser, 1841), p. 1.

*T*he Mind

CHAPTER 12

Do We Survive Death?

Bertrand Russell

In this essay, the great British philosopher Bertrand Russell (1872–1970) argues that, unfortunately, we do not survive death.

Russell's major works include *A Critical Exposition of the Philosophy of Leibniz* (1900), *The Problems of Philosophy* (1912), *A Free Man's Worship* (1923), *Sceptical Essays* (1928), *A History of Western Philosophy* (1946), *The Philosophy of Logical Atomism* (1949), *Authority and the Individual* (1949), and *The Autobiography of Bertrand Russell* (in three volumes, 1967, 1968, and 1969).

This piece was first published in 1936 in a book entitled The Mysteries of Life and Death. *The article by Bishop Barnes to which Russell refers appeared in the same work.*

Before we can profitably discuss whether we shall continue to exist after death, it is well to be clear as to the sense in which a man is the same person as he was yesterday. Philosophers used to think that there were definite substances, the soul and the body, that each lasted on from day to day, that a soul, once created, continued to exist throughout all future time, whereas a body ceased temporarily from death till the resurrection of the body.

Source: Bertrand Russell, *Why I Am Not a Christian* (New York: Simon and Schuster, 1957), pp. 88–93. Reprinted with permission of Simon & Schuster Adult Publishing Group, Taylor & Francis Books, Ltd., and the Bertrand Russell Peace Foundation. Copyright © 1957, 1985 by George Allen & Unwin, Ltd.

The part of this doctrine which concerns the present life is pretty certainly false. The matter of the body is continually changing by processes of nutriment and wastage. Even if it were not, atoms in physics are no longer supposed to have continuous existence; there is no sense in saying: this is the same atom as the one that existed a few minutes ago. The continuity of a human body is a matter of appearance and behavior, not of substance.

The same thing applies to the mind. We think and feel and act, but there is not, in addition to thoughts and feelings and actions, a bare entity, the mind or the soul, which does or suffers these occurrences. The mental continuity of a person is a continuity of habit and memory: there was yesterday one person whose feelings I can remember, and that person I regard as myself of yesterday; but, in fact, myself of yesterday was only certain mental occurrences which are now remembered and are regarded as part of the person who now recollects them. All that constitutes a person is a series of experiences connected by memory and by certain similarities of the sort we call habit.

If, therefore, we are to believe that a person survives death, we must believe that the memories and habits which constitute the person will continue to be exhibited in a new set of occurrences.

No one can prove that this will not happen. But it is easy to see that it is very unlikely. Our memories and habits are bound up with the structure of the brain, in much the same way in which a river is connected with the riverbed. The water in the river is always changing, but it keeps to the same course because previous rains have worn a channel. In like manner, previous events have worn a channel in the brain, and our thoughts flow along this channel. This is the cause of memory and mental habits. But the brain, as a structure, is dissolved at death, and memory therefore may be expected to be also dissolved. There is no more reason to think otherwise than to expect a river to persist in its old course after an earthquake has raised a mountain where a valley used to be.

All memory, and therefore (one may say) all minds, depend upon a property which is very noticeable in certain kinds of material structures but exists little if at all in other kinds. This is the property of forming habits as a result of frequent similar occurrences. For example: a bright light makes the pupils of the eyes contract; and if you repeatedly flash a light in a man's eyes and beat a gong at the same time, the gong alone will, in the end, cause his pupils to contract. This is a fact about the brain and nervous system—that is to say, about a certain material structure. It will be found that exactly similar facts explain our response to language and our use of it, our memories and the emotions they arouse, our moral or immoral habits of behavior, and indeed everything that constitutes our mental personality, except the part determined by heredity. The part determined by heredity is handed on to our posterity but cannot, in the individual, survive the disintegration of the body. Thus both the hereditary and the acquired parts of a personality are, so far as our experience goes, bound up with the characteristics of certain bodily structures. We all know that memory may be obliterated by an injury to the brain, that a virtuous person may be rendered vicious by encephalitis lethargica, and that a clever child can be turned into an idiot by lack of iodine. In view of such familiar facts, it seems scarcely probable that the mind survives the total destruction of brain structure which occurs at death.

It is not rational arguments but emotions that cause belief in a future life.

The most important of these emotions is fear of death, which is instinctive and biologically useful. If we genuinely and wholeheartedly believed in the future life, we should cease completely to fear death. The effects would be curious, and probably such as most of us would deplore. But our human and subhuman ancestors have fought and exterminated their enemies throughout many geological ages and have profited by courage; it is therefore an advantage to the victors in the struggle for life to be able, on occasion, to overcome the natural fear of death. Among animals and savages, instinctive pugnacity suffices for this purpose; but at a certain stage of development, as the Mohammedans first proved, belief in Paradise has considerable military value as reinforcing natural pugnacity. We should therefore admit that militarists are wise in encouraging the belief in immortality, always supposing that this belief does not become so profound as to produce indifference to the affairs of the world.

Another emotion which encourages the belief in survival is admiration of the excellence of man. As the Bishop of Birmingham says, "His mind is a far finer instrument than anything that had appeared earlier—he knows right and wrong. He can build Westminster Abbey. He can make an airplane. He can calculate the distance of the sun. . . . Shall, then, man at death perish utterly? Does that incomparable instrument, his mind, vanish when life ceases?"

The Bishop proceeds to argue that "the universe has been shaped and is governed by an intelligent purpose," and that it would have been unintelligent, having made man, to let him perish.

To this argument there are many answers. In the first place, it has been found, in the scientific investigation of nature, that the intrusion of moral or aesthetic values has always been an obstacle to discovery. It used to be thought that the heavenly bodies must move in circles because the circle is the most perfect curve, that species must be immutable because God would only create what was perfect and what therefore stood in no need of improvement, that it was useless to combat epidemics except by repentance because they were sent as a punishment for sin, and so on. It has been found, however, that, so far as we can discover, nature is indifferent to our values and can only be understood by ignoring our notions of good and bad. The Universe may have a purpose, but nothing that we know suggests that, if so, this purpose has any similarity to ours.

Nor is there in this anything surprising. Dr. Barnes tells us that man "knows right and wrong." But, in fact, as anthropology shows, men's views of right and wrong have varied to such an extent that no single item has been permanent. We cannot say, therefore, that man knows right and wrong, but only that some men do. Which men? Nietzsche argued in favor of an ethic profoundly different from Christ's, and some powerful governments have accepted his teaching. If knowledge of right and wrong is to be an argument for immortality, we must first settle whether to believe Christ or Nietzsche, and then argue that Christians are immortal, but Hitler and Mussolini are not, or vice versa. The decision will obviously be made on the battlefield, not in the study. Those who have the best poison gas will have the ethic of the future and will therefore be the immortal ones.

Our feelings and beliefs on the subject of good and evil are, like everything else about us, natural facts, developed in the struggle for existence and not having any divine or supernatural origin. In one of Aesop's fables, a lion is shown pictures of huntsmen catching lions and remarks that, if he had painted them, they would have shown lions catching huntsmen. Man, says Dr. Barnes, is a fine fellow because he can make airplanes. A little while ago there was a popular song about the cleverness of flies in walking upside down on the ceiling, with the chorus: "Could Lloyd George do it? Could Mr. Baldwin do it? Could Ramsay Mac do it? Why, no." On this basis a very telling argument could be constructed by a theologically-minded fly, which no doubt the other flies would find most convincing.

Moreover, it is only when we think abstractly that we have such a high opinion of man. Of men in the concrete, most of us think the vast majority very bad. Civilized states spend more than half their revenue on killing each other's citizens. Consider the long history of the activities inspired by moral fervor: human sacrifices, persecutions of heretics, witch-hunts, pogroms leading up to wholesale extermination by poison gases . . . Are these abominations, and the ethical doctrines by which they are prompted, really evidence of an intelligent Creator? And can we really wish that the men who practiced them should live forever? The world in which we live can be understood as a result of muddle and accident; but if it is the outcome of deliberate purpose, the purpose must have been that of a fiend. For my part, I find accident a less painful and more plausible hypothesis.

CHAPTER 13

Split Brains and Personal Identity

Derek Parfit

The British philosopher Derek Parfit (1942–) describes some startling results in neuroscience and asks what they mean for our conception of ourselves.

Parfit's *Reasons and Persons* (1984) will be remembered as one of the great philosophical works of the twentieth century.

It was the split-brain cases which drew me into philosophy. Our knowledge of these cases depends on the results of various psychological tests, as described by Donald MacKay.[1] These tests made use of two facts. We control each of our arms, and see what is in each half of our visual fields, with only one of our hemispheres. When someone's hemispheres have been disconnected, psychologists can thus present to this person two different written questions in the two halves of his visual field, and can receive two different answers written by this person's two hands.

Here is a simplified imaginary version of the kind of evidence that such tests provide. One of these people looks fixedly at the

---

[1] See Donald MacKay, "Divided Brains—Divided Minds?" in *Mindwaves,* eds. Colin Blakemore and Susan Greenfield (New York: Blackwell, 1987), pp. 5–16.

Source: This essay appears as "Divided Minds and the Nature of Persons" by Derek Parfit, in *Mindwaves,* ed. Colin Blakemore and Susan Greenfield (New York: Blackwell, 1987), pp. 19–26. Reprinted by permission of Blackwell Publishing Ltd.

centre of a wide screen, whose left half is red and right half is blue. On each half in a darker shade are the words, "How many colours can you see?" With both hands the person writes, "Only one." The words are now changed to read, "Which is the only colour that you can see?" With one of his hands the person writes "Red," with the other he writes "Blue."

If this is how such a person responds, I would conclude that he is having two visual sensations—that he does, as he claims, see both red and blue. But in seeing each colour he is not aware of seeing the other. He has two streams of consciousness, in each of which he can see only one colour. In one stream he sees red, and at the same time, in his other stream, he sees blue. More generally, he could be having at the same time two series of thoughts and sensations, in having each of which he is unaware of having the other.

This conclusion has been questioned. It has been claimed by some that there are not *two* streams of consciousness, on the ground that the sub-dominant hemisphere is a part of the brain whose functioning involves no consciousness. If this were true, these cases would lose most of their interest. I believe that it is not true, chiefly because, if a person's dominant hemisphere is destroyed, this person is able to react in the way in which, in the split-brain cases, the sub-dominant hemisphere reacts, and we do not believe that such a person is just an automaton, without consciousness. The sub-dominant hemisphere is, of course, much less developed in certain ways, typically having the linguistic abilities of a three-year-old. But three-year-olds are conscious. This supports the view that, in split-brain cases, there *are* two streams of consciousness.

Another view is that, in these cases, there are two persons involved, sharing the same body. Like Professor MacKay, I believe that we should reject this view. My reason for believing this is, however, different. Professor MacKay denies that there are two persons involved because he believes that there is only one person involved. I believe that, in a sense, the number of persons involved is none.

The Ego Theory and the Bundle Theory

To explain this sense I must, for a while, turn away from the split-brain cases. There are two theories about what persons are, and what is involved in a person's continued existence over time. On the *Ego Theory*, a person's continued existence cannot be explained except as the continued existence of a particular *Ego*, or *subject of experiences*. An Ego

Theorist claims that, if we ask what unifies someone's consciousness at any time—what makes it true, for example, that I can now both see what I am typing and hear the wind outside my window—the answer is that these are both experiences which are being had by me, this person, at this time. Similarly, what explains the unity of a person's whole life is the fact that all of the experiences in this life are had by the same person, or subject of experiences. In its best-known form, the *Cartesian view,* each person is a persisting purely mental thing—a soul, or spiritual substance.

The rival view is the *Bundle Theory.* Like most styles in art—Gothic, baroque, rococo, etc.—this theory owes its name to its critics. But the name is good enough. According to the Bundle Theory, we can't explain either the unity of consciousness at any time, or the unity of a whole life, by referring to a person. Instead we must claim that there are long series of different mental states and events—thoughts, sensations, and the like—each series being what we call one life. Each series is unified by various kinds of causal relation, such as the relations that hold between experiences and later memories of them. Each series is thus like a bundle tied up with string.

In a sense, a Bundle Theorist denies the existence of persons. An outright denial is of course absurd. As Reid protested in the eighteenth century, "I am not thought, I am not action, I am not feeling; I am something which thinks and acts and feels." I am not a series of events, but a person. A Bundle Theorist admits this fact, but claims it to be only a fact about our grammar, or our language. There are persons or subjects in this language-dependent way. If, however, persons are believed to be more than this—to be separately existing things, distinct from our brains and bodies, and the various kinds of mental states and events—the Bundle Theorist denies that there are such things.

The first Bundle Theorist was Buddha, who taught "anatta," or the *No Self view.* Buddhists concede that selves or persons have "nominal existence," by which they mean that persons are merely combinations of other elements. Only what exists by itself, as a separate element, has instead what Buddhists call "actual existence." Here are some quotations from Buddhist texts:

> At the beginning of their conversation the king politely asks the monk his name, and receives the following reply: "Sir, I am known as 'Nagasena'; my fellows in the religious life address me as 'Nagasena.' Although my parents gave me the name . . . it is just an appellation, a form of speech, a description, a conventional usage. 'Nagasena' is only a name, for no person is found here."

A sentient being does exist, you think, O Mara? You are misled by a false conception. This bundle of elements is void of Self. In it there is no sentient being. Just as a set of wooden parts receives the name of carriage, so do we give to elements the name of fancied being.

Buddha has spoken thus: "O Brethren, actions do exist, and also their consequences, but the person that acts does not. There is no one to cast away this set of elements, and no one to assume a new set of them. There exists no Individual, it is only a conventional name given to a set of elements."[2]

Buddha's claims are strikingly similar to the claims advanced by several Western writers. Since these writers knew nothing of Buddha, the similarity of these claims suggests that they are not merely part of one cultural tradition, in one period. They may be, as I believe they are, true.

What We Believe Ourselves to Be

Given the advances in psychology and neurophysiology, the Bundle Theory may now seem to be obviously true. It may seem uninteresting to deny that there are separately existing Egos, which are distinct from brains and bodies and the various kinds of mental states and events. But this is not the only issue. We may be convinced that the Ego Theory is false, or even senseless. Most of us, however, even if we are not aware of this, also have certain beliefs about what is involved in our continued existence over time. And these beliefs would only be justified if something like the Ego Theory was true. Most of us therefore have false beliefs about what persons are, and about ourselves.

These beliefs are best revealed when we consider certain imaginary cases, often drawn from science fiction. One such case is *teletransportation*. Suppose that you enter a cubicle in which, when you press a button, a scanner records the states of all of the cells in your brain and body, destroying both while doing so. This information is then transmitted at the speed of light to some other planet, where a replicator produces a perfect organic copy of you. Since the brain of your Replica is exactly like yours, it will seem to remember living your life up to the moment when you pressed the button, its character will be just like yours, and it will be in every other way psychologically

---

[2] For the sources of these and similar quotations, see my [Parfit's] *Reasons and Persons* (Oxford: Oxford Univ. Press, 1984), pp. 502–3, 532.

continuous with you. This psychological continuity will not have its normal cause, the continued existence of your brain, since the causal chain will run through the transmission by radio of your "blueprint."

Several writers claim that, if you chose to be teletransported, believing this to be the fastest way of travelling, you would be making a terrible mistake. This would not be a way of travelling, but a way of dying. It may not, they concede, be quite as bad as ordinary death. It might be some consolation to you that, after your death, you will have this Replica, which can finish the book that you are writing, act as parent to your children, and so on. But, they insist, this Replica won't be you. It will merely be someone else, who is exactly like you. This is why this prospect is nearly as bad as ordinary death.

Imagine next a whole range of cases, in each of which, in a single operation, a different proportion of the cells in your brain and body would be replaced with exact duplicates. At the near end of this range, only 1 or 2 per cent would be replaced; in the middle, 40 or 60 per cent; near the far end, 98 or 99 per cent. At the far end of this range is pure teletransportation, the case in which all of your cells would be "replaced."

When you imagine that some proportion of your cells will be replaced with exact duplicates, it is natural to have the following beliefs. First, if you ask, "Will I survive? Will the resulting person be me?," there must be an answer to this question. Either you will survive, or you are about to die. Second, the answer to this question must be either a simple "Yes" or a simple "No." The person who wakes up either will or will not be you. There cannot be a third answer, such as that the person waking up will be half you. You can imagine yourself later being half-conscious. But if the resulting person will be fully conscious, he cannot be half you. To state these beliefs together: to the question, "Will the resulting person be me?," there must always *be* an answer, which must be all-or-nothing.

There seem good grounds for believing that, in the case of teletransportation, your Replica would not be you. In a slight variant of this case, your Replica might be created while you were still alive, so that you could talk to one another. This seems to show that, if 100 per cent of your cells were replaced, the result would merely be a Replica of you. At the other end of my range of cases, where only 1 per cent would be replaced, the resulting person clearly *would* be you. It therefore seems that, in the cases in between, the resulting person must be either you, or merely a Replica. It seems that one of these must be true, and that it makes a great difference which is true.

How We Are Not What We Believe

If these beliefs were correct, there must be some critical percentage, somewhere in this range of cases, up to which the resulting person would be you, and beyond which he would merely be your Replica. Perhaps, for example, it would be you who would wake up if the proportion of cells replaced were 49 per cent, but if just a few more cells were also replaced, this would make all the difference, causing it to be someone else who would wake up.

That there must be some such critical percentage follows from our natural beliefs. But this conclusion is most implausible. How could a few cells make such a difference? Moreover, if there is such a critical percentage, no one could ever discover where it came. Since in all these cases the resulting person would believe that he was you, there could never be any evidence about where, in this range of cases, he would suddenly cease to be you.

On the Bundle Theory, we should reject these natural beliefs. Since you, the person, are not a separately existing entity, we can know exactly what would happen without answering the question of what will happen to you. Moreover, in the cases in the middle of my range, it is an empty question whether the resulting person would be you, or would merely be someone else who is exactly like you. These are not here two different possibilities, one of which must be true. These are merely two different descriptions of the very same course of events. If 50 per cent of your cells were replaced with exact duplicates, we could call the resulting person you, or we could call him merely your Replica. But since these are not here different possibilities, this is a mere choice of words.

As Buddha claimed, the Bundle Theory is hard to believe. It is hard to accept that it could be an empty question whether one is about to die, or will instead live for many years.

What we are being asked to accept may be made clearer with this analogy. Suppose that a certain club exists for some time, holding regular meetings. The meetings then cease. Some years later, several people form a club with the same name, and the same rules. We can ask, "Did these people revive the very same club? Or did they merely start up another club which is exactly similar?" Given certain further details, this would be another empty question. We could know just what happened without answering this question. Suppose that someone said: "But there must be an answer. The club meeting later must either be, or not be, the very same club." This would show that this person didn't understand the nature of clubs.

In the same way, if we have any worries about my imagined cases, we don't understand the nature of persons. In each of my cases, you would know that the resulting person would be both psychologically and physically exactly like you, and that he would have some particular proportion of the cells in your brain and body—90 per cent, or 10 per cent, or, in the case of teletransportation, 0 per cent. Knowing this, you know everything. How could it be a real question what would happen to you, unless you are a separately existing Ego, distinct from a brain and body, and the various kinds of mental state and event? If there are no such Egos, there is nothing else to ask a real question about.

Accepting the Bundle Theory is not only hard; it may also affect our emotions. As Buddha claimed, it may undermine our concern about our own futures. This effect can be suggested by redescribing this change of view. Suppose that you are about to be destroyed, but will later have a Replica on Mars. You would naturally believe that this prospect is about as bad as ordinary death, since your Replica won't be you. On the Bundle Theory, the fact that your Replica won't be you just consists in the fact that, though it will be fully psychologically continuous with you, this continuity won't have its normal cause. But when you object to teletransportation you are not objecting merely to the abnormality of this cause. You are objecting that this cause won't get *you* to Mars. You fear that the abnormal cause will fail to produce a further and all-important fact, which is different from the fact that your Replica will be psychologically continuous with you. You do not merely want there to be psychological continuity between you and some future person. You want to *be* this future person. On the Bundle Theory, there is no such special further fact. What you fear will not happen, in this imagined case, *never* happens. You want the person on Mars to be you in a specially intimate way in which no future person will ever be you. This means that, judged from the standpoint of your natural beliefs, even ordinary survival is about as bad as teletransportation. *Ordinary survival is about as bad as being destroyed and having a Replica.*

How the Split-Brain Cases
Support the Bundle Theory

The truth of the Bundle Theory seems to me, in the widest sense, as much a scientific as a philosophical conclusion. I can imagine kinds of evidence which would have justified believing in the existence of separately existing Egos, and believing that the continued existence of these Egos is what explains the continuity of each mental life. But there is in fact very little evidence in favour of this Ego Theory, and much for the alternative Bundle Theory.

Some of this evidence is provided by the split-brain cases. On the Ego Theory, to explain what unifies our experiences at any one time, we should simply claim that these are all experiences which are being had by the same person. Bundle Theorists reject this explanation. This disagreement is hard to resolve in ordinary cases. But consider the simplified split-brain case that I described. We show to my imagined patient a placard whose left half is blue and right half is red. In one of this person's two streams of consciousness, he is aware of seeing only blue, while at the same time, in his other stream, he is aware of seeing only red. Each of these two visual experiences is combined with other experiences, like that of being aware of moving one of his hands. What unifies the experiences, at any time, in each of this person's two streams of consciousness? What unifies his awareness of seeing only red with his awareness of moving one hand? The answer cannot be that these experiences are being had by the same person. This answer cannot explain the unity of each of this person's two streams of consciousness, since it ignores the disunity between these streams. This person is now having all of the experiences in both of his two streams. If this fact was what unified these experiences, this would make the two streams one.

These cases do not, I have claimed, involve two people sharing a single body. Since there is only one person involved, who has two streams of consciousness, the Ego Theorist's explanation would have to take the following form. He would have to distinguish between persons and subjects of experiences, and claim that, in split-brain cases, there are *two* of the latter. What unifies the experiences in one of the person's two streams would have to be the fact that these experiences are all being had by the same subject of experiences. What unifies the experiences in this person's other stream would have to be the fact that they are being had by another subject of experiences. When this explanation takes this form, it becomes much less plausible. While we could assume that "subject of experiences," or "Ego," simply meant "person," it was easy to believe that there are subjects of experiences. But if there can be subjects of experiences that are not persons, and if in the life of a split-brain patient there are at any time two different subjects of experiences—two different Egos—why should we believe that there really are such things? This does not amount to a refutation. But it seems to me a strong argument against the Ego Theory.

As a Bundle Theorist, I believe that these two Egos are idle cogs. There is another explanation of the unity of consciousness, both in ordinary cases and in split-brain cases. It is simply a fact that ordinary people are, at any time, aware of having several different experiences. This awareness of several different experiences can be helpfully compared with one's awareness, in short-term memory, of several different experiences. Just as there can be a single memory of just having had several experiences, such as hearing a bell strike three times, there can be a single state of awareness both of hearing the fourth striking of this bell, and of seeing, at the same time, ravens flying past the bell-tower.

Unlike the Ego Theorist's explanation, this explanation can easily be extended to cover split-brain cases. In such cases there is, at any time, not one state of awareness of several different experiences, but two such states. In the case I described, there is one state of awareness of both seeing only red and of moving one hand, and there is another state of awareness of both seeing only blue and moving the other hand. In claiming that there are two such states of awareness, we are not postulating the existence of unfamiliar entities, two separately existing Egos which are not the same as the single person whom the case involves. This explanation appeals to a pair of mental states which would have to be described anyway in a full description of this case.

I have suggested how the split-brain cases provide one argument for one view about the nature of persons. I should mention another such argument, provided by an imagined extension of these cases, first discussed at length by David Wiggins.[3]

In this imagined case a person's brain is divided, and the two halves are transplanted into a pair of different bodies. The two resulting people live quite separate lives. This imagined case shows that personal identity is not what matters. If I was about to divide, I should conclude that neither of the resulting people will be me. I will have ceased to exist. But this way of ceasing to exist is about as good—or as bad—as ordinary survival.

Some of the features of Wiggins's imagined case are likely to remain technically impossible. But the case cannot be dismissed, since its most striking feature, the division of one stream of consciousness into separate streams, has already happened. This is a second way in which the actual split-brain cases have great theoretical importance. They challenge some of our deepest assumptions about ourselves.[4]

---

[3] At the end of his *Identity and Spatio-temporal Continuity* (Oxford: Blackwell, 1967).
[4] I discuss these assumptions further in part 3 of my [Parfit's] *Reasons and Persons.*

CHAPTER 14

Where Am I?

Daniel C. Dennett

Philosophers rarely write good science fiction, and science fiction writers rarely write good philosophy. But here, Daniel Dennett does a splendid job of doing both. We may think we know what a person is, but we're less sure as Dennett throws us into a delightfully bizarre science-fiction scenario.

Daniel Dennett (1942–) is University Professor and Co-director of the Center of Cognitive Studies at Tufts University in Boston. Due to his wit and style, Dennett is one of the best-selling authors in philosophy. His books include *Breaking the Spell: Religion as a Natural Phenomenon* (2006) and *Science and Religion: Are They Compatible?* (with Alvin Plantinga, 2011).

Now that I've won my suit under the Freedom of Information Act, I am at liberty to reveal for the first time a curious episode in my life that may be of interest not only to those engaged in research in the philosophy of mind, artificial intelligence and neuroscience but also to the general public.

Several years ago I was approached by Pentagon officials who asked me to volunteer for a highly dangerous and secret mission. In collaboration with NASA and Howard Hughes, the Department of Defense was spending billions to develop a Supersonic Tunneling

Source: Daniel C. Dennett, "Where Am I?" *Brainstorms: Philosophical Essays on Mind and Psychology* (Cambridge, MA: The MIT Press, 1981), pp. 310–323. Copyright © 1978 by Bradford Books, Publishers.

Underground Device, or STUD. It was supposed to tunnel through the earth's core at great speed and deliver a specially designed atomic warhead "right up the Reds' missile silos," as one of the Pentagon brass put it.

The problem was that in an early test they had succeeded in lodging a warhead about a mile deep under Tulsa, Oklahoma, and they wanted me to retrieve it for them. "Why me?" I asked. Well, the mission involved some pioneering applications of current brain research, and they had heard of my interest in brains and of course my Faustian curiosity and great courage and so forth. . . . Well, how could I refuse? The difficulty that brought the Pentagon to my door was that the device I'd been asked to recover was fiercely radioactive, in a new way. According to monitoring instruments, something about the nature of the device and its complex interactions with pockets of material deep in the earth had produced radiation that could cause severe abnormalities in certain tissues of the brain. No way had been found to shield the brain from these deadly rays, which were apparently harmless to other tissues and organs of the body. So it had been decided that the person sent to recover the device should *leave his brain behind.* It would be kept in a safe place where it could execute its normal control functions by elaborate radio links. Would I submit to a surgical procedure that would completely remove my brain, which would then be placed in a life-support system at the Manned Spacecraft Center in Houston? Each input and output pathway, as it was severed, would be restored by a pair of microminiaturized radio transceivers, one attached precisely to the brain, the other to the nerve stumps in the empty cranium. No information would be lost, all the connectivity would be preserved. At first I was a bit reluctant. Would it really work? The Houston brain surgeons encouraged me. "Think of it," they said, "as a mere *stretching* of the nerves. If your brain were just moved over an *inch* in your skull, that would not alter or impair your mind. We're simply going to make the nerves indefinitely elastic by splicing radio links into them."

I was shown around the life-support lab in Houston and saw the sparkling new vat in which my brain would be placed, were I to agree. I met the large and brilliant support team of neurologists, hematologists, biophysicists, and electrical engineers, and after several days of discussions and demonstrations, I agreed to give it a try. I was subjected to an enormous array of blood tests, brain scans, experiments, interviews, and the like. They took down my autobiography at great length, recorded tedious lists of my beliefs, hopes, fears, and tastes.

They even listed my favorite stereo recordings and gave me a crash session of psychoanalysis.

The day for surgery arrived at last and of course I was anesthetized and remember nothing of the operation itself. When I came out of anesthesia, I opened my eyes, looked around, and asked the inevitable, the traditional, the lamentably hackneyed post-operative question: "Where am I?" The nurse smiled down at me. "You're in Houston," she said, and I reflected that this still had a good chance of being the truth one way or another. She handed me a mirror. Sure enough, there were the tiny antennae poking up through their titanium ports cemented into my skull.

"I gather the operation was a success," I said. "I want to go see my brain." They led me (I was a bit dizzy and unsteady) down a long corridor and into the life-support lab. A cheer went up from the assembled support team, and I responded with what I hoped was a jaunty salute. Still feeling lightheaded, I was helped over to the life-support vat. I peered through the glass. There, floating in what looked like ginger-ale, was undeniably a human brain, though it was almost covered with printed circuit chips, plastic tubules, electrodes, and other paraphernalia. "Is that mine?" I asked. "Hit the output transmitter switch there on the side of the vat and see for yourself," the project director replied. I moved the switch to OFF, and immediately slumped, groggy and nauseated, into the arms of the technicians, one of whom kindly restored the switch to its ON position. While I recovered my equilibrium and composure, I thought to myself: "Well, here I am, sitting on a folding chair, staring through a piece of plate glass at my own brain. . . . But wait," I said to myself, "shouldn't I have thought, 'Here I am, suspended in a bubbling fluid, being stared at by my own eyes'?" I tried to think this latter thought. I tried to project it into the tank, offering it hopefully to my brain, but I failed to carry off the exercise with any conviction. I tried again. "Here am *I*, Daniel Dennett, suspended in a bubbling fluid, being stared at by my own eyes." No, it just didn't work. Most puzzling and confusing. Being a philosopher of firm physicalist conviction, I believed unswervingly that the tokening of my thoughts was occurring somewhere in my brain: yet, when I thought "Here I am," where the thought occurred to me was *here*, outside the vat, where I, Dennett, was standing staring at my brain.

I tried and tried to think myself into the vat, but to no avail. I tried to build up to the task by doing mental exercises. I thought to myself, "The sun is shining *over there*," five times in rapid succession, each time mentally ostending a different place: in order, the sun-lit corner of the lab, the visible front lawn of the hospital, Houston, Mars, and Jupiter. I found I had little difficulty in getting my "there's" to hop all over the celestial map with their proper references. I could loft a "there" in an instant through the farthest reaches of space, and then aim the next "there" with pinpoint accuracy at the upper left quadrant of a freckle on my arm. Why was I having such trouble with "here"? "Here in Houston" worked well enough, and so did "here in the lab," and even "here in this part of the lab," but "here in the vat" always seemed merely an unmeant mental mouthing. I tried closing my eyes while thinking it. This seemed to help, but still I couldn't manage to pull it off, except perhaps for a fleeting instant. I couldn't be sure. The discovery that I couldn't be sure was also unsettling. How did I know *where* I meant by "here" when I thought "here"? Could I *think* I meant one place when in fact I meant another? I didn't see how that could be admitted without untying the few bonds of intimacy between a person and his own mental life that had survived the onslaught of the brain scientists and philosophers, the physicalists and behaviorists. Perhaps I was incorrigible about where I *meant* when I said "here." But in my present circumstances it seemed that either I was doomed by sheer force of mental habit to thinking systematically false indexical thoughts, or where a person is (and hence where his thoughts are tokened for purposes of semantic analysis) is not necessarily where his brain, the physical seat of his soul, resides. Nagged by confusion, I attempted to orient myself by falling back on a favorite philosopher's ploy. I began naming things.

"Yorick," I said aloud to my brain, "you are my brain. The rest of my body, seated in this chair, I dub 'Hamlet.'" So here we all are: Yorick's my brain, Hamlet's my body, and I am Dennett. *Now*, where am I? And when I think "where am I?" where's that thought tokened? Is it tokened in my brain, lounging about in the vat, or right here between my ears where it *seems* to be tokened? Or nowhere? Its *temporal* coordinates give me no trouble; must it not have spatial coordinates as well? I began making a list of the alternatives.

(1) *Where Hamlet goes, there goes Dennett.* This principle was easily refuted by appeal to the familiar brain transplant thought-experiments so enjoyed by philosophers. If Tom and Dick switch brains, Tom is the fellow with Dick's former body—just ask him; he'll claim to be Tom, and tell you the most intimate details of Tom's autobiography. It was clear enough, then, that my current body and I could part company, but not likely that I could be separated from my brain. The rule of

thumb that emerged so plainly from the thought experiments was that in a brain-transplant operation, one wanted to be the *donor*, not the recipient. Better to call such an operation a body-transplant, in fact. So perhaps the truth was,

(2) *Where Yorick goes, there goes Dennett.* This was not at all appealing, however. How could I be in the vat and not about to go anywhere, when I was so obviously outside the vat looking in and beginning to make guilty plans to return to my room for a substantial lunch? This begged the question I realized, but it still seemed to be getting at something important. Casting about for some support for my intuition, I hit upon a legalistic sort of argument that might have appealed to Locke.

Suppose, I argued to myself, I were now to fly to California, rob a bank, and be apprehended. In which state would I be tried: In California, where the robbery took place, or in Texas, where the brains of the outfit were located? Would I be a California felon with an out-of-state brain, or a Texas felon remotely controlling an accomplice of sorts in California? It seemed possible that I might beat such a rap just on the undecidability of that jurisdictional question, though perhaps it would be deemed an inter-state, and hence Federal, offense. In any event, suppose I were convicted. Was it likely that California would be satisfied to throw Hamlet into the brig, knowing that Yorick was living the good life and luxuriously taking the waters in Texas? Would Texas incarcerate Yorick, leaving Hamlet free to take the next boat to Rio? This alternative appealed to me. Barring capital punishment or other cruel and unusual punishment, the state would be obliged to maintain the life-support system for Yorick though they might move him from Houston to Leavenworth, and aside from the unpleasantness of the opprobrium, I, for one, would not mind at all and would consider myself a free man under those circumstances. If the state has an interest in forcibly relocating persons in institutions, it would fail to relocate me in any institution by locating Yorick there. If this were true, it suggested a third alternative.

(3) *Dennett is wherever he thinks he is.* Generalized, the claim was as follows: At any given time a person has a *point of view*, and the location of the point of view (which is determined internally by the content of the point of view) is also the location of the person.

Such a proposition is not without its perplexities, but to me it seemed a step in the right direction. The only trouble was that it seemed to place one in a heads-I-win/tails-you-lose situation of unlikely infallibility as regards location. Hadn't I myself often been wrong about where I was, and at least as often uncertain? Couldn't one get lost? Of course, but getting lost *geographically* is not the only way one might get lost. If one were lost in the woods one could attempt to reassure oneself with the consolation that at least one knew where one was: one was right *here* in the familiar surroundings of one's own body. Perhaps in this case one would not have drawn one's attention to much to be thankful for. Still, there were worse plights imaginable, and I wasn't sure I wasn't in such a plight right now.

Point of view clearly had something to do with personal location, but it was itself an unclear notion. It was obvious that the content of one's point of view was not the same as or determined by the content of one's beliefs or thoughts. For example, what should we say about the point of view of the Cinerama viewer who shrieks and twists in his seat as the roller-coaster footage overcomes his psychic distancing? Has he forgotten that he is safely seated in the theater? Here I was inclined to say that the person is experiencing an illusory shift in point of view. In other cases, my inclination to call such shifts illusory was less strong. The workers in laboratories and plants who handle dangerous materials by operating feedback-controlled mechanical arms and hands undergo a shift in point of view that is crisper and more pronounced than anything Cinerama can provoke. They can feel the heft and slipperiness of the containers they manipulate with their metal fingers. They know perfectly well where they are and are not fooled into false beliefs by the experience, yet it is as if they were inside the isolation chamber they are peering into. With mental effort, they can manage to shift their point of view back and forth, rather like making a transparent Neckar cube or an Escher drawing change orientation before one's eyes. It does seem extravagant to suppose that in performing this bit of mental gymnastics, they are transporting *themselves* back and forth.

Still their example gave me hope. If I was in fact in the vat in spite of my intuitions, I might be able to train myself to adopt that point of view even as a matter of habit. I should dwell on images of myself comfortably floating in my vat, beaming volitions to that familiar body *out there*. I reflected that the ease or difficulty of this task was presumably independent of the truth about the location of one's brain. Had I been practicing before the operation, I might now be finding it second nature. You might now yourself try such a *tromp l'oeil*. Imagine you have written an inflammatory letter which has been published in the *Times,* the result of which is that the Government has chosen to impound your brain for a probationary period of three years in its Dangerous

Brain Clinic in Bethesda, Maryland. Your body of course is allowed freedom to earn a salary and thus to continue its function of laying up income to be taxed. At this moment, however, your body is seated in an auditorium listening to a peculiar account by Daniel Dennett of his own similar experience. Try it. Think yourself to Bethesda, and then hark back longingly to your body, far away, and yet *seeming* so near. It is only with long-distance restraint (yours? the Government's?) that you can control your impulse to get those hands clapping in polite applause before navigating the old body to the rest room and a well-deserved glass of evening sherry in the lounge. The task of imagination is certainly difficult, but if you achieve your goal the results might be consoling.

Anyway, there I was in Houston, lost in thought as one might say, but not for long. My speculations were soon interrupted by the Houston doctors, who wished to test out my new prosthetic nervous system before sending me off on my hazardous mission. As I mentioned before, I was a bit dizzy at first, and not surprisingly, although I soon habituated myself to my new circumstances (which were, after all, well nigh indistinguishable from my old circumstances). My accommodation was not perfect, however, and to this day I continue to be plagued by minor coordination difficulties. The speed of light is fast, but finite, and as my brain and body move farther and farther apart, the delicate interaction of my feedback systems is thrown into disarray by the time lags. Just as one is rendered close to speechless by a delayed or echoic hearing of one's speaking voice so, for instance, I am virtually unable to track a moving object with my eyes whenever my brain and my body are more than a few miles apart. In most matters my impairment is scarcely detectable, though I can no longer hit a slow curve ball with the authority of yore. There are some compensations of course. Though liquor tastes as good as ever, and warms my gullet while corroding my liver, I can drink it in any quantity I please, without becoming the slightest bit inebriated, a curiosity some of my close friends may have noticed (though I occasionally have *feigned* inebriation, so as not to draw attention to my unusual circumstances). For similar reasons, I take aspirin orally for a sprained wrist, but if the pain persists I ask Houston to administer codeine to me *in vitro*. In times of illness the phone bill can be staggering.

But to return to my adventure. At length, both the doctors and I were satisfied that I was ready to undertake my subterranean mission. And so I left my brain in Houston and headed by helicopter for Tulsa. Well, in any case, that's the way it seemed to me. That's how I would

put it, just off the top of my head as it were. On the trip I reflected
further about my earlier anxieties and decided that my first postoper-
ative speculations had been tinged with panic. The matter was not
nearly as strange or metaphysical as I had been supposing. Where was
I? In two places, clearly: both inside the vat and outside it. Just as one
can stand with one foot in Connecticut and the other in Rhode Island,
I was in two places at once. I had become one of those scattered individuals we used to hear so much about. The more I considered this
answer, the more obviously true it appeared. But, strange to say, the
more true it appeared, the less important the question to which it
could be the true answer seemed. A sad, but not unprecedented, fate
for a philosophical question to suffer. This answer did not completely
satisfy me, of course. There lingered some question to which I should
have liked an answer, which was neither "Where are all my various and
sundry parts?" nor "What is my current point of view?" Or at least
there seemed to be such a question. For it did seem undeniable that
in some sense *I* and not merely *most of me* was descending into the
earth under Tulsa in search of an atomic warhead.

When I found the warhead, I was certainly glad I had left my
brain behind, for the pointer on the specially built Geiger counter I
had brought with me was off the dial. I called Houston on my ordinary radio and told the operation control center of my position and
my progress. In return, they gave me instructions for dismantling the
vehicle, based upon my on-site observations. I had set to work with my
cutting torch when all of a sudden a terrible thing happened. I went
stone deaf. At first I thought it was only my radio earphones that had
broken, but when I tapped on my helmet, I heard nothing. Apparently the auditory transceivers had gone on the fritz. I could no
longer hear Houston or my own voice, but I could speak, so I started
telling them what had happened. In mid-sentence, I knew something
else had gone wrong. My vocal apparatus had become paralyzed.
Then my right hand went limp—another transceiver had gone. I was
truly in deep trouble. But worse was to follow. After a few more minutes, I went blind. I cursed my luck, and then I cursed the scientists
who had led me into this grave peril. There I was, deaf, dumb, and
blind, in a radioactive hole more than a mile under Tulsa. Then the
last of my cerebral radio links broke, and suddenly I was faced with a
new and even more shocking problem: whereas an instant before I
had been buried alive in Oklahoma, now I was disembodied in Houston. My recognition of my new status was not immediate. It took me
several very anxious minutes before it dawned on me that my poor

body lay several hundred miles away, with heart pulsing and lungs respirating, but otherwise as dead as the body of any heart transplant donor, its skull packed with useless, broken electronic gear. The shift in perspective I had earlier found well nigh impossible now seemed quite natural. Though I could think myself back into my body in the tunnel under Tulsa, it took some effort to sustain the illusion. For surely it was an illusion to suppose I was still in Oklahoma: I had lost all contact with that body.

It occurred to me then, with one of those rushes of revelation of which we should be suspicious, that I had stumbled upon an impressive demonstration of the immateriality of the soul based upon physicalist principles and premises. For as the last radio signal between Tulsa and Houston died away, had I not changed location from Tulsa to Houston at the speed of light? And had I not accomplished this without any increase in mass? What moved from A to B at such speed was surely myself, or at any rate my soul or mind—the massless center of my being and home of my consciousness. My *point of view* had lagged somewhat behind, but I had already noted the indirect bearing of point of view on personal location. I could not see how a physicalist philosopher could quarrel with this except by taking the dire and counter-intuitive route of banishing all talk of persons. Yet the notion of personhood was so well entrenched in everyone's world view, or so it seemed to me, that any denial would be as curiously unconvincing, as systematically disingenuous, as the Cartesian negation, "non sum."

The joy of philosophic discovery thus tided me over some very bad minutes or perhaps hours as the helplessness and hopelessness of my situation became more apparent to me. Waves of panic and even nausea swept over me, made all the more horrible by the absence of their normal body-dependent phenomenology. No adrenalin rush of tingles in the arms, no pounding heart, no premonitory salivation. I did feel a dread sinking feeling in my bowels at one point, and this tricked me momentarily into the false hope that I was undergoing a reversal of the process that landed me in this fix—a gradual undisembodiment. But the isolation and uniqueness of that twinge soon convinced me that it was simply the first of a plague of phantom body hallucinations that I, like any other amputee, would be all too likely to suffer.

My mood then was chaotic. On the one hand, I was fired up with elation at my philosophic discovery and was wracking my brain (one of the few familiar things I could still do), trying to figure out how to communicate my discovery to the journals; while on the other, I was bitter, lonely, and filled with dread and uncertainty. Fortunately, this did not last long, for my technical support team sedated me into a dreamless sleep from which I awoke, hearing with magnificent fidelity the familiar opening strains of my favorite Brahms piano trio. So that was why they had wanted a list of my favorite recordings! It did not take me long to realize that I was hearing the music without ears. The output from the stereo stylus was being fed through some fancy rectification circuitry directly into my auditory nerve. I was mainlining Brahms, an unforgettable experience for any stereo buff. At the end of the record it did not surprise me to hear the reassuring voice of the project director speaking into a microphone that was now my prosthetic ear. He confirmed my analysis of what had gone wrong and assured me that steps were being taken to re-embody me. He did not elaborate, and after a few more recordings, I found myself drifting off to sleep. My sleep lasted, I later learned, for the better part of a year, and when I awoke, it was to find myself fully restored to my senses. When I looked into the mirror, though, I was a bit startled to see an unfamiliar face. Bearded and a bit heavier, bearing no doubt a family resemblance to my former face, and with the same look of spritely intelligence and resolute character, but definitely a new face. Further self-explorations of an intimate nature left me no doubt that this was a new body and the project director confirmed my conclusions. He did not volunteer any information on the past history of my new body and I decided (wisely, I think in retrospect) not to pry. As many philosophers unfamiliar with my ordeal have more recently speculated, the acquisition of a new body leaves one's *person* intact. And after a period of adjustment to a new voice, new muscular strengths and weaknesses, and so forth, one's *personality* is by and large also preserved. More dramatic changes in personality have been routinely observed in people who have undergone extensive plastic surgery, to say nothing of sex change operations, and I think no one contests the survival of the person in such cases. In any event I soon accommodated to my new body, to the point of being unable to recover any of its novelties to my consciousness or even memory. The view in the mirror soon became utterly familiar. That view, by the way, still revealed antennae, and so I was not surprised to learn that my brain had not been moved from its haven in the life-support lab.

I decided that good old Yorick deserved a visit. I and my new body, whom we might as well call Fortinbras, strode into the familiar lab to another round of applause from the technicians, who were of course congratulating themselves, not me. Once more I stood before the vat and contemplated poor Yorick, and on a whim I once again cavalierly flicked off the output transmitter switch. Imagine my surprise when nothing unusual happened. No fainting spell, no nausea, no noticeable change. A technician hurried to restore the switch to ON, but still I felt nothing. I demanded an explanation, which the project director hastened to provide. It seems that before they had even operated on the first occasion, they had constructed a computer duplicate of my brain, reproducing both the complete information processing structure and the computational speed of my brain in a giant computer program. After the operation, but before they had dared to send me off on my mission to Oklahoma, they had run this computer system and Yorick side by side. The incoming signals from Hamlet were sent simultaneously to Yorick's transceivers and to the computer's array of inputs. And the outputs from Yorick were not only beamed back to Hamlet, my body; they were recorded and checked against the simultaneous output of the computer program, which was called "Hubert" for reasons obscure to me. Over days and even weeks, the outputs were identical and synchronous, which of course did not *prove* that they had succeeded in copying the brain's functional structure, but the empirical support was greatly encouraging.

Hubert's input, and hence activity, had been kept parallel with Yorick's during my disembodied days. And now, to demonstrate this, they had actually thrown the master switch that put Hubert for the first time in on-line control of my body—not Hamlet, of course, but Fortinbras. (Hamlet, I learned, had never been recovered from its underground tomb and could be assumed by this time to have largely returned to the dust. At the head of my grave still lay the magnificent bulk of the abandoned device, with the word STUD emblazoned on its side in large letters—a circumstance which may provide archeologists of the next century with a curious insight into the burial rites of their ancestors.)

The laboratory technicians now showed me the master switch, which had two positions, labeled B, for Brain (they didn't know my brain's name was Yorick) and H, for Hubert. The switch did indeed point to H, and they explained to me that if I wished, I could switch it back to B. With my heart in my mouth (and my brain in its vat), I did this. Nothing happened. A click, that was all. To test their claim, and with the master switch now set at B, I hit Yorick's output transmitter switch on the vat and sure enough, I began to faint. Once the output switch was turned back on and I had recovered my wits, so to speak,

I continued to play with the master switch, flipping it back and forth. I found that with the exception of the transitional click, I could detect no trace of a difference. I could switch in mid-utterance, and the sentence I had begun speaking under the control of Yorick was finished without a pause or hitch of any kind under the control of Hubert. I had a spare brain, a prosthetic device which might some day stand me in very good stead, were some mishap to befall Yorick. Or alternatively, I could keep Yorick as a spare and use Hubert. It didn't seem to make any difference which I chose, for the wear and tear and fatigue on my body did not have any debilitating effect on either brain, whether or not it was actually causing the motions of my body, or merely spilling its output into thin air.

The one truly unsettling aspect of this new development was the prospect, which was not long in dawning on me, of someone detaching the spare—Hubert or Yorick, as the case might be—from Fortinbras and hitching it to yet another body—some Johnny-come-lately Rosencrantz or Guildenstern. Then (if not before) there would be *two* people, that much was clear. One would be me, and the other would be a sort of super-twin brother. If there were two bodies, one under the control of Hubert and the other being controlled by Yorick, then which would the world recognize as the true Dennett? And whatever the rest of the world decided, which one would be *me*? Would I be the Yorick-brained one, in virtue of Yorick's causal priority and former intimate relationship with the original Dennett body, Hamlet? That seemed a bit legalistic, a bit too redolent of the arbitrariness of consanguinity and legal possession, to be convincing at the metaphysical level. For, suppose that before the arrival of the second body on the scene, I had been keeping Yorick as the spare for years, and letting Hubert's output drive my body—that is, Fortinbras—all that time. The Hubert-Fortinbras couple would seem then by squatter's rights (to combat one legal intuition with another) to be the true Dennett and the lawful inheritor of everything that was Dennett's. This was an interesting question, certainly, but not nearly so pressing as another question that bothered me. My strongest intuition was that in such an eventuality *I* would survive so long as *either* brain-body couple remained intact, but I had mixed emotions about whether I should want both to survive.

I discussed my worries with the technicians and the project director. The prospect of two Dennetts was abhorrent to me, I explained, largely for social reasons. I didn't want to be my own rival for the affections of my wife, nor did I like the prospect of the two Dennetts sharing my modest professor's salary. Still more vertiginous and distasteful, though, was the idea of knowing *that much* about another person, while he had the very same goods on me. How could we ever face each other? My colleagues in the lab argued that I was ignoring the bright side of the matter. Weren't there many things I wanted to do but, being only one person, had been unable to do? Now one Dennett could stay at home and be the professor and family man, while the other could strike out on a life of travel and adventure— missing the family of course, but happy in the knowledge that the other Dennett was keeping the home fires burning. I could be faithful and adulterous at the same time. I could even cuckold myself—to say nothing of other more lurid possibilities my colleagues were all too ready to force upon my overtaxed imagination. But my ordeal in Oklahoma (or was it Houston?) had made me less adventurous, and I shrank from this opportunity that was being offered (though of course I was never quite sure it was being offered to *me* in the first place).

There was another prospect even more disagreeable—that the spare, Hubert or Yorick as the case might be, would be detached from any input from Fortinbras and just left detached. Then, as in the other case, there would be two Dennetts, or at least two claimants to my name and possessions, one embodied in Fortinbras, and the other sadly, miserably disembodied. Both selfishness and altruism bade me take steps to prevent this from happening. So I asked that measures be taken to ensure that no one could ever tamper with the transceiver connections or the master switch without my (our? no, *my*) knowledge and consent. Since I had no desire to spend my life guarding the equipment in Houston, it was mutually decided that all the electronic connections in the lab would be carefully locked: both those that controlled the life-support system for Yorick and those that controlled the power supply for Hubert would be guarded with fail-safe devices, and I would take the only master switch, outfitted for radio remote control, with me wherever I went. I carry it strapped around my waist and—wait a moment—*here it is*. Every few months I reconnoiter the situation by switching channels. I do this only in the presence of friends of course, for if the other channel were, heaven forbid, either dead or otherwise occupied, there would have to be somebody who had my interests at heart to switch it back, to bring me back from the void. For while I could feel, see, hear and otherwise sense whatever befell my body, subsequent to such a switch, I'd be unable to control it. By the way, the two positions on the switch are intentionally unmarked, so I never have the faintest idea whether I am switching from Hubert to Yorick or *vice versa*. (Some of you may think that in this case I really don't know *who* I am, let alone where I am. But such reflections no longer make much of a dent on my essential Dennett-ness, on my own sense of who I am. If it is true that in one sense I don't know who I am then that's another one of your philosophical truths of underwhelming significance.)

In any case, every time I've flipped the switch so far, nothing has happened. *So let's give it a try. . . .*

"THANK GOD! I THOUGHT YOU'D NEVER FLIP THAT SWITCH! You can't imagine how horrible it's been these last two weeks—but now you know, it's your turn in purgatory. How I've longed for this moment! You see, about two weeks ago—excuse me, ladies and gentlemen, but I've got to explain this to my . . . um, brother, I guess you could say, but he's just told you the facts, so you'll understand—about two weeks ago our two brains drifted just a bit out of synch. I don't know whether *my* brain is now Hubert or Yorick, any more than you do, but in any case, the two brains drifted apart, and of course once the process started, it snowballed, for I was in a slightly different receptive state for the input we both received, a difference that was soon magnified. In no time at all the illusion that I was in control of my body—our body—was completely dissipated. There was nothing I could do—no way to call you. YOU DIDN'T EVEN KNOW I EXISTED! It's been like being carried around in a cage, or better, like being possessed—hearing my own voice say things I didn't mean to say, watching in frustration as my own hands performed deeds I hadn't intended. You'd scratch our itches, but not the way I would have, and you kept me awake, with your tossing and turning. I've been totally exhausted, on the verge of a nervous breakdown, carried around helplessly by your frantic round of activi-ties, sustained only by the knowledge that some day you'd throw the switch.

"Now it's your turn, but at least you'll have the comfort of knowing *I* know you're in there. Like an expectant mother, I'm eating—or at any rate tasting, smelling, seeing—for *two* now, and I'll try to make it easy for you. Don't worry. Just as soon as this collo-quium is over, you and I will fly to Houston, and we'll see what can be done to get one of us another body. You can have a female body—your body could be any color you like. But let's think it over. I tell you what—to be fair, if we both want this body, I promise I'll let the project director flip a coin to settle which of us gets to keep it and which then gets to choose a new body. That should guarantee justice, shouldn't it? In any case, I'll take care of you, I promise. These people are my witnesses.

"Ladies and gentlemen, this talk we have just heard is not exactly the talk *I* would have given, but I assure you that everything he said was perfectly true. And now if you'll excuse me, I think I'd—we'd—better sit down."

CHAPTER 15

The Mind–Brain Identity Theory

David Armstrong

The Australian philosopher David Armstrong (1926–) was an early defender of the idea that the mind is the brain. Armstrong's books include *A Materialist Theory of the Mind* (1968), *Universals* (1989), and *Truth and Truthmakers* (2004).

Men have minds, that is to say, they perceive, they have sensations, emotions, beliefs, thoughts, purposes, and desires. What is it to have a mind? What is it to perceive, to feel emotion, to hold a belief, or to have a purpose? In common with many other modern philosophers, I think that the best clue we have to the nature of mind is furnished by the discoveries and hypotheses of modern science concerning the nature of man.

What does modern science have to say about the nature of man? There are, of course, all sorts of disagreements and divergencies in the views of individual scientists. But I think it is true to say that one view is steadily gaining ground, so that it bids fair to become established scientific doctrine. This is the view that we can give a complete account

Source: "The Nature of Mind" in *The Nature of Mind and Other Essays* by D. M. Armstrong (University of Queensland Press, 1980). Reprinted with permission of the University of Queensland Press.

of man *in purely physico-chemical terms.* This view has received a tremendous impetus in the last decade from the new subject of molecular biology, a subject which promises to unravel the physical and chemical mechanisms which lie at the basis of life. Before that time, it received great encouragement from pioneering work in neuro-physiology pointing to the likelihood of a purely electro-chemical account of the working of the brain. I think it is fair to say that those scientists who still reject the physico-chemical account of man do so primarily for philosophical, or moral, or religious reasons, and only secondarily, and half-heartedly, for reasons of scientific detail. This is not to say that in the future new evidence and new problems may not come to light which will force science to reconsider the physico-chemical view of man. But at present the drift of scientific thought is clearly set towards the physico-chemical hypothesis. And we have nothing better to go on than the present.

For me, then, and for many philosophers who think like me, the moral is clear. We must try to work out an account of the nature of mind which is compatible with the view that man is nothing but a physico-chemical mechanism.

And in this paper I shall be concerned to do just this: to sketch (in barest outline) what may be called a Materialist or Physicalist account of the mind.

But before doing this I should like to go back and consider a criticism of my position which must inevitably occur to some. What reason have I, it may be asked, for taking my stand on science? Even granting that I am right about what is the currently dominant scientific view of man, why should we concede science a special authority to decide questions about the nature of man? What of the authority of philosophy, of religion, of morality, or even of literature and art? Why do I set the authority of science above all these? Why this 'scientism'?

It seems to me that the answer to this question is very simple. If we consider the search for truth, in all its fields, we find that it is only in science that men versed in their subject can, after investigation that is more or less prolonged, and which may in some cases extend beyond a single human lifetime, reach substantial agreement about what is the case. It is only as a result of scientific investigation that we ever seem to reach an intellectual consensus about controversial matters.

In the Epistle Dedicatory to his *De Corpore* Hobbes wrote of William Harvey, the discoverer of the circulation of the blood, that he was 'the only man I know, that conquering envy, hath established a new doctrine in his life-time.'

Before Copernicus, Galileo, and Harvey, Hobbes remarks, 'there was nothing certain in natural philosophy.' And, we might add, with the exception of mathematics, there was nothing certain in any other learned discipline.

These remarks of Hobbes are incredibly revealing. They show us what a watershed in the intellectual history of the human race the seventeenth century was. Before that time inquiry proceeded, as it were, in the dark. Men could not hope to see their doctrine *established*, that is to say, accepted by the vast majority of those properly versed in the subject under discussion. There was no intellectual consensus. Since that time, it has become a commonplace to see new doctrines, sometimes of the most far-reaching kind, established to the satisfaction of the learned, often within the lifetime of their first proponents. Science has provided us with a method of deciding disputed questions. This is not to say, of course, that the consensus of those who are learned and competent in a subject cannot be mistaken. Of course such a consensus can be mistaken. Sometimes it has been mistaken. But, granting fallibility, what better authority have we than such a consensus?

Now this is of the utmost importance. For in philosophy, in religion, in such disciplines as literary criticism, in moral questions in so far as they are thought to be matters of truth and falsity, there has been a notable failure to achieve an intellectual consensus about disputed questions among the learned. Must we not then attach a peculiar authority to the discipline that can achieve a consensus? And if it presents us with a certain vision of the nature of man, is this not a powerful reason for accepting that vision?

I will not take up here the deeper question *why* it is that the methods of science have enabled us to achieve an intellectual consensus about so many disputed matters. That question, I think, could receive no brief or uncontroversial answer. I am resting my argument on the simple and uncontroversial fact that, as a result of scientific investigation, such a consensus has been achieved.

It may be replied—it often is replied—that while science is all very well in its own sphere—the sphere of the physical, perhaps—there are matters of fact on which it is not competent to pronounce. And among such matters, it may be claimed, is the question what is the whole nature of man. But I cannot see that this reply has much force. Science has provided us with an island of truths, or, perhaps one should say, a raft of truths, to bear us up on the sea of our disputatious ignorance. There may have to be revisions and refinements, new results may set old findings in a new perspective, but what science has given us will not be altogether superseded. Must we not therefore appeal to these relative certainties for guidance when we come to consider uncertainties elsewhere? Perhaps science cannot help us to decide whether or not there is a God, whether or not human beings have immortal souls, or whether or not the will is free. But if science cannot assist us, what can? I conclude that it is the scientific vision of man, and not the philosophical or religious or artistic or moral vision of man, that is the best clue we have to the nature of man. And it is rational to argue from the best evidence we have.

Having in this way attempted to justify my procedure, I turn back to my subject: the attempt to work out an account of mind, or, if you prefer, of mental process, within the framework of the physico-chemical, or, as we may call it, the Materialist view of man.

Now there is one account of mental process that is at once attractive to any philosopher sympathetic to a Materialist view of man: this is Behaviourism. Formulated originally by a psychologist, J. B. Watson, it attracted widespread interest and considerable support from scientifically oriented philosophers. Traditional philosophy had tended to think of the mind as a rather mysterious inward arena that lay behind, and was responsible for, the outward or physical behaviour of our bodies. Descartes thought of this inner arena as a *spiritual substance,* and it was this conception of the mind as spiritual object that Gilbert Ryle attacked, apparently in the interest of Behaviourism, in his important book *The Concept of Mind.* He ridiculed the Cartesian view as the dogma of 'the ghost in the machine.' The mind was not something behind the behaviour of the body, it was simply part of that physical behaviour. My anger with you is not some modification of a spiritual substance which somehow brings about aggressive behaviour; rather it is the aggressive behaviour itself; my addressing strong words to you, striking you, turning my back on you, and so on. Thought is not an inner process that lies behind, and brings about, the words I speak and write: it is my speaking and writing. The mind is not an inner arena, it is outward act.

It is clear that such a view of mind fits in very well with a completely Materialistic or Physicalist view of man. If there is no need to draw a distinction between mental processes and their expression in physical behaviour, but if instead the mental processes are identified with their so-called 'expressions,' then the existence of mind stands in no conflict with the view that man is nothing but a physico-chemical mechanism.

However, the version of Behaviourism that I have just sketched is a very crude version, and its crudity lays it open to obvious objections. One obvious difficulty is that it is our common experience that there can be mental processes going on although there is no behaviour occurring that could possibly be treated as expressions of these processes. A man may be angry, but give no bodily sign; he may think, but say or do nothing at all.

In my view, the most plausible attempt to refine Behaviourism with a view to meeting this objection was made by introducing the notion of *a disposition to behave*. (Dispositions to behave play a particularly important part in Ryle's account of the mind.) Let us consider the general notion of disposition first. Brittleness is a disposition, a disposition possessed by materials like glass. Brittle materials are those which, when subjected to relatively small forces, break or shatter easily. But breaking and shattering easily is not brittleness, rather it is the *manifestation* of brittleness. Brittleness itself is the tendency or liability of the material to break or shatter easily. A piece of glass may never shatter or break throughout its whole history, but it is still the case that it is brittle: it is liable to shatter or break if dropped quite a small way or hit quite lightly. Now a disposition to *behave* is simply a tendency or liability of a person to behave in a certain way under certain circumstances. The brittleness of glass is a disposition that the glass retains throughout its history, but clearly there could also be dispositions that come and go. The dispositions to behave that are of interest to the Behaviourist are, for the most part, of this temporary character.

Now how did Ryle and others use the notion of a disposition to behave to meet the obvious objection to Behaviourism that there can be mental processes going on although the subject is engaging in no relevant behaviour? Their strategy was to argue that in such cases, although the subject was not behaving in any relevant way, he or she was *disposed* to behave in some relevant way. The glass does not shatter, but it is still brittle. The man does not behave, but he does have a disposition to behave. We can say he thinks although he does not speak or act because at that time he was disposed to speak or act in a certain way. *If* he had been asked, perhaps, he would have spoken or acted. We can say he is angry although he does not behave angrily, because he is disposed so to behave. *If* only one more word had been addressed to him, he would have burst out. And so on. In this way it was hoped that Behaviourism could be squared with the obvious facts.

It is very important to see just how these thinkers conceived of dispositions. I quote from Ryle

> To possess a dispositional property *is not to be in a particular state, or to undergo a particular change;* it is to be bound or liable to be in a particular state, or to undergo a particular change, when a particular condition is realised. (*The Concept of Mind,* p. 43, my italics.)

So to explain the breaking of a lightly struck glass on a particular occasion by saying it was brittle is, on this view of dispositions, simply to say that the glass broke because it is the sort of thing that regularly breaks when quite lightly struck. The breaking was the normal behaviour, or not abnormal behaviour, of such a thing. The brittleness is not to be conceived of as a *cause* for the breakage, or even, more vaguely, a *factor* in bringing about the breaking. Brittleness is just the fact that things of that sort break easily.

But although in this way the Behaviourists did something to deal with the objection that mental processes can occur in the absence of behaviour, it seems clear, now that the shouting and the dust have died, that they did not do enough. When I think, but my thoughts do not issue in any action, it seems as obvious as anything is obvious that there is something actually going on in me which constitutes my thought. It is not simply that I would speak or act if some conditions that are unfulfilled were to be fulfilled. Something is currently going on, in the strongest and most literal sense of 'going on,' and this something is my thought. Rylean Behaviourism denies this, and so it is unsatisfactory as a theory of mind. Yet I know of no version of Behaviourism that is more satisfactory. The moral for those of us who wish to take a purely physicalistic view of man is that we must look for some other account of the nature of mind and of mental processes.

But perhaps we need not grieve too deeply about the failure of Behaviourism to produce a satisfactory theory of mind. Behaviourism is a profoundly unnatural account of mental processes. If somebody speaks and acts in certain ways it is natural to speak of this speech and action as the *expression* of his thought. It is not at all natural to speak of his speech and action as identical with his thought. We naturally think of the thought as something quite distinct from the speech and action which, under suitable circumstances, brings the speech and action about. Thoughts are not to be identified with behaviour, we think, they lie behind behaviour. A man's behaviour constitutes the *reason* we have for attributing certain mental processes to him, but the behaviour cannot be identified with the mental processes.

This suggests a very interesting line of thought about the mind. Behaviourism is certainly wrong, but perhaps it is not altogether wrong. Perhaps the Behaviourists are wrong in identifying the mind and mental occurrences with behaviour, but perhaps they are right in thinking that our notion of a mind and of individual mental states is *logically tied to behaviour*. For perhaps what we mean by a mental state is some state of the person which, under suitable circumstances, *brings about* a certain range of behaviour. Perhaps mind can be defined not as behaviour, but rather as the inner *cause* of certain behaviour. Thought is not speech under suitable circumstances, rather it is something within the person which, in suitable circumstances, brings about speech. And, in fact, I believe that this is the true account, or, at any rate, a true first account, of what we mean by a mental state.

How does this line of thought link up with a purely physicalist view of man? The position is, I think, that while it does not make such a physicalist view inevitable, it does make it *possible*. It does not entail, but it is compatible with, a purely physicalist view of man. For if our notion of the mind and mental states is nothing but that of a cause within the person of certain ranges of behaviour, then it becomes a scientific question, and not a question of logical analysis, what in fact the intrinsic nature of that cause is. The cause might be, as Descartes thought it was, a spiritual substance working through the pineal gland to produce the complex bodily behaviour of which men are capable. It might be breath, or specially smooth and mobile atoms dispersed throughout the body; it might be many other things. But in fact the verdict of modern science seems to be that the sole cause of mind-betokening behaviour in man and the higher animals is the physico-chemical workings of the central nervous system. And so, assuming we have correctly characterised our concept of a mental state as nothing but the cause of certain sorts of behaviour, then we can identify these mental states with purely physical states of the central nervous system.

At this point we may stop and go back to the Behaviourists' dispositions. We saw that, according to them, the brittleness of glass or, to take another example, the elasticity of rubber, is not a state of the glass or the rubber, but is simply the fact that things of that sort behave in the way they do. But now let us consider how a scientist would think about brittleness or elasticity. Faced with the phenomenon of breakage under relatively small impacts, or the phenomenon of stretching when a force is applied followed by contraction when the force is removed, he will assume that there is some current *state* of the glass or the rubber which is responsible for the characteristic behaviour of samples of these two materials. At the beginning he will not know what this state is, but he will endeavour to find out, and he may succeed in finding out. And when he has found out he will very likely make remarks of this sort: 'We have discovered that the brittleness of glass is in fact a certain sort of pattern in the molecules of the glass.' That is to say, he will *identify* brittleness with the state of the glass that is responsible for the liability of the glass to break. For him, a disposition of an object is a state of the object. What makes the state of brittleness is the fact that it gives rise to the characteristic manifestations of brittleness. But the disposition itself is distinct from its manifestations: it is the state of the glass that gives rise to these manifestations in suitable circumstances.

You will see that this way of looking at dispositions is very different from that of Ryle and the Behaviourists. The great difference is this: if we treat dispositions as actual states, as I have suggested that scientists do, even if states whose intrinsic nature may yet have to be discovered, then we can say that dispositions are actual *causes,* or causal factors, which, in suitable circumstances, actually bring about those happenings which are the manifestations of the disposition. A certain molecular constitution of glass which constitutes its brittleness is actually *responsible* for the fact that, when the glass is struck, it breaks.

Now I shall not argue the matter here, because the detail of the argument is technical and difficult, but I believe that the view of dispositions as states, which is the view that is natural to science, is the correct one. I believe it can be shown quite strictly that, to the extent that we admit the notion of dispositions at all, we are committed to the view that they are actual *states* of the object that has the disposition. I may add that I think that the same holds for the closely connected notions of capacities and powers. Here I will simply assume this step in my argument.

But perhaps it can be seen that the rejection of the idea that mind is simply a certain range of man's behaviour in favour of the view that mind is rather the inner *cause* of that range of man's behaviour is bound up with the rejection of the Rylean view of dispositions in favour of one that treats disposition as states of objects and so as having actual causal power. The Behaviourists were wrong to identify the mind with behaviour. They were not so far off the mark when they tried to deal with cases where mental happenings occur in the absence of behaviour by saying that these are dispositions to behave. But in order to reach a correct view, I am suggesting, they would have to conceive of these dispositions as actual *states* of the person who has the disposition, states that have actual power to bring about behaviour in suitable circumstances. But to do this is to abandon the central inspiration of Behaviourism: that in talking about the mind we do not have to go behind outward behaviour to inner states.

And so two separate but interlocking lines of thought have pushed me in the same direction. The first line of thought is that it goes profoundly against the grain to think of the mind as behaviour. The mind is, rather, that which stands behind and brings about our complex behaviour. The second line of thought is that the Behaviourists' dispositions, properly conceived, are really states that underlie behaviour, and, under suitable circumstances, bring about behaviour. Putting these two together, we reach the conception of a mental state as *a state of the person apt for producing certain ranges of behaviour*. This formula: a mental state is a state of the person apt for producing certain ranges of behaviour, I believe to be a very illuminating way of looking at the concept of a mental state. I have found it very fruitful in the search for detailed logical analyses of the individual mental concepts.

Now, I do not think that Hegel's dialectic has much to tell us about the nature of reality. But I think that human thought often moves in a dialectical way, from thesis to antithesis and then to the synthesis. Perhaps thought about the mind is a case in point. I have already said that classical philosophy tended to think of the mind as an inner arena of some sort. This we may call the Thesis. Behaviourism moved to the opposite extreme: the mind was seen as outward behaviour. This is the Antithesis. My proposed Synthesis is that the mind is properly conceived as an inner principle, but a principle that is identified in terms of the outward behaviour it is apt for bringing about. This way of looking at the mind and mental states does not itself entail a Materialist or Physicalist view of man, for nothing is said in this analysis about the intrinsic nature of these mental states. But if we have, as I have asserted that we do have, general scientific grounds for thinking that man is nothing but a physical mechanism, we can go on to argue that the mental states are in fact nothing but physical states of the central nervous system.

Along these lines, then, I would look for an account of the mind that is compatible with a purely Materialist theory of man. I have tried to carry out this programme in detail in *A Materialist Theory of the Mind*. There are, as may be imagined, all sorts of powerful objections that can be made to this view. But in the rest of this paper I propose to do only one thing. I will develop one very important objection to my view of the mind—an objection felt by many philosophers—and then try to show how the objection should be met.

The view that our notion of mind is nothing but that of an inner principle apt for bringing about certain sorts of behaviour may be thought to share a certain weakness with Behaviourism. Modern philosophers have put the point about Behaviourism by saying that although Behaviourism may be a satisfactory account of the mind from an *other-person point of view,* it will not do as a *first-person* account. To explain. In our encounters with other people, all we ever observe is their behaviour: their actions, their speech, and so on. And so, if we simply consider other people, Behaviourism might seem to do full justice to the facts. But the trouble about Behaviourism is that it seems so unsatisfactory as applied to our *own* case. In our own case, we seem to be aware of so much more than mere behaviour.

Suppose that now we conceive of the mind as an inner principle apt for bringing about certain sorts of behaviour. This again fits the other-person cases very well. Bodily behaviour of a very sophisticated sort is observed, quite different from the behaviour that ordinary physical objects display. It is inferred that this behaviour must spring from a very special sort of inner cause in the object that exhibits this behaviour. This inner cause is christened 'the mind,' and those who take a physicalist view of man argue that it is simply the central nervous system of the body observed. Compare this with the case of glass. Certain characteristic behaviour is observed: the breaking and shattering of the material when acted upon by relatively small forces. A special inner state of the glass is postulated to explain this behaviour. Those who take a purely physicalist view of glass then argue that this state is a *natural* state of the glass. It is, perhaps, an arrangement of its molecules, and not, say, the peculiarly malevolent disposition of the demons that dwell in glass.

But when we turn to our own case, the position may seem less plausible. We are conscious, we have experiences. Now can we say that to be conscious, to have experiences, is simply for something to go on within us apt for the causing of certain sorts of behaviour? Such an account does not seem to do any justice to the phenomena. And so it seems that our account of the mind, like Behaviourism, will fail to do justice to the first-person case.

In order to understand the objection better it may be helpful to consider a particular case. If you have driven for a very long distance without a break, you may have had experience of a curious state of automatism, which can occur in these conditions. One can suddenly 'come to' and realise that one has driven for long distances without being aware of what one was doing, or indeed, without being aware of anything. One has kept the car on the road, used the brake and the clutch perhaps, yet all without any awareness of what one was doing.

Now, if we consider this case it is obvious that *in some sense* mental processes are still going on when one is in such an automatic state. Unless one's will was still operating in some way, and unless one was still perceiving in some way, the car would not still be on the road. Yet, of course, *something* mental is lacking. Now, I think, when it is alleged that an account of mind as an inner principle apt for the production of certain sorts of behaviour leaves out consciousness or experience, what is alleged to have been left out is just whatever is missing in the automatic driving case. It is conceded that an account of mental processes as states of the person apt for the production of certain sorts of behaviour may very possibly be adequate to deal with such cases as that of automatic driving. It may be adequate to deal with most of the mental processes of animals, who perhaps spend a good deal of their lives in this state of automatism. But, it is contended, it cannot deal with the consciousness that we normally enjoy.

I will now try to sketch an answer to this important and powerful objection. Let us begin in an apparently unlikely place, and consider the way that an account of mental processes of the sort I am giving would deal with *sense-perception*.

Now psychologists, in particular, have long realised that there is a very close logical tie between sense-perception and *selective behaviour*. Suppose we want to decide whether an animal can perceive the difference between red and green. We might give the animal a choice between two pathways, over one of which a red light shines and over the other of which a green light shines. If the animal happens by chance to choose the green pathway we reward it; if it happens to choose the other pathway we do not reward it. If, after some trials, the animal systematically takes the green-lighted pathway, and if we become assured that the only relevant differences in the two pathways are the differences in the colour of the lights, we are entitled to say that the animal can see this colour difference. Using its eyes, it selects between red-lighted and green-lighted pathways. So we say it can see the difference between red and green.

Now a Behaviourist would be tempted to say that the animal's regularly selecting the green-lighted pathway *was* its perception of the colour difference. But this is unsatisfactory, because we all want to say that perception is something that goes on within the person or animal—within its mind—although, of course, this mental event is normally *caused* by the operation of the environment upon the organism. Suppose, however, that we speak instead of *capacities* for selective behaviour towards the current environment, and suppose we think of these capacities, like dispositions, as actual inner states of the organism. We can then think of the animal's perception as a state within the animal apt, if the animal is so impelled, for selective behaviour between the red- and green-lighted pathways.

In general, we can think of perceptions as inner states or events apt for the production of certain sorts of selective behaviour towards our environment. To perceive is like acquiring a key to a door. You do not have to use the key: you can put it in your pocket and never bother about the door. But if you do want to open the door the key may be essential. The blind man is a man who does not acquire certain keys, and, as a result, is not able to operate in his environment in the way that somebody who has his sight can operate. It seems, then, a very promising view to take of perceptions that they are inner states defined by the sorts of selective behaviour that they enable the perceiver to exhibit, if so impelled.

Now how is this discussion of perception related to the question of consciousness or experience, the sort of thing that the driver who is in a state of automatism has not got, but which we normally do have? Simply this. My proposal is that consciousness, in this sense of the word, is nothing but *perception or awareness of the state of our own mind*. The driver in a state of automatism perceives, or is aware of, the road. If he did not, the car would be in a ditch. But he is not currently aware of his awareness of the road. He perceives the road, but he does not perceive his perceiving, or anything else that is going on in his mind. He is not, as we normally are, conscious of what is going on in his mind.

And so I conceive of consciousness or experience, in this sense of the words, in the way that Locke and Kant conceived it, as like perception. Kant, in a striking phrase, spoke of 'inner sense.' We cannot directly observe the minds of others, but each of us has the power to observe directly our own minds, and 'perceive' what is going on there.

The driver in the automatic state is one whose 'inner eye' is shut: who is not currently aware of what is going on in his own mind.

Now if this account is along the right lines, why should we not give an account of this inner observation along the same lines as we have already given of perception? Why should we not conceive of it as an inner state, a state in this case directed towards other inner states and not to the environment, which enables us, if we are so impelled, to behave in a selective way *towards our own states of mind*? One who is aware, or conscious, of his thoughts or his emotions is one who has the capacity to make discriminations between his different mental states. His capacity might be exhibited in words. He might say that he was in an angry state of mind when, and only when, he *was* in an angry state of mind. But such verbal behaviour would be the mere *expression* or *result* of the awareness. The awareness itself would be an inner state: the sort of inner state that gave the man a capacity for such behavioural expressions.

So I have argued that consciousness of our own mental state may be assimilated to *perception* of our own mental state, and that, like other perceptions, it may then be conceived of as an inner state or event giving a capacity for selective behaviour, in this case selective behaviour towards our own mental state. All this is meant to be simply a logical analysis of consciousness, and none of it entails, although it does not rule out, a purely physicalist account of what these inner states are. But if we are convinced, on general scientific grounds, that a purely physical account of man is likely to be the true one, then there seems to be no bar to our identifying these inner states with purely physical states of the central nervous system. And so consciousness of our own mental state becomes simply the scanning of one part of our central nervous system by another. Consciousness is a self-scanning mechanism in the central nervous system.

As I have emphasised before, I have done no more than sketch a programme for a philosophy of mind. There are all sorts of expansions and elucidations to be made, and all sorts of doubts and difficulties to be stated and overcome. But I hope I have done enough to show that a purely physicalist theory of the mind is an exciting and plausible intellectual option.

CHAPTER 16

*B*at Sonar

Thomas Nagel

Thomas Nagel (1937–) is famous for arguing that if any being is conscious, then there must be something that it is like to *be* that being. Could we know what it is like to be an animal quite alien to us? And if we could not, what does this imply about the nature of subjective experiences?

Thomas Nagel is University Professor of Philosophy at New York University. His books include *The View from Nowhere* (1986) and *Secular Philosophy and the Religious Temperament: Essays 2002–2008* (2010).

I assume we all believe that bats have experience. After all, they are mammals, and there is no more doubt that they have experience than that mice or pigeons or whales have experience. I have chosen bats instead of wasps or flounders because if one travels too far down the phylogenetic tree, people gradually shed their faith that there is experience there at all. Bats, although more closely related to us than those other species, nevertheless present a range of activity and a sensory apparatus so different from ours that the problem I want to pose is exceptionally vivid. . . . Even without the benefit of philosophical reflection, anyone who has spent some time in an enclosed space with an excited bat knows what it is to encounter a fundamentally *alien* form of life.

Source: From *Philosophical Review,* Vol. LXXXIII, No. 4 (October 1974), pp. 435–450.

I have said that the essence of the belief that bats have experience is that there is something that it is like to be a bat. Now we know that most bats (the microchiroptera, to be precise) perceive the external world primarily by sonar, or echolocation, detecting the reflections, from objects within range, of their own rapid, subtly modulated, high-frequency shrieks. Their brains are designed to correlate the outgoing impulses with the subsequent echoes, and the information thus acquired enables bats to make precise discriminations of distance, size, shape, motion, and texture comparable to those we make by vision. But bat sonar, though clearly a form of perception, is not similar in its operation to any sense that we possess, and there is no reason to suppose that it is subjectively like anything we can experience or imagine. This appears to create difficulties for the notion of what it is like to be a bat. We must consider whether any method will permit us to extrapolate to the inner life of the bat from our own case, and if not, what alternative methods there may be for understanding the notion.

Our own experience provides the basic material for our imagination, whose range is therefore limited. It will not help to try to imagine that one has webbing on one's arms, which enables one to fly around at dusk and dawn catching insects in one's mouth; that one has very poor vision, and perceives the surrounding world by a system of reflected high-frequency sound signals; and that one spends the day hanging upside down by one's feet in an attic. Insofar as I can imagine this (which is not very far), it tells me only what it would be like for *me* to behave as a bat behaves. But that is not the question. I want to know what it is like for a *bat* to be a bat. Yet if I try to imagine this, I am restricted to the resources of my own mind, and those resources are inadequate to the task. I cannot perform it either by imagining additions to my present experience, or by imagining segments gradually subtracted from it, or by imagining some combination of additions, subtractions, and modifications.

To the extent that I could look and behave like a wasp or a bat without changing my fundamental structure, my experiences would not be anything like the experiences of those animals. On the other hand, it is doubtful that any meaning can be attached to the supposition that I should possess the internal neurophysiological constitution of a bat. Even if I could by gradual degrees be transformed into a bat, nothing in my present constitution enables me to imagine what the experiences of such a future stage of myself thus metamorphosed would be like. The best evidence would come from the experiences of bats, if we only knew what they were like.

So if extrapolation from our own case is involved in the idea of what it is like to be a bat, the extrapolation must be incompletable. We cannot form more than a schematic conception of what it *is* like. For example, we may ascribe general *types* of experience on the basis of the animal's structure and behavior. Thus we describe bat sonar as a form of three-dimensional forward perception; we believe that bats feel some versions of pain, fear, hunger, and lust, and that they have other, more familiar types of perception besides sonar. But we believe that these experiences also have in each case a specific subjective character, which it is beyond our ability to conceive. And if there is conscious life elsewhere in the universe, it is likely that some of it will not be describable even in the most general experiential terms available to us. (The problem is not confined to exotic cases, however, for it exists between one person and another. The subjective character of the experience of a person deaf and blind from birth is not accessible to me, for example, nor presumably is mine to him. This does not prevent us each from believing that the other's experience has such a subjective character.) . . .

. . . Reflection on what it is like to be a bat seems to lead us, therefore, to the conclusion that there are facts that do not consist in the truth of propositions expressible in a human language. We can be compelled to recognize the existence of such facts without being able to state or comprehend them.

I shall not pursue this subject, however. Its bearing on the topic before us (namely, the mind–body problem) is that it enables us to make a general observation about the subjective character of experience. Whatever may be the status of facts about what it is like to be a human being, or a bat, or a Martian, these appear to be facts that embody a particular point of view.

I am not adverting here to the alleged privacy of experience to its possessor. The point of view in question is not one accessible only to a single individual. Rather it is a *type*. It is often possible to take up a point of view other than one's own, so the comprehension of such facts is not limited to one's own case. There is a sense in which phenomenological facts are perfectly objective: one person can know or say of another what the quality of the other's experience is. They are subjective, however, in the sense that even this objective ascription of experience is possible only for someone sufficiently similar to the object of ascription to be able to adopt his point of view—to understand the ascription in the first person as well as in the third, so to speak. The more different from oneself the other experiencer is, the less success one can expect with this enterprise. In our own case we occupy the relevant point of view, but we will have as much difficulty understanding our own experience properly if we approach it from another point of view as we would if we tried to understand the experience of another species without taking up *its* point of view.

This bears directly on the mind–body problem. For if the facts of experience—facts about what it is like *for* the experiencing organism— are accessible only from one point of view, then it is a mystery how the true character of experiences could be revealed in the physical operation of that organism. The latter is a domain of objective facts *par excellence*—the kind that can be observed and understood from many points of view and by individuals with differing perceptual systems. . . .

CHAPTER 17

Facing Up to the Problem of Consciousness

David Chalmers

The biggest difference between a human being and a toaster might be that the human being is capable of conscious experience. And without consciousness, we might as well be toasters—our lives would have no inner quality. Understanding consciousness is central to understanding ourselves and our place in the world.

In this selection, David Chalmers advocates treating experience as a fundamental part of the universe, rather than as being explicable in terms of something else. Dr. Chalmers is Distinguished Professor of Philosophy and Director for the Centre of Consciousness at the Australian National University in Canberra, Australia. He wrote *The Conscious Mind* (1996) and *The Character of Consciousness* (2011), as well as over fifty scholarly articles.

1. Introduction

Consciousness poses the most baffling problems in the science of the mind. There is nothing that we know more intimately than conscious experience, but there is nothing that is harder to explain. All sorts of mental phenomena have yielded to scientific investigation in recent years, but consciousness has stubbornly resisted. Many have tried to

Source: David Chalmers, "Facing Up to the Problem of Consciousness," *Journal of Consciousness Studies,* 2 (1995), 200–219. Copyright © 1995 by David Chalmers.

explain it, but the explanations always seem to fall short of the target. Some have been led to suppose that the problem is intractable, and that no good explanation can be given.

To make progress on the problem of consciousness, we have to confront it directly. In this paper, I first isolate the truly hard part of the problem, separating it from more tractable parts and giving an account of why it is so difficult to explain. I critique some recent work that uses reductive methods to address consciousness, and argue that these methods inevitably fail to come to grips with the hardest part of the problem. Once this failure is recognized, the door to further progress is opened. In the second half of the paper, I argue that if we move to a new kind of nonreductive explanation, a naturalistic account of consciousness can be given. . . .

2. The Easy Problems and the Hard Problem

There is not just one problem of consciousness. "Consciousness" is an ambiguous term, referring to many different phenomena. Each of these phenomena needs to be explained, but some are easier to explain than others. At the start, it is useful to divide the associated problems of consciousness into "hard" and "easy" problems. The easy problems of consciousness are those that seem directly susceptible to the standard methods of cognitive science, whereby a phenomenon is explained in terms of computational or neural mechanisms. The hard problems are those that seem to resist those methods.

The easy problems of consciousness include those of explaining the following phenomena:

- the ability to discriminate, categorize, and react to environmental stimuli;
- the integration of information by a cognitive system;
- the reportability of mental states;
- the ability of a system to access its own internal states;
- the focus of attention;
- the deliberate control of behavior;
- the difference between wakefulness and sleep.

All of these phenomena are associated with the notion of consciousness. For example, one sometimes says that a mental state is conscious when it is verbally reportable, or when it is internally accessible. Sometimes a system is said to be conscious of some information when it has the ability to react on the basis of that information, or, more strongly, when it attends to that information, or when it can integrate that information and exploit it in the sophisticated control of behavior. We sometimes say that an action is conscious precisely when it is deliberate. Often, we say that an organism is conscious as another way of saying that it is awake.

There is no real issue about whether *these* phenomena can be explained scientifically. All of them are straightforwardly vulnerable to explanation in terms of computational or neural mechanisms. To explain access and reportability, for example, we need only specify the mechanism by which information about internal states is retrieved and made available for verbal report. To explain the integration of information, we need only exhibit mechanisms by which information is brought together and exploited by later processes. For an account of sleep and wakefulness, an appropriate neurophysiological account of the processes responsible for organisms' contrasting behavior in those states will suffice. In each case, an appropriate cognitive or neurophysiological model can clearly do the explanatory work.

If these phenomena were all there was to consciousness, then consciousness would not be much of a problem. Although we do not yet have anything close to a complete explanation of these phenomena, we have a clear idea of how we might go about explaining them. This is why I call these problems the easy problems. Of course, 'easy' is a relative term. Getting the details right will probably take a century or two of difficult empirical work. Still, there is every reason to believe that the methods of cognitive science and neuroscience will succeed.

The really hard problem of consciousness is the problem of *experience*. When we think and perceive, there is a whir of information-processing, but there is also a subjective aspect. As Nagel has put it, there is *something it is like* to be a conscious organism. This subjective aspect is experience. When we see, for example, we *experience* visual sensations: the felt quality of redness, the experience of dark and light, the quality of depth in a visual field. Other experiences go along with perception in different modalities: the sound of a clarinet, the smell of mothballs. Then there are bodily sensations, from pains to orgasms; mental images that are conjured up internally; the felt quality of emotion, and the experience of a stream of conscious thought. What unites all of these states is that there is something it is like to be in them. All of them are states of experience.

It is undeniable that some organisms are subjects of experience. But the question of how it is that these systems are subjects of experience is perplexing. Why is it that when our cognitive systems engage in visual and auditory information-processing, we have visual or auditory experience: the quality of deep blue, the sensation of middle C? How can we explain why there is something it is like to entertain a mental image, or to experience an emotion? It is widely agreed that experience arises from a physical basis, but we have no good explanation of why and how it so arises. Why should physical processing give rise to a rich inner life at all? It seems objectively unreasonable that it should, and yet it does.

If any problem qualifies as *the* problem of consciousness, it is this one. In this central sense of "consciousness," an organism is conscious if there is something it is like to be that organism, and a mental state is conscious if there is something it is like to be in that state. Sometimes terms such as "phenomenal consciousness" and "qualia" are also used here, but I find it more natural to speak of "conscious experience" or simply "experience." Another useful way to avoid confusion is to reserve the term "consciousness" for the phenomena of experience, using the less loaded term "awareness" for the more straightforward phenomena described earlier. If such a convention were widely adopted, communication would be much easier; as things stand, those who talk about "consciousness" are frequently talking past each other.

The ambiguity of the term "consciousness" is often exploited by both philosophers and scientists writing on the subject. It is common to see a paper on consciousness begin with an invocation of the mystery of consciousness, noting the strange intangibility and ineffability of subjectivity, and worrying that so far we have no theory of the phenomenon. Here, the topic is clearly the hard problem—the problem of experience. In the second half of the paper, the tone becomes more optimistic, and the author's own theory of consciousness is outlined. Upon examination, this theory turns out to be a theory of one of the more straightforward phenomena—of reportability, of introspective access, or whatever. At the close, the author declares that consciousness has turned out to be tractable after all, but the reader is left feeling like the victim of a bait-and-switch. The hard problem remains untouched.

3. Functional Explanation

Why are the easy problems easy, and why is the hard problem hard? The easy problems are easy precisely because they concern the explanation of cognitive *abilities* and *functions*. To explain a cognitive function, we need only specify a mechanism that can perform the function.

The methods of cognitive science are well-suited for this sort of explanation, and so are well-suited to the easy problems of consciousness. By contrast, the hard problem is hard precisely because it is not a problem about the performance of functions. The problem persists even when the performance of all the relevant functions is explained. (Here "function" is not used in the narrow teleological sense of something that a system is designed to do, but in the broader sense of any causal role in the production of behavior that a system might perform.)

To explain reportability, for instance, is just to explain how a system could perform the function of producing reports on internal states. To explain internal access, we need to explain how a system could be appropriately affected by its internal states and use information about those states in directing later processes. To explain integration and control, we need to explain how a system's central processes can bring information contents together and use them in the facilitation of various behaviors. These are all problems about the explanation of functions.

How do we explain the performance of a function? By specifying a *mechanism* that performs the function. Here, neurophysiological and cognitive modeling are perfect for the task. If we want a detailed low-level explanation, we can specify the neural mechanism that is responsible for the function. If we want a more abstract explanation, we can specify a mechanism in computational terms. Either way, a full and satisfying explanation will result. Once we have specified the neural or computational mechanism that performs the function of verbal report, for example, the bulk of our work in explaining reportability is over.

In a way, the point is trivial. It is a *conceptual* fact about these phenomena that their explanation only involves the explanation of various functions, as the phenomena are *functionally definable*. All it *means* for reportability to be instantiated in a system is that the system has the capacity for verbal reports of internal information. All it means for a system to be awake is for it to be appropriately receptive to information from the environment and for it to be able to use this information in directing behavior in an appropriate way. To see that this sort of thing is a conceptual fact, note that someone who says "you have explained the performance of the verbal report function, but you have not explained reportability" is making a trivial conceptual mistake about reportability. All it could *possibly* take to explain reportability is an explanation of how the relevant function is performed; the same goes for the other phenomena in question.

Throughout the higher-level sciences, reductive explanation works in just this way. To explain the gene, for instance, we needed to

specify the mechanism that stores and transmits hereditary information from one generation to the next. It turns out that DNA performs
this function; once we explain how the function is performed, we have
explained the gene. To explain life, we ultimately need to explain how
a system can reproduce, adapt to its environment, metabolize, and so
on. All of these are questions about the performance of functions, and
so are well-suited to reductive explanation. The same holds for most
problems in cognitive science. To explain learning, we need to explain
the way in which a system's behavioral capacities are modified in light
of environmental information, and the way in which new information
can be brought to bear in adapting a system's actions to its environment. If we show how a neural or computational mechanism does the
job, we have explained learning. We can say the same for other cognitive phenomena, such as perception, memory, and language. Sometimes the relevant functions need to be characterized quite subtly, but
it is clear that insofar as cognitive science explains these phenomena
at all, it does so by explaining the performance of functions.

When it comes to conscious experience, this sort of explanation
fails. What makes the hard problem hard and almost unique is that it
goes *beyond* problems about the performance of functions. To see
this, note that even when we have explained the performance of all
the cognitive and behavioral functions in the vicinity of experience—
perceptual discrimination, categorization, internal access, verbal
report—there may still remain a further unanswered question: *Why is
the performance of these functions accompanied by experience?* A simple
explanation of the functions leaves this question open.

There is no analogous further question in the explanation of
genes, or of life, or of learning. If someone says "I can see that you
have explained how DNA stores and transmits hereditary information
from one generation to the next, but you have not explained how it is
a *gene*," then they are making a conceptual mistake. All it means to be
a gene is to be an entity that performs the relevant storage and transmission function. But if someone says "I can see that you have
explained how information is discriminated, integrated, and reported,
but you have not explained how it is *experienced*," they are not making
a conceptual mistake. This is a nontrivial further question.

This further question is the key question in the problem of consciousness. Why doesn't all this information-processing go on "in the
dark," free of any inner feel? Why is it that when electromagnetic wave-
forms impinge on a retina and are discriminated and categorized by
a visual system, this discrimination and categorization is experienced

as a sensation of vivid red? We know that conscious experience *does* arise when these functions are performed, but the very fact that it arises is the central mystery. There is an *explanatory gap* between the functions and experience, and we need an explanatory bridge to cross it. A mere account of the functions stays on one side of the gap, so the materials for the bridge must be found elsewhere.

This is not to say that experience *has* no function. Perhaps it will turn out to play an important cognitive role. But for any role it might play, there will be more to the explanation of experience than a simple explanation of the function. Perhaps it will even turn out that in the course of explaining a function, we will be led to the key insight that allows an explanation of experience. If this happens, though, the discovery will be an *extra* explanatory reward. There is no cognitive function such that we can say in advance that explanation of that function will *automatically* explain experience.

To explain experience, we need a new approach. The usual explanatory methods of cognitive science and neuroscience do not suffice. These methods have been developed precisely to explain the performance of cognitive functions, and they do a good job of it. But as these methods stand, they are *only* equipped to explain the performance of functions. When it comes to the hard problem, the standard approach has nothing to say.

4. Some Case Studies

In the last few years, a number of works have addressed the problems of consciousness within the framework of cognitive science and neuroscience. This might suggest that the analysis above is faulty, but in fact a close examination of the relevant work only lends the analysis further support. When we investigate just which aspects of consciousness these studies are aimed at, and which aspects they end up explaining, we find that the ultimate target of explanation is always one of the easy problems. I will illustrate this with two representative examples.

The first is the "neurobiological theory of consciousness" outlined by Crick and Koch (1990; see also Crick 1994). This theory centers on certain 35–75 hertz neural oscillations in the cerebral cortex; Crick and Koch hypothesize that these oscillations are the basis of consciousness. This is partly because the oscillations seem to be correlated with awareness in a number of different modalities—within the visual and olfactory systems, for example—and also because they suggest a mechanism by which the *binding* of information contents might be achieved. Binding is the process whereby separately represented pieces of information about a single entity are brought together to be used by later processing, as when information about the color and shape of a perceived object is integrated from separate visual pathways. Following others, Crick and Koch hypothesize that binding may be achieved by the synchronized oscillations of neuronal groups representing the relevant contents. When two pieces of information are to be bound together, the relevant neural groups will oscillate with the same frequency and phase.

The details of how this binding might be achieved are still poorly understood, but suppose that they can be worked out. What might the resulting theory explain? Clearly it might explain the binding of information contents, and perhaps it might yield a more general account of the integration of information in the brain. Crick and Koch also suggest that these oscillations activate the mechanisms of working memory, so that there may be an account of this and perhaps other forms of memory in the distance. The theory might eventually lead to a general account of how perceived information is bound and stored in memory, for use by later processing.

Such a theory would be valuable, but it would tell us nothing about why the relevant contents are experienced. Crick and Koch suggest that these oscillations are the neural *correlates* of experience. This claim is arguable—does not binding also take place in the processing of unconscious information?—but even if it is accepted, the *explanatory* question remains: Why do the oscillations give rise to experience? The only basis for an explanatory connection is the role they play in binding and storage, but the question of why binding and storage should themselves be accompanied by experience is never addressed. If we do not know why binding and storage should give rise to experience, telling a story about the oscillations cannot help us. Conversely, if we *knew* why binding and storage gave rise to experience, the neurophysiological details would be just the icing on the cake. Crick and Koch's theory gains its purchase by *assuming* a connection between binding and experience, and so can do nothing to explain that link.

I do not think that Crick and Koch are ultimately claiming to address the hard problem, although some have interpreted them otherwise. A published interview with Koch gives a clear statement of the limitations on the theory's ambitions.

> Well, let's first forget about the really difficult aspects, like subjective feelings, for they may not have a scientific solution. The subjective state of play, of pain, of pleasure, of seeing blue, of

smelling a rose—there seems to be a huge jump between the materialistic level, of explaining molecules and neurons, and the subjective level. Let's focus on things that are easier to study—like visual awareness. You're now talking to me, but you're not looking at me, you're looking at the cappuccino, and so you are aware of it. You can say, "It's a cup and there's some liquid in it." If I give it to you, you'll move your arm and you'll take it—you'll respond in a meaningful manner. That's what I call awareness. (What Is Consciousness? *Discover,* November 1992, p. 96.)

The second example is an approach at the level of cognitive psychology. This is Bernard Baars' global workspace theory of consciousness, presented in his book *A Cognitive Theory of Consciousness.* According to this theory, the contents of consciousness are contained in a *global workspace,* a central processor used to mediate communication between a host of specialized nonconscious processors. When these specialized processors need to broadcast information to the rest of the system, they do so by sending this information to the workspace, which acts as a kind of communal blackboard for the rest of the system, accessible to all the other processors.

Baars uses this model to address many aspects of human cognition, and to explain a number of contrasts between conscious and unconscious cognitive functioning. Ultimately, however, it is a theory of *cognitive accessibility,* explaining how it is that certain information contents are widely accessible within a system, as well as a theory of informational integration and reportability. The theory shows promise as a theory of awareness, the functional correlate of conscious experience, but an explanation of experience itself is not on offer.

One might suppose that according to this theory, the contents of experience are precisely the contents of the workspace. But even if this is so, nothing internal to the theory *explains* why the information within the global workspace is experienced. The best the theory can do is to say that the information is experienced because it is *globally accessible.* But now the question arises in a different form: Why should global accessibility give rise to conscious experience? As always, this bridging question is unanswered. . . .

5. The Extra Ingredient

We have seen that there are systematic reasons why the usual methods of cognitive science and neuroscience fail to account for conscious experience. These are simply the wrong sort of methods: nothing that they give to us can yield an explanation. To account for conscious experience, we need an *extra ingredient* in the explanation. This makes for a challenge to those who are serious about the hard problem of consciousness: What is your extra ingredient, and why should *that* account for conscious experience?

There is no shortage of extra ingredients to be had. Some propose an injection of chaos and nonlinear dynamics. Some think that the key lies in nonalgorithmic processing. Some appeal to future discoveries in neurophysiology. Some suppose that the key to the mystery will lie at the level of quantum mechanics. It is easy to see why all these suggestions are put forward. None of the old methods work, so the solution must lie with *something* new. Unfortunately, these suggestions all suffer from the same old problems.

Nonalgorithmic processing, for example, is put forward by Penrose (1989; 1994) because of the role it might play in the process of conscious mathematical insight. The arguments about mathematics are controversial, but even if they succeed and an account of nonalgorithmic processing in the human brain is given, it will still only be an account of the *functions* involved in mathematical reasoning and the like. For a nonalgorithmic process as much as an algorithmic process, the question is left unanswered: Why should this process give rise to experience? In answering *this* question, there is no special role for nonalgorithmic processing.

The same goes for nonlinear and chaotic dynamics. These might provide a novel account of the dynamics of cognitive functioning, quite different from that given by standard methods in cognitive science. But from dynamics, one only gets more dynamics. The question about experience here is as mysterious as ever. The point is even clearer for new discoveries in neurophysiology. These new discoveries may help us make significant progress in understanding brain function, but for any neural process we isolate, the same question will always arise. It is difficult to imagine what a proponent of new neurophysiology expects to happen, over and above the explanation of further cognitive functions. It is not as if we will suddenly discover a phenomenal glow inside a neuron! . . .

At the end of the day, the same criticism applies to *any* purely physical account of consciousness. For any physical process we specify there will be an unanswered question: Why should this process give rise to experience? Given any such process, it is conceptually coherent that it could be instantiated in the absence of experience. It follows that no mere account of the physical process will tell us why experience arises. The emergence of experience goes beyond what can be derived from physical theory.

6. Nonreductive Explanation

At this point some are tempted to give up, holding that we will never have a theory of conscious experience. McGinn (1989), for example, argues that the problem is too hard for our limited minds; we are "cognitively closed" with respect to the phenomenon. Others have argued that conscious experience lies outside the domain of scientific theory altogether.

I think this pessimism is premature. This is not the place to give up; it is the place where things get interesting. When simple methods of explanation are ruled out, we need to investigate the alternatives. Given that reductive explanation fails, *nonreductive* explanation is the natural choice.

Although a remarkable number of phenomena have turned out to be explicable wholly in terms of entities simpler than themselves, this is not universal. In physics, it occasionally happens that an entity has to be taken as *fundamental.* Fundamental entities are not explained in terms of anything simpler. Instead, one takes them as basic, and gives a theory of how they relate to everything else in the world. For example, in the nineteenth century it turned out that electromagnetic processes could not be explained in terms of the wholly mechanical processes that previous physical theories appealed to, so Maxwell and others introduced electromagnetic charge and electromagnetic forces as new fundamental components of a physical theory. To explain electromagnetism, the ontology of physics had to be expanded. New basic properties and basic laws were needed to give a satisfactory account of the phenomena.

Other features that physical theory takes as fundamental include mass and space-time. No attempt is made to explain these features in terms of anything simpler. But this does not rule out the possibility of a theory of mass or of space-time. There is an intricate theory of how these features interrelate, and of the basic laws they enter into. These basic principles are used to explain many familiar phenomena concerning mass, space, and time at a higher level.

I suggest that a theory of consciousness should take experience as fundamental. We know that a theory of consciousness requires the addition of *something* fundamental to our ontology, as everything in physical theory is compatible with the absence of consciousness.

We might add some entirely new nonphysical feature, from which experience can be derived, but it is hard to see what such a feature would be like. More likely, we will take experience itself as a fundamental feature of the world, alongside mass, charge, and space-time. If we take experience as fundamental, then we can go about the business of constructing a theory of experience.

Where there is a fundamental property, there are fundamental laws. A nonreductive theory of experience will add new principles to the furniture of the basic laws of nature. These basic principles will ultimately carry the explanatory burden in a theory of consciousness. Just as we explain familiar high-level phenomena involving mass in terms of more basic principles involving mass and other entities, we might explain familiar phenomena involving experience in terms of more basic principles involving experience and other entities.

In particular, a nonreductive theory of experience will specify basic principles telling us how experience depends on physical features of the world. These *psychophysical* principles will not interfere with physical laws, as it seems that physical laws already form a closed system. Rather, they will be a supplement to a physical theory. A physical theory gives a theory of physical processes, and a psychophysical theory tells us how those processes give rise to experience. We know that experience depends on physical processes, but we also know that this dependence cannot be derived from physical laws alone. The new basic principles postulated by a nonreductive theory give us the extra ingredient that we need to build an explanatory bridge.

Of course, by taking experience as fundamental, there is a sense in which this approach does not tell us why there is experience in the first place. But this is the same for any fundamental theory. Nothing in physics tells us why there is matter in the first place, but we do not count this against theories of matter. Certain features of the world need to be taken as fundamental by any scientific theory. A theory of matter can still explain all sorts of facts about matter, by showing how they are consequences of the basic laws. The same goes for a theory of experience.

This position qualifies as a variety of dualism, as it postulates basic properties over and above the properties invoked by physics. But it is an innocent version of dualism, entirely compatible with the scientific view of the world. Nothing in this approach contradicts anything in physical theory; we simply need to add further *bridging* principles to explain how experience arises from physical processes. There is nothing particularly spiritual or mystical about this theory—its overall shape is like that of a physical theory, with a few fundamental entities connected by fundamental laws. It expands the ontology slightly, to be sure, but Maxwell did the same thing. Indeed, the overall structure of this position is entirely naturalistic, allowing that ultimately the universe comes down to a network of basic entities obeying simple laws, and allowing that there may ultimately be a theory of consciousness cast in terms of such laws. If the position is to have a name, a good choice might be *naturalistic dualism.*

If this view is right, then in some ways a theory of consciousness will have more in common with a theory in physics than a theory in biology. Biological theories involve no principles that are fundamental in this way, so biological theory has a certain complexity and messiness to it; but theories in physics, insofar as they deal with fundamental principles, aspire to simplicity and elegance. The fundamental laws of nature are part of the basic furniture of the world, and physical theories are telling us that this basic furniture is remarkably simple. If a theory of consciousness also involves fundamental principles, then we should expect the same. The principles of simplicity, elegance, and even beauty that drive physicists' search for a fundamental theory will also apply to a theory of consciousness. . . .

Bibliography

Baars, B. J. 1988. *A Cognitive Theory of Consciousness.* Cambridge: Cambridge University Press.

Crick, F. 1994. *The Astonishing Hypothesis: The Scientific Search for the Soul.* New York: Scribners.

Crick, F. and Koch, C. 1990. Toward a neurobiological theory of consciousness. *Seminars in the Neurosciences* 2:263–275.

McGinn, C. 1989. Can we solve the mind-body problem? *Mind* 98:349–66.

Penrose, R. 1989. *The Emperor's New Mind.* Oxford: Oxford University Press.

Penrose, R. 1994. *Shadows of the Mind.* Oxford: Oxford University Press.

CHAPTER 18

The Myth of the Computer

John R. Searle

John R. Searle (1932–) is famous for arguing that computers cannot think. Minds and machines, in his view, are utterly different kinds of things.

Professor Searle has been at Berkeley for more than fifty years. His many books include *Minds, Brains, and Science* (1984), *The Mystery of Consciousness* (1997), *Freedom and Neurobiology* (2006), and *Making the Social World: The Structure of Human Civilization* (2011).

Our ordinary ways of talking about ourselves and other people, of justifying our behavior and explaining that of others, express a certain conception of human life that is so close to us, so much a part of common sense that we can hardly see it. It is a conception according to which each person has (or perhaps is) a mind; the contents of the mind—beliefs, fears, hopes, motives, desires, etc.—cause and therefore explain our actions; and the continuity of our minds is the source of our individuality and identity as persons.

In the past couple of centuries we have also become convinced that this common-sense psychology is grounded in the brain, that

Source: From John R. Searle, "The Myth of the Computer," *The New York Review of Books,* April 29, 1982, pp. 3–5. Reprinted with permission from *The New York Review of Books.* © 1982. This was originally a review of Douglas R. Hofstadter and Daniel C. Dennett's *The Mind's I* (New York: Basic Books, 1981); most of the references to Hofstadter and Dennett have been removed.

these mental states and events are somehow, we are not quite sure how, going on in the neurophysiological processes of the brain. So this leaves us with two levels at which we can describe and explain human beings: a level of common-sense psychology, which seems to work well enough in practice but which is not scientific; and a level of neurophysiology, which is certainly scientific but which even the most advanced specialists know very little about.

But couldn't there be a third possibility, a science of human beings that was not introspective common-sense psychology but was not neurophysiology either? This has been the great dream of the human sciences in the twentieth century, but so far all of the efforts have been, in varying degrees, failures. The most spectacular failure was behaviorism, but in my intellectual lifetime I have lived through exaggerated hopes placed on and disappointed by games theory, cybernetics, information theory, generative grammar, structuralism, and Freudian psychology, among others. Indeed it has become something of a scandal of twentieth-century intellectual life that we lack a science of the human mind and human behavior, that the methods of the natural sciences have produced such meager results when applied to human beings.

The latest candidate or family of candidates to fill the gap is called cognitive science, a collection of related investigations into the human mind involving psychology, philosophy, linguistics, anthropology, and artificial intelligence. Cognitive science is really the name of a family of research projects and not a theory, but many of its practitioners think that the heart of cognitive science is a theory of the mind based on artificial intelligence (AI). According to this theory minds are just computer programs of certain kinds. . . .

The theory, which is fairly widely held in cognitive science, can be summarized in three propositions.

1. Mind as Program. What we call minds are simply very complex digital computer programs. Mental states are simply computer states and mental processes are computational processes. Any system whatever that had the right program, with the right input and output, would have to have mental states and processes in the same literal sense that you and I do, because that is all there is to mental states and processes, that is all that you and I have. The programs in question are "self-updating" or "self-designing" "systems of representations."

2. The Irrelevance of the Neurophysiology of the Brain. In the study of the mind actual biological facts about actual human and animal brains are irrelevant because the mind is an "abstract sort of thing" and human brains just happen to be among the indefinitely large number of kinds of computers that can have minds. Our minds happen to be embodied in our brains, but there is no essential connection between the mind and the brain. Any other computer with the right program would also have a mind. . . .

3. The Turing Test as the Criterion of the Mental. The conclusive proof of the presence of mental states and capacities is the ability of a system to pass the Turing test, the test devised by Alan Turing. If a system can convince a competent expert that it has mental states then it really has those mental states. If, for example, a machine could "converse" with a native Chinese speaker in such a way as to convince the speaker that it understood Chinese then it would literally understand Chinese. . . .

We might call this collection of theses "strong artificial intelligence" (strong AI). These theses are certainly not obviously true and they are seldom explicitly stated and defended.

Let us inquire first into how plausible it is to suppose that specific biochemical powers of the brain are really irrelevant to the mind. It is an amazing fact, by the way, that in twenty-seven pieces about the mind the editors [Hofstadter and Dennett] have not seen fit to include any whose primary aim is to tell us how the brain actually works, and this omission obviously derives from their conviction that since "mind is an abstract sort of thing" the specific neurophysiology of the brain is incidental. This idea derives part of its appeal from the editors' keeping their discussion at a very abstract general level about "consciousness" and "mind" and "soul," but if you consider specific mental states and processes—being thirsty, wanting to go to the bathroom, worrying about your income tax, trying to solve math puzzles, feeling depressed, recalling the French word for "butterfly"—then it seems at least a little odd to think that the brain is so irrelevant.

Take thirst, where we actually know a little bit about how it works. Kidney secretions of renin synthesize a substance called angiotensin. This substance goes into the hypothalamus and triggers a series of neuron firings. As far as we know these neuron firings are a very large part of the cause of thirst. Now obviously there is more to be said, for example, about the relations of the hypothalamic responses to the rest of the brain, about other things going on in the hypothalamus, and about the possible distinctions between the feeling of thirst and the urge to drink. Let us suppose we have filled out the story with the rest of the biochemical causal account of thirst.

Now the theses of the mind as program and the irrelevance of the brain would tell that what matters about this story is not the specific biochemical properties of the angiotensin or the hypothalamus but only the formal computer programs that the whole sequence instantiates. Well, let's try that out as a hypothesis and see how it works. A computer can simulate the formal properties of the sequence of chemical and electrical phenomena in the production of thirst just as much as it can simulate the formal properties of anything else—we can simulate thirst just as we can simulate hurricanes, rainstorms, five-alarm fires, internal combustion engines, photosynthesis, lactation, or the flow of currency in a depressed economy. But no one in his right mind thinks that a computer simulation of a five-alarm fire will burn down the neighborhood, or that a computer simulation of an internal combustion engine will power a car, or that computer simulations of lactation and photosynthesis will produce milk and sugar. To my amazement, however, I have found that a large number of people suppose that computer simulations of mental phenomena, whether at the level of brain processes or not, literally produce mental phenomena.

Again, let's try it out. Let's program our favorite PDP-10 computer with the formal program that simulates thirst. We can even program it to print out at the end "Boy, am I thirsty!" or "Won't someone please give me a drink?" etc. Now would anyone suppose that we thereby have even the slightest reason to suppose that the computer is literally thirsty? Or that any simulation of any other mental phenomena, such as understanding stories, feeling depressed, or worrying about itemized deductions, must therefore produce the real thing? The answer, alas, is that a large number of people are committed to an ideology that requires them to believe just that. So let us carry the story a step further.

The PDP-10 is powered by electricity and perhaps its electrical properties can reproduce some of the actual causal powers of the electrochemical features of the brain in producing mental states. We certainly couldn't rule out that eventuality a priori. But remember: the thesis of strong AI is that the mind is "independent of any particular embodiment" because the mind is just a program and the program can be run on a computer made of anything whatever provided it is stable enough and complex enough to carry the program. The actual physical computer could be an ant colony (one of their examples), a collection of beer cans, streams of toilet paper with small stones placed on the squares, men sitting on high stools with green eye shades—anything you like.

So let us imagine our thirst-simulating program running on a computer made entirely of old beer cans, millions (or billions) of old beer cans that are rigged up to levers and powered by windmills. We can imagine that the program simulates the neuron firings at the synapses by having beer cans bang into each other, thus achieving a strict correspondence between neuron firings and beer-can bangings. And at the end of the sequence a beer can pops up on which is written "I am thirsty." Now, to repeat the question, does anyone suppose that this Rube Goldberg apparatus is literally thirsty in the sense in which you and I are? . . .

Digital computer programs by definition consist of sets of purely formal operations on formally specified symbols. The ideal computer does such things as print a 0 on the tape, move one square to the left, erase a 1, move back to the right, etc. It is common to describe this as "symbol manipulation" or, to use the term favored by Hofstadter and Dennett, the whole system is a "self-updating representational system"; but these terms are at least a bit misleading since as far as the computer is concerned the symbols don't symbolize anything or represent anything. They are just formal counters.

The computer attaches no meaning, interpretation, or content to the formal symbols; and qua computer it couldn't, because if we tried to give the computer an interpretation of its symbols we could only give it more uninterpreted symbols. The interpretation of the symbols is entirely up to the programmers and users of the computer. For example, on my pocket calculator if I print "3 × 3 = ," the calculator will print "9" but it has no idea that "3" means 3 or that "9" means 9 or that anything means anything. We might put this point by saying that the computer has a syntax but no semantics. The computer manipulates formal symbols but attaches no meaning to them, and this simple observation will enable us to refute the thesis of mind as program.

Suppose that we write a computer program to simulate the understanding of Chinese so that, for example, if the computer is asked questions in Chinese the program enables it to give answers in Chinese; if asked to summarize stories in Chinese it can give such summaries; if asked questions about the stories it has been given it will answer such questions.

Now suppose that I, who understand no Chinese at all and can't even distinguish Chinese symbols from some other kinds of symbols, am locked in a room with a number of cardboard boxes full of Chinese symbols. Suppose that I am given a book of rules in English that instruct me how to match these Chinese symbols with each other. The rules say such things as that the "squiggle-squiggle" sign is to be followed by the "squoggle-squoggle" sign. Suppose that people outside the room pass in more Chinese symbols and that following the instructions in the book I pass Chinese symbols back to them. Suppose that unknown to me the people who pass me the symbols call them "questions," and the book of instructions that I work from they call "the program"; the symbols I give back to them they call "answers to the questions" and me they call "the computer." Suppose that after a while the programmers get so good at writing the programs and I get so good at manipulating the symbols that my answers are indistinguishable from those of native Chinese speakers. I can pass the Turing test for understanding Chinese. But all the same I still don't understand a word of Chinese and neither does any other digital computer because all the computer has is what I have: a formal program that attaches no meaning, interpretation, or content to any of the symbols.

What this simple argument shows is that no formal program by itself is sufficient for understanding, because it would always be possible in principle for an agent to go through the steps in the program and still not have the relevant understanding. And what works for Chinese would also work for other mental phenomena. I could, for example, go through the steps of the thirst-simulating program without feeling thirsty. The argument also, en passant, refutes the Turing test because it shows that a system, namely me, could pass the Turing test without having the appropriate mental states. . . .

The details of how the brain works are immensely complicated and largely unknown, but some of the general principles of the relations between brain functioning and computer programs can be stated quite simply. First, we know that brain processes cause mental phenomena. Mental states are caused by and realized in the structure of the brain. From this it follows, that any system that produced mental states would have to have powers equivalent to those of the brain. Such a system might use a different chemistry, but whatever its chemistry it would have to be able to cause what the brain causes. We know from the Chinese room argument that digital computer programs by themselves are never sufficient to produce mental states. Now since brains do produce minds, and since programs by themselves can't produce minds, it follows that the way the brain does it can't be by simply instantiating a computer program. (Everything, by the way, instantiates some program or other, and brains are no exception. So in that trivial sense brains, like everything else, are digital computers.) And it also follows that if you wanted to build a machine to produce mental states, a thinking machine, you couldn't do it solely in virtue of the fact that your machine ran a certain kind of computer program. The thinking machine couldn't work solely in virtue of being a digital computer but would have to duplicate the specific causal powers of the brain.

Freedom

CHAPTER 19

A Defense of Free Will Skepticism

Derk Pereboom

Most people think it's obvious that human beings have free will. They also think it's obvious that, if human beings did not have free will, then this would be a bad thing. Derk Pereboom, a professor at Cornell University, disagrees on both counts. Pereboom defends a view called *hard incompatibilism*. The "incompatibilism" part denies that an action could be both freely chosen and determined by forces outside of one's control—in other words, freedom and determinism are incompatible. But Pereboom does not claim that all of our actions are determined by forces outside of our control. Rather, he is a "hard" incompatibilist because he believes that, however our actions are caused, they are not free in any sense that would allow us to be morally responsible in performing them. And this state of affairs, Pereboom argues, is not bad.

1. Outline of Hard Incompatibilism

Spinoza maintained that due to certain general facts about the nature of the universe, we human beings do not have the sort of free will required for moral responsibility. I agree. More exactly, he argues that it is because causal determinism is true that we lack this sort of free will; he is thus a *hard determinist*. By contrast, the position I defend is agnostic about causal determinism. I contend, like Spinoza, that we would not have the sort of free will required for moral responsibility if causal determinism were true, but also that indeterministic theories do not significantly improve the prospects for this sort of free will. Consequently, we need to take seriously the verdict that we lack the sort of free will required for moral responsibility. I call the resulting skeptical view about free will *hard incompatibilism*. In addition, I argue that a conception of life without this sort of free will need not exclude morality or our sense of meaning in life, and in some respects it could even be beneficial.

2. Against Compatibilism

The case for hard incompatibilism involves arguing against two competing positions. The first of these is *compatibilism,* which claims that free will of the type required for moral responsibility is compatible with determinism. Compatibilists typically maintain, in addition, that we do in fact have this sort of free will. The second is *libertarianism,* which contends that although the sort of free will required for moral responsibility is not compatible with determinism, it turns out that determinism is false, and we do have this kind of free will.

Compatibilists typically attempt to formulate conditions on agency intended to provide an account of what it is to be morally responsible for an action. These conditions are compatibilist in that they allow for an agent to be morally responsible for an action even when she is causally determined to act as she does. For instance, Hume and his followers specify that morally responsible action be caused by desires that flow from the agent's "durable and constant" character, and that the agent not be constrained to act, at least in the sense that the action not result from an irresistible desire. Harry Frankfurt proposes that moral responsibility requires that the agent have endorsed and produced her will to perform the action in the right way. More specifically, she must have a second-order desire— that is, a desire to have a particular desire—to will to perform it, and her will must be her will because she has this second-order desire. John Fischer argues that morally responsible action must result from a rational consideration of the reasons at issue; among other things, the agent must be receptive to the reasons present in a situation, and she must be responsive to them to the degree that in at least some situations in which the reasons are different, she would have done otherwise. Finally, Jay Wallace proposes that moral responsibility requires that the agent have the general ability to grasp, apply, and regulate her behavior by moral reasons. Each of these compatibilists intends for his conditions to be sufficient for an agent's moral responsibility when they are supplemented by some fairly uncontroversial additional necessary conditions, such as the provision that the agent understands that killing is morally wrong.

In my view, the best type of challenge to the compatibilist begins with the intuition that if someone is causally determined to act by other agents, for example, by scientists who manipulate her brain, then she is not morally responsible for that action. This intuition remains strong even if she meets the compatibilist conditions on moral responsibility just canvassed. The following "four-case argument" first of all develops examples of actions that involve such manipulation, in which these compatibilist conditions on moral responsibility are satisfied. Manipulation cases, taken individually, indicate that it is possible for an agent not to be morally responsible even if the compatibilist conditions are satisfied, and that as a result these conditions are inadequate. But the argument has additional force, by way of setting out three such cases, each progressively more like a fourth scenario which the compatibilist would regard as realistic, in which the action is causally determined in a natural way. An additional challenge for the compatibilist is to point out a relevant difference between any two adjacent cases that would show why the agent might be morally responsible in the later example but not in the earlier one. I argue that this can't be done. So I contend that the agent's non-responsibility generalizes from the first two manipulation examples to the ordinary case.

In each of the four cases, Professor Plum decides to kill Ms. White for the sake of some personal advantage, and succeeds in doing so. We design the cases so that his act of murder conforms to the prominent compatibilist conditions. Plum's action meets the Humean conditions, since for him purely selfish reasons typically weigh heavily—much too heavily as judged from the moral point of view, while in addition the desire that motivates him to act is nevertheless not irresistible for him, and in this sense he is not constrained to act. It fits the condition proposed by Frankfurt: Plum's effective desire (i.e., his will) to murder White conforms appropriately to his second-order desires for which effective desires he will have. That is, he not only wills to murder her, but he also wants to will to do so. The action also satisfies the reasons-responsiveness condition advocated by Fischer: Plum's desires are modified by, and some of them arise from, his rational consideration of the reasons he has, and if he knew that the bad consequences for himself that would result from killing White would be much more severe than they are actually likely to be, he would have refrained from killing her for this reason. In addition, this action meets the condition advanced by Wallace: Plum retains the general ability to grasp, apply, and regulate his behavior by moral reasons. When egoistic reasons that count against acting morally are relatively weak, he will usually regulate his behavior by moral reasons instead. This ability provides him with the capacity to revise and develop his moral character over time, as Alfred Mele requires. Now, supposing that causal determinism is true, is it plausible that Plum is morally responsible for his action?

Each of the four cases features different ways in which Plum's murder of White might be causally determined by factors beyond his control.

> Case 1: A team of neuroscientists is able to manipulate Professor Plum's mental state at any moment through the use of radio-like technology. In this case, they do so by pressing a button just before he begins to reason about his situation. This causes Plum's reasoning process to be egoistic, which the neuroscientists know will deterministically result in his decision to kill White. Plum does not think and act contrary to character since his reasoning processes are not infrequently egoistic. His effective first-order desire to kill White conforms to his second-order desires. The process of deliberation from which his action results is reasons-responsive; in particular, this type of process would have resulted in his refraining from killing White in some situations in which the reasons were different. Still, his reasoning is not in general exclusively egoistic, since he often regulates his behavior by moral reasons, especially when the egoistic reasons are relatively weak. He is also not constrained, in the sense that he does not act because of an irresistible desire—the neuroscientists do not induce a desire of this kind.

In Case 1, Plum's action satisfies all the compatibilist conditions we just examined. But intuitively, he is not morally responsible for the murder, because his action is causally determined by what the neuroscientists do, which is beyond his control. Consequently, it would seem that these compatibilist conditions are not sufficient for moral responsibility—even if all taken together.

A compatibilist might resist this conclusion by arguing that although in Case 1 the process resulting in the action satisfies all of the prominent compatibilist conditions, yet Plum's relevant states are directly produced by the manipulators at the time of the action—he is locally manipulated—and this is the aspect of the story that undermines his moral responsibility. In reply, if the neuroscientists did all of their manipulating during one time interval and, after some length of time, the relevant states were produced in him, would he only then be morally responsible? It is my sense that such a time lag, all by itself, would make no difference to whether an agent is responsible.

So let us now consider a scenario in which the manipulation takes place long before the action:

> Case 2: Plum is like an ordinary human being, except that neuroscientists have programmed him at the beginning of his life so that his reasoning is frequently but not always egoistic (as in Case 1), with the consequence that in the particular circumstances in which he now finds himself, he is causally determined to engage in the egoistic reasons-responsive process of deliberation and to have the set of first- and second-order desires that result in his decision to kill White. Plum has the general ability to regulate his behavior by moral reasons, but in his circumstances, due to the egoistic character of his reasoning, he is causally determined to make his decision. At the same time, he does not act because of an irresistible desire.

Here again, although Plum meets each of the compatibilist conditions, it is intuitive that he is not morally responsible. Thus Case 2 also shows that the prominent compatibilist conditions, either separately or in conjunction, are not sufficient for moral responsibility. Again, it would seem unprincipled to claim that here, by contrast with Case 1, Plum is morally responsible because the length of time between the programming and the action is now great enough. Here also it would seem that he is not morally responsible because he is causally determined to decide and act by forces beyond his control.

Imagine next a scenario more similar yet to an ordinary situation:

> Case 3: Plum is an ordinary human being, except that he was causally determined by the rigorous training practices of his household and community in such a way that his reasoning processes are often but not exclusively rationally egoistic (as in Cases 1 and 2). This training took place when he was too young to have the ability to prevent or alter the practices that determined this aspect of his character. This training, together with his particular current circumstances, causally determines him to engage in the egoistic reasons-responsive process of deliberation and to have the first- and second-order desires that result in his decision to kill White. Plum has the general ability to regulate his

behavior by moral reasons, but in his circumstances, due to the egoistic nature of his reasoning processing, he is causally determined to make his decision. Here again his action is not due to an irresistible desire.

If a compatibilist wishes to contend that Plum is morally responsible in Case 3, he needs to point to a feature of these circumstances that would explain why he is morally responsible here but not in Case 2. But it seems that there is no such feature. In each of these examples, Plum meets all the prominent compatibilist conditions for morally responsible action, so a divergence in judgment about moral responsibility between these examples will not be supported by a difference in whether these conditions are satisfied. Causal determination by factors beyond his control most plausibly explains the absence of moral responsibility in Case 2, and we are constrained to conclude that Plum is not morally responsible in Case 3 for the same reason.

Thus it appears that Plum's exemption from responsibility in Cases 1 and 2 generalizes to the nearer-to-normal Case 3. Does it generalize all the way to the ordinary case?

Case 4: Physicalist determinism is true—everything in the universe is physical, and everything that happens is causally determined by virtue of the past states of the universe in conjunction with the laws of nature. Plum is an ordinary human being, raised in normal circumstances, and again his reasoning processes are frequently but not exclusively egoistic (as in Cases 1–3). His decision to kill White results from his reasons-responsive process of deliberation, and he has the specified first- and second-order desires. Again, he has the general ability to grasp, apply, and regulate his behavior by moral reasons, and his action is not due to an irresistible desire.

Given that we need to deny moral responsibility in Case 3, could Plum be responsible in this more ordinary case? There would seem to be no differences between Case 3 and Case 4 that could serve to justify the claim that Plum is not responsible in Case 3 but is in Case 4. One distinguishing feature of Case 4 is that the causal determination of Plum's crime is not brought about by other agents. However, the claim that this is a relevant difference is implausible. Imagine a further example that is exactly the same as, say, Case 1 or Case 2, except that Plum's states are induced by a spontaneously generated machine —a machine that has no intelligent designer. Here also Plum would not be morally responsible.

The best explanation for the intuition that Plum is not morally responsible in the first three cases is that his action is produced by a deterministic causal process that traces back to factors beyond his control. Because his action is also causally determined in this way in Case 4, we should conclude that here again he is not morally responsible. So by this argument, Plum's non-responsibility in Case 1 generalizes to non-responsibility in Case 4. We should conclude that if an action results from any deterministic causal process that traces back to factors beyond the agent's control, then she will lack the control required to be morally responsible for it.

3. Agent-Causal Libertarianism and an Objection from Our Best Physical Theories

A number of different libertarian theories have been proposed, but let us examine the agent causal version, since it is particularly intuitive and attractive. This view claims that we agents possess a special causal power—a power for an agent, fundamentally as a substance, to cause a decision, and thereby to settle which of a number of competing possible decisions occurs, without being causally determined to do so. But can this position be reconciled with what we would expect given our best physical theories? When an agent makes a free decision, she causes the decision without being causally determined. On the path to action that results from this undetermined decision, changes in the physical world, for example in the agent's brain or some other part of her body, are produced. But if the physical world were generally governed by deterministic laws, it seems that here we would encounter divergences from these laws. For the changes in the physical world that result from the undetermined decision would themselves not be causally determined, and they would thus not be governed by the deterministic laws. For this reason, agent-causal libertarianism is not plausibly reconciled with the physical world's being governed by deterministic laws.

On the standard interpretation of quantum mechanics, however, the physical world is not in fact deterministic, but is rather governed by probabilistic statistical laws. Some philosophers have defended the claim that agent-causal libertarianism can be reconciled with physical laws of this sort. However, wild coincidences would arise on this suggestion. Consider actions whose physical component has a 0.32 probability of occurring. It would not violate the statistical laws in the sense of being logically incompatible with them if, for a large number of instances, the physical components in this class were not actually realized close to 32% of the time. Rather, the force of the statistical law is that for a large number of instances it is correct to *expect* physical components in this class to be realized close to 32% of the time. Are free choices on the agent-causal libertarian model compatible with what the statistical law leads us to expect about them? If they were, then for a large enough number of instances the possible actions in our class would almost certainly be freely chosen close to 32% of the time. But if the occurrence of these physical components were settled by the choices of agent-causes, then their actually being chosen close to 32% of the time would amount to a wild coincidence. The proposal that agent-caused free choices do not diverge from what the statistical laws predict for the physical components of our actions would run so sharply counter to what we would expect as to make it incredible.

At this point, the libertarian might propose that there actually do exist divergences from the probabilities that we would expect without the presence of agent-causes, and that these divergences are to be found at the interface between the agent-cause and that which it directly affects—an interface which is likely to be found in the brain. The problem for this proposal, however, is that we have no evidence that such divergences occur. This difficulty, all by itself, provides a strong reason to reject this approach.

On the other hand, nothing we've said conclusively rules out the claim that because we are agent causes, there exist such divergences. We do not have a complete understanding of the human neural system, and it may turn out that some human neural structures are significantly different from anything else in nature we understand, and that they serve to ground agent-causation. This approach may be the best one for libertarians to pursue. But at this point we have no evidence that it will turn out to be correct. So given the kinds of difficulties we've encountered for libertarianism and compatibilism, it makes sense to take seriously the remaining skeptical option, according to which we do not have the sort of free will required for moral responsibility.

4. Hard Incompatibilism and Wrongdoing

Accepting hard incompatibilism demands giving up our ordinary view of ourselves as blameworthy for immoral actions and praiseworthy for actions that are morally exemplary. At this point one might object that giving up our belief in moral responsibility would have very harmful consequences, perhaps so harmful that thinking and acting as if hard incompatibilism is true is not a feasible option. Thus even if the claim that we are morally responsible turns out to be false, there may yet be weighty practical reasons to believe that we are, or at least to treat people as if they were.

For instance, one might think that if we gave up the belief that people are blameworthy, we could no longer legitimately judge any actions as wrong or even bad, or as right or good. But this seems mistaken. Even if we came to believe that some perpetrator of genocide was not morally responsible because of some degenerative brain disease he had, we would still maintain that his actions were morally wrong, and that it was extremely bad that he acted as he did. So, in general, denying blameworthiness would not at the same time threaten judgments of wrongness or badness, and, likewise, denying praiseworthiness would not undermine assessments of rightness or goodness.

Perhaps treating wrongdoers as blameworthy is often required for effective moral education and improvement. If we resolved never to treat people as blameworthy, one might fear that we would be left with insufficient leverage to reform immoral behavior. Still, this option would have us treat people as blameworthy—by, for example, expressing anger toward them because of what they have done—when they do not deserve it, which would seem prima facie morally wrong. If people are not morally responsible for immoral behavior, treating them as if they were would seem to be unfair. However, it is possible to achieve moral reform by methods that would not be threatened by this sort of unfairness, and in ordinary situations such practices could arguably be as successful as those that presuppose moral responsibility. Instead of treating people as if they deserve blame, the hard incompatibilist can turn to moral admonition and encouragement, which presuppose only that the offender has done wrong. These methods can effectively communicate a sense of right and wrong, and they can help to reform the wrongdoer.

But does this position have resources adequate for contending with criminal behavior? Here it would appear to be at a disadvantage, and if so, practical considerations might yield strong reasons to treat criminals as if they were morally responsible. First of all, if the free will skeptic is right, a retributivist justification for criminal punishment would be unavailable, for it asserts that the criminal deserves pain or deprivation just for committing the crime, while hard incompatibilism denies this claim. And retributivism is one of the most naturally compelling ways to justify criminal punishment.

By contrast, a theory that justifies criminal punishment on the ground that punishment educates criminals morally is not threatened by hard incompatibilism specifically. However, we lack significant empirical evidence that punishing criminals brings about moral education, and without such evidence, it would be wrong to punish them in order to achieve this goal. In general, it is wrong to harm a person for the sake of realizing some good in the absence of impressive evidence that the harm will produce the good. Moreover, even if we had impressive evidence that punishment was effective in morally educating criminals, we should prefer non-punitive ways of achieving this result, if they are available—whether or not criminals are morally responsible.

Deterrence theories try to justify punishment on the grounds that it deters future crime. The two most-discussed deterrence theories, the utilitarian version and the one that grounds the right to punish on the right to self-defense, are not undermined by hard incompatibilism. Still, they are questionable on other grounds. The utilitarian theory, which claims that punishment is justified because it maximizes utility (i.e., the quantity of happiness or pleasure minus the quantity of unhappiness or pain), faces well-known challenges. It would seem at times to require punishing the innocent when doing so would maximize utility; in certain situations it would appear to prescribe punishment that is unduly severe; and it would authorize harming people merely as means to the well-being, in this case the safety, of others. The sort of deterrence theory that grounds the right to punish in the right of individuals to defend themselves against immediate threats is also objectionable. For when a criminal is sentenced to punishment he is most often not an immediate threat to anyone, since he is then in the custody of the law, and this fact about his circumstances distinguishes him from those who can legitimately be harmed on the basis of the right of self-defense.

There is, however, a resilient theory of crime prevention that is consistent with hard incompatibilism. This view draws an analogy between the treatment of criminals and the treatment of carriers of dangerous diseases. Ferdinand Schoeman argues that if we have the right to quarantine carriers of serious communicable diseases to protect people, then for the same reason we also have the right to isolate the criminally dangerous. Notice that quarantining a person can be justified when she is not morally responsible for being dangerous to others. If a child is infected with a deadly contagious virus that was transmitted to her before she was born, quarantine can still be legitimate. Now imagine that a serial killer poses a grave danger to a community. Even if he is not morally responsible for his crimes (say because no one is ever morally responsible), it would be as legitimate to isolate him as it is to quarantine a non-responsible carrier of a serious communicable disease.

Clearly, it would be morally wrong to treat carriers of communicable diseases more severely than is required to protect people from the resulting threat. Similarly, it would be wrong to treat criminals more harshly than is required to protect society against the danger posed by them. Furthermore, just as it would be wrong to quarantine someone whose disease was less than severe, so it would be wrong to lock someone up whose crime was less than severe. In addition, I suspect that a theory modelled on quarantine would not justify measures of the sort whose legitimacy is most in doubt, such as the death penalty or confinement in the worst prisons we have. Moreover, it would demand a degree of concern for the rehabilitation and well-being of the criminal that would alter much of current practice. Just as society must seek to cure the diseased it quarantines, so it would be required to try to rehabilitate the criminals it detains. In addition, if a criminal cannot be rehabilitated, and if protection of society demands his indefinite confinement, there would be no justification for making his life more miserable than needed to guard against the danger he poses.

5. Meaning in Life

If hard incompatibilism is true, could we legitimately retain a sense of achievement for what makes our lives fulfilled, happy, satisfactory, or worthwhile, and our hold onto our hopes for making these sorts of achievements in our lives? It might be argued that if hard incompatibilism is true, there can be no genuine achievements, for an agent cannot have an achievement for which she is not also praiseworthy. However, achievement, and our hope for achievement, is not as closely connected to praiseworthiness as this objection supposes. If an agent hopes to achieve success in some project, and if she accomplishes what she hoped for, intuitively this outcome would be an achievement of hers even if she is not praiseworthy for it—although at the same time the sense in which it is her achievement may be diminished. For example, if someone hopes that her efforts as a teacher will result in well-educated children, and they do, there remains a clear sense in which she has achieved what she hoped for —even if it turns out she is not praiseworthy for anything she does.

One might think that hard incompatibilism would instill an attitude of resignation to whatever the future holds in store, and would thereby undermine any hope or motivation for achievement. But this isn't clearly right. Even if what we know about our behavioral dispositions and our environment gives us reason to believe that our futures will turn out in a particular way, it can often be reasonable to hope that they will turn out differently. For this to be so, it may sometimes be important that we lack complete knowledge of our dispositions and environmental conditions. For instance, imagine that someone aspires to become a successful politician, but he is concerned that his fear of public speaking will get in the way. He does not know whether this fear will in fact frustrate his ambition, since it is open for him that he will overcome this problem, perhaps due to a disposition for resolute self-discipline in transcending obstacles of this sort. As a result, he might reasonably hope that he will get over his fear and succeed in his ambition. Given hard incompatibilism, if he in fact does overcome his problem and succeeds in political life, this will not be an achievement of his in as robust a sense as we might naturally suppose, but it will be his achievement in a substantial sense nonetheless.

Still, one might contend that, although the skeptical view leaves room for a limited foundation of the sense of self-worth, this perspective can nevertheless be damaging to our view of ourselves, to our sense of achievement and self-worth. But, in response, first note that our sense of self-worth—our sense that we have value and that our lives are worth living—is to a non-trivial extent due to features not produced by our will, let alone by free will. People place great value on natural beauty, native athletic ability, and intelligence, none of which have their source in our volition. To be sure, we also value efforts that are voluntary in the sense that they are willed by us—in productive work and altruistic behavior, and indeed, in the formation of moral character. However, does it matter very much to us that these voluntary efforts are also *freely* willed?

Consider how someone comes to have a good moral character. It is not implausible that it is formed to a significant degree as a result of upbringing, and moreover, the belief that this is so is widespread. Parents typically regard themselves as having failed in raising their children if they turn out with immoral dispositions, and parents often take great care to bring their children up to prevent such a result.

Accordingly, people often come to believe that they have the good moral character they do largely because they were raised with love and skill. But those who come to believe this about themselves seldom experience dismay because of it. People tend not to become dispirited upon coming to understand that their good moral character is not their own doing, and that they do not deserve a great deal of praise or respect for it. By contrast, they often come to feel more fortunate and thankful. Suppose, however, that there are some who would be overcome with dismay. Would it be justified or even desirable for them to foster the illusion that they nevertheless deserve praise and respect for producing their moral character? I suspect that most would eventually be able to accept the truth without incurring much loss. All of this, I think, would also hold for those who come to believe that they do not deserve praise and respect for producing their moral character because they are not, in general, morally responsible.

6. Emotions, Reactive Attitudes, and Personal Relationships

Peter Strawson argues that the justification for judgments of blameworthiness and praiseworthiness has its foundation in what he calls the *reactive attitudes,* reactions to how people voluntarily behave—attitudes such as moral resentment, guilt, gratitude, forgiveness, and love. Moreover, because moral responsibility has this kind of foundation, the truth or falsity of determinism is irrelevant to whether we are justified in regarding agents as morally responsible. This is because these reactive attitudes are required for the kinds of interpersonal relationships that make our lives meaningful, and so even if we could give up the reactive attitudes we would never have sufficient practical reason to do so. Strawson believes that it is in fact psychologically impossible for us to give up the reactive attitudes altogether, but in a limited range of cases we can adopt what he calls the "objective attitude," a cold and calculating stance towards others, which he describes as follows:

> To adopt the objective attitude to another human being is to see him, perhaps, as an object of social policy; as a subject for what, in a wide range of sense, might be called treatment; as something certainly to be taken account, perhaps precautionary account, of; to be managed or handled or cured or trained; perhaps simply to be avoided. . . . The objective attitude may be emotionally toned in many ways: it may include repulsion or fear, it may

include pity or love, though not all kinds of love. But it cannot include the range of reactive feelings and attitudes which belong to involvement or participation with others in interpersonal human relationships; it cannot include resentment, gratitude, forgiveness, anger, or the sort of love which two adults can sometimes be said to feel reciprocally, for each other. (Strawson 1962)

If determinism did imperil the reactive attitudes, and we were able to relinquish them, Strawson suggests that we would face the prospect of adopting this objective attitude toward everyone, as a result of which our interpersonal relationships would be damaged. Since we have extremely good practical reasons for maintaining these relationships, we would never have sufficient practical reason to adopt the objective attitude in most cases, and hence we would never have sufficient reason to give up our reactive attitudes, and thus to stop regarding people as morally responsible.

If we persistently maintained an objective attitude toward others, I agree that our relationships would be threatened. However, I deny that it would be appropriate to adopt this stance if we came to believe the skeptical view about free will. Certain reactive attitudes would be undercut, because some of them, such as moral resentment and indignation, would have the false presupposition that the person who is the object of the attitude is morally responsible. But I claim that the reactive attitudes that we would want to retain either are not threatened by hard incompatibilism in this way, or else have analogues or aspects that would not have false presuppositions. The attitudes that would survive do not amount to the objective attitude, and they would be sufficient to sustain good human relationships.

It is plausible that to a certain degree moral resentment and indignation are beyond our power to affect. Even supposing that a free will skeptic is thoroughly committed to morality and rationality, and that she is admirably in control of her emotions, she might still be unable to eliminate these attitudes. Instead we might expect people to be morally resentful in certain circumstances, and we would not regard them as morally responsible for it. But we also have the ability to prevent, temper, and sometimes to dispel moral resentment, and given a belief in hard incompatibilism, we might attempt such measures for the sake of morality and rationality. Modifications of this sort, assisted by the skeptical conviction, might well be good for interpersonal relationships.

Forgiveness might appear to presuppose that the person being forgiven is blameworthy, and if this is so, this attitude would also be undercut. But certain key features of forgiveness would not be endangered, and they are sufficient to sustain the role forgiveness has in relationships. Suppose a friend repeatedly mistreats you, and because of this you decide to end your relationship with him. However, he then apologizes to you, indicating his recognition that his actions were wrong, his wish that he had not mistreated you, and his commitment to refrain from the immoral behavior. Because of this you decide not to end the friendship. In this case, the feature of forgiveness that is consistent with the skeptical view is the willingness to cease to regard past immoral behavior as a reason to weaken or end a relationship. The aspect of forgiveness that would be undermined is the willingness to disregard the friend's blameworthiness. But since she has given up the belief that we are morally responsible, the hard incompatibilist no longer needs a willingness to disregard blameworthiness to sustain good relationships.

One might object that hard incompatibilism threatens the self-directed attitudes of guilt and repentance, and that this would be especially bad for relationships. In the absence of guilt and repentance, we would not only be incapable of restoring relationships damaged because we have done wrong, but we would also be kept from restoring our moral integrity. For without the attitudes of guilt and repentance, we would lack the psychological mechanisms that can play these roles. But note first that it is because guilt essentially involves a belief that one is blameworthy that this attitude would be threatened by hard incompatibilism. It is for this reason that repentance would also seem to be (indirectly) threatened, for feeling guilty would appear to be required to motivate repentance. Imagine, however, that you have acted immorally; still because you endorse the skeptical view, you deny that you are blameworthy. Instead, you acknowledge that you were the agent of wrongdoing, you feel sorrow on account of having done wrong, and you deeply regret having acted as you did. In addition, because you are committed to doing what is right and to your own moral improvement, you resolve not to act in this way again. None of these measures are jeopardized by hard incompatibilism.

Gratitude would appear to presuppose that the person to whom one is grateful is morally responsible for a beneficial act, as a result of which this attitude would also be endangered. But as in the case of forgiveness, certain aspects of this attitude would be unaffected, and these aspects can provide what is needed for good relationships. Gratitude involves, first of all, being thankful toward a person who has acted beneficially. It is true that being thankful toward someone usually involves the belief that she is praiseworthy for some action. Still, one can also be thankful to a small child for some kindness, without believing that she is morally responsible for it. This aspect of thankfulness could be retained even without the presupposition of praiseworthiness. Typically gratitude also involves joy as a response to what someone has done. But no feature of hard incompatibilism undermines being joyful and expressing joy when others are, for example, considerate or generous in one's behalf. Expressing joy can bring about the sense of harmony and goodwill often produced by gratitude, and thus here the skeptical position is not at a disadvantage.

Would the kind of love that mature adults have for each other in good relationships be imperiled, as Strawson's line of argument suggests? Consider first whether for loving someone it is important that the person who is loved has and exercises free will in the sense required for moral responsibility. Parents love their children rarely, if ever, for the reason that they possess this sort of free will, or decide to do what is right by free will, or deserve to be loved due to freely-willed choices. Moreover, when adults love each other, it is also very seldom, if at all, for these sorts of reasons. Besides moral character and behavior, features such as intelligence, appearance, style, and resemblance to others in one's personal history all might play a part. Suppose morally admirable qualities are particularly important in occasioning, enriching, and maintaining love. Even if there is an aspect of love that we conceive as a deserved response to morally admirable qualities, it is unlikely that love would even be diminished if we came to believe that these qualities are not produced or sustained by freely-willed decisions. Such admirable qualities are loveable whether or not we deserve praise for having them.

One might contend that we want to be freely loved by others—to be loved by them as a result of their free will. Against this, the love parents have for their children typically comes about independently of the parents' will altogether, and we don't think that love of this sort is deficient. Robert Kane recognizes this fact about parents' love, and he acknowledges that romantic love is similar in this respect. However, he maintains that there is a kind of love we very much want that would not exist if all love were causally determined by factors beyond our control. The plausibility of Kane's claim might be enhanced by reflecting on how you would react upon discovering that someone you love was causally determined to love you by, say, a benevolent manipulator.

Setting aside *free* will for a moment, when does the will play any role at all in engendering love? When a relationship is disintegrating, people will at times decide to try to restore the love they once had for one another. When a student finds herself in conflict with a room-mate from the outset, she might choose to take steps to improve the relationship. When a marriage is arranged, the partners may decide to do what they can to love each other. In these kinds of circum-stances we might want others to make a decision that might produce or maintain love. But this is not to say that we would want that deci-sion to be freely willed in the sense required for moral responsibility. For it is not clear that value would be added by the decision's being free in this sense. Moreover, although in some circumstances we might want others to make decisions of this sort, we would typically prefer love that did not require such decisions. This is so not only for intimate romantic relationships—where it is quite obvious—but also for friendships and relationships between parents and children.

Suppose Kane's view could be defended, and we did want love that is freely willed in the sense required for moral responsibility. If we in fact desired love of this kind, then we would want a kind of love that is impossible if we lack the sort of free will required for moral responsibility. Still, the sorts of love not threatened by the skeptical view are sufficient for good relationships. If we can aspire to the kind of love parents typically have for their children, or the type romantic lovers share, or the sort had by friends who are deeply devoted to each other, and whose friendship became close through their interac-tions, then the possibility of fulfillment through interpersonal rela-tionships remains intact.

Accepting hard incompatibilism, therefore, would not under-mine interpersonal relationships. It might challenge certain attitudes that typically have a role in such relationships. Moral resentment, indig-nation and guilt would likely be irrational, since these attitudes would have presuppositions believed to be false. But these attitudes are either not required for good relationships, or they have analogues that could play their typical role. Moreover, love—the reactive attitude most essen-tial to good interpersonal relationships—does not seem threatened at all. Love of another involves, fundamentally, wishing for the other's good, taking on her aims and desires, and a desire to be together with her, and none of this is endangered by the skeptical position.

7. The Good in Hard Incompatibilism

Hard incompatibilism also promises substantial benefits for human life. Of all the attitudes associated with the assumption that we are morally responsible, anger seems most closely connected with it. Discussions about moral responsibility most often focus not on how we judge morally exemplary agents, but rather on how we regard those who are morally deficient. Examples designed to elicit a strong intuition that an agent is morally responsible most often feature an especially heinous action, and the intuition usually involves sympathetic anger. It may be, then, that our attachment to the assumption that we are morally responsible derives to a significant degree from the role anger plays in our emotional lives. Perhaps we feel that giving up the assumption of responsibility is threatening because the rationality of anger would be undercut as a result.

The kind of anger at issue is the sort that is directed toward a person who is believed to have behaved immorally—it comprises both moral resentment and indignation. Let us call this attitude *moral anger*. Not all anger is moral anger. One type of non-moral anger is directed toward someone because his abilities are lacking in some respect or because he has performed poorly in some situation. We are sometimes angry with machines for malfunctioning. At times our anger has no object. Still, most human anger is moral anger.

Moral anger comprises a significant part of our moral lives as we ordinarily conceive them. It motivates us to resist abuse, discrimination, and oppression. At the same time, expression of moral anger often has harmful effects, failing to contribute to the well-being either of those toward whom it is directed or of those expressing the anger. Often its expression is intended to cause little else than emotional or physical pain. Consequently, it has a tendency to damage relationships, impair the functioning of organizations, and unsettle societies. In extreme cases, it can motivate people to torture and kill.

The realization that expression of moral anger can be damaging gives rise to a strong demand that it be morally justified when it occurs. The demand to morally justify behavior that is harmful is generally a very strong one, and expressions of moral anger are often harmful. This demand is made more urgent by the fact that we are often attached to moral anger, and that we frequently enjoy expressing it. Most commonly we justify expression of moral anger by arguing that wrongdoers deserve it, and we believe that they deserve it because they are morally responsible for what they do. If hard incompatibilism is true, however, justification of this sort is undermined. Yet this may be a good thing.

Accepting hard incompatibilism is not likely to modify our attitudes to the extent that the expression of moral anger ceases to be a problem for us. However, moral anger is often sustained and magnified by the belief that its object is morally responsible for immoral behavior. Destructive moral anger in relationships is nurtured in this way by the assumption that the other is blameworthy. The anger that fuels ethnic conflicts, for example, is almost always fostered by the conviction that a group of people deserves blame for past wrongs. Hard incompatibilism advocates giving up such beliefs because they are false. As a result, moral anger might decrease, and its expressions subside.

Would the benefits that would result if moral anger were modified in this way compensate for the losses that would ensue? Moral anger motivates us to oppose wrongful behavior. Would we lose the motivation to oppose immorality? If for hard incompatibilist reasons the assumption that wrongdoers are blameworthy is withdrawn, the belief that they have in fact behaved immorally would not be threatened. Even if those who commit genocide are not morally responsible, their actions are nonetheless clearly horribly immoral, and a conviction that this is so would remain untouched. This, together with a commitment to oppose wrongdoing, would permit a resolve to resist abuse, discrimination, and oppression. Accepting hard incompatibilism would thus allow us to retain the benefits moral anger can also provide, while at the same time challenging its destructive effects.

CHAPTER 20

*C*ompatibilism Defended

W. T. Stace

W. T. Stace (1886–1967) of Princeton University is not read much today. However, his vigorous defense of compatibilism—the idea that a human act can be both free and determined—is a classic.

I shall first discuss the problem of free will, for it is certain that if there is no free will there can be no morality. Morality is concerned with what men ought and ought not to do. But if a man has no freedom to choose what he will do, if whatever he does is done under compulsion, then it does not make sense to tell him that he ought not to have done what he did and that he ought to do something different. All moral precepts would in such case be meaningless. Also if he acts always under compulsion, how can he be held morally responsible for his actions? How can he, for example, be punished for what he could not help doing?

It is to be observed that those learned professors of philosophy or psychology who deny the existence of free will do so only in their professional moments and in their studies and lecture rooms. For when it comes to doing anything practical, even of the most trivial kind, they invariably behave as if they and others were free. They inquire from you at dinner whether you will choose this dish or that

---

Source: W. T. Stace, *Religion and the Modern Mind,* pp. 279–287. Copyright © 1952 by W. T. Stace, renewed 1980 by Blanche Stace. Reprinted by permission of Harper-Collins Publishers, Inc.

dish. They will ask a child why he told a lie, and will punish him for not having chosen the way of truthfulness. All of which is inconsistent with a disbelief in free will. This should cause us to suspect that the problem is not a real one; and this, I believe, is the case. The dispute is merely verbal, and is due to nothing but a confusion about the meanings of words. It is what is now fashionably called a semantic problem.

How does a verbal dispute arise? Let us consider a case which, although it is absurd in the sense that no one would ever make the mistake which is involved in it, yet illustrates the principle which we shall have to use in the solution of the problem. Suppose that someone believed that the word "man" means a certain sort of five-legged animal; in short that "five-legged animal" is the correct *definition* of man. He might then look around the world, and rightly observing that there are no five-legged animals in it, he might proceed to deny the existence of men. This preposterous conclusion would have been reached because he was using an incorrect definition of "man." All you would have to do to show him his mistake would be to give him the correct definition; or at least to show him that his definition was wrong. Both the problem and its solution would, of course, be entirely verbal. The problem of free will, and its solution, I shall maintain, is verbal in exactly the same way. The problem has been created by the fact that learned men, especially philosophers, have assumed an incorrect definition of free will, and then finding that there is nothing in the world which answers to their definition, have denied its existence. As far as logic is concerned, their conclusion is just as absurd as that of the man who denies the existence of men. The only difference is that the mistake in the latter case is obvious and crude, while the mistake which the deniers of free will have made is rather subtle and difficult to detect.

Throughout the modern period, until quite recently, it was assumed, both by the philosophers who denied free will and by those who defended it, that *determinism is inconsistent with free will.* If a man's actions were wholly determined by chains of causes stretching back into the remote past, so that they could be predicted beforehand by a mind which knew all the causes, it was assumed that they could not in that case be free. This implies that a certain definition of actions done from free will was assumed, namely that they are actions *not* wholly determined by causes or predictable beforehand. Let us shorten this by saying that free will was defined as meaning indeterminism. This is the incorrect definition which has led to the denial of free will. As soon as we see what the true definition is we shall find that the question whether the world is deterministic, as Newtonian science implied, or in a measure indeterministic, as current physics teaches, is wholly irrelevant to the problem.

Of course there is a sense in which one can define a word arbitrarily in any way one pleases. But a definition may nevertheless be called correct or incorrect. It is correct if it accords with a *common usage* of the word defined. It is incorrect if it does not. And if you give an incorrect definition, absurd and untrue results are likely to follow. For instance, there is nothing to prevent you from arbitrarily defining a man as a five-legged animal, but this is incorrect in the sense that it does not accord with the ordinary meaning of the word. Also it has the absurd result of leading to a denial of the existence of men. This shows that *common usage is the criterion for deciding whether a definition is correct or not.* And this is the principle which I shall apply to free will. I shall show that indeterminism is not what is meant by the phrase "free will" *as it is commonly used.* And I shall attempt to discover the correct definition by inquiring how the phrase is used in ordinary conversation.

Here are a few samples of how the phrase might be used in ordinary conversation. It will be noticed that they include cases in which the question whether a man acted with free will is asked in order to determine whether he was morally and legally responsible for his acts.

JONES: I once went without food for a week.
SMITH: Did you do that of your own free will?
JONES: No. I did it because I was lost in a desert and could find no food.

But suppose that the man who had fasted was Mahatma Gandhi. The conversation might then have gone:

GANDHI: I once fasted for a week.
SMITH: Did you do that of your own free will?
GANDHI: Yes. I did it because I wanted to compel the British Government to give India its independence.

Take another case. Suppose that I had stolen some bread, but that I was as truthful as George Washington. Then, if I were charged with the crime in court, some exchange of the following sort might take place:

JUDGE: Did you steal the bread of your own free will?
STACE: Yes. I stole it because I was hungry.

Or in different circumstances the conversation might run:

JUDGE: Did you steal of your own free will?

STACE: No. I stole because my employer threatened to beat me if I did not.

At a recent murder trial in Trenton some of the accused had signed confessions, but afterwards asserted that they had done so under police duress. The following exchange might have occurred:

JUDGE: Did you sign this confession of your own free will?

PRISONER: No. I signed it because the police beat me up.

Now suppose that a philosopher had been a member of the jury. We could imagine this conversation taking place in the jury room.

FOREMAN OF THE JURY: The prisoner says he signed the confession because he was beaten, and not of his own free will.

PHILOSOPHER: This is quite irrelevant to the case. There is no such thing as free will.

FOREMAN: Do you mean to say that it makes no difference whether he signed because his conscience made him want to tell the truth or because he was beaten?

PHILOSOPHER: None at all. Whether he was caused to sign by a beating or by some desire of his own—the desire to tell the truth, for example—in either case his signing was causally determined, and therefore in neither case did he act of his own free will. Since there is no such thing as free will, the question whether he signed of his own free will ought not to be discussed by us.

The foreman and the rest of the jury would rightly conclude that the philosopher must be making some mistake. What sort of a mistake could it be? There is only one possible answer. The philosopher must be using the phrase "free will" in some peculiar way of his own which is not the way in which men usually use it when they wish to determine a question of moral responsibility. That is, he must be using an incorrect definition of it as implying action not determined by causes.

Suppose a man left his office at noon, and were questioned about it. Then we might hear this:

JONES: Did you go out of your own free will?

SMITH: Yes. I went out to get my lunch.

But we might hear:

JONES: Did you leave your office of your own free will?
SMITH: No. I was forcibly removed by the police.

We have now collected a number of cases of actions which, in the ordinary usage of the English language, would be called cases in which people have acted of their own free will. We should also say in all these cases that they *chose* to act as they did. We should also say that they could have acted otherwise, if they had chosen. For instance, Mahatma Gandhi was not compelled to fast; he chose to do so. He could have eaten if he had wanted to. When Smith went out to get his lunch, he chose to do so. He could have stayed and done some more work, if he had wanted to. We have also collected a number of cases of the opposite kind. They are cases in which men were not able to exercise their free will. They had no choice. They were compelled to do as they did. The man in the desert did not fast of his own free will. He had no choice in the matter. He was compelled to fast because there was nothing for him to eat. And so with the other cases. It ought to be quite easy, by an inspection of these cases, to tell what we ordinarily mean when we say that a man did or did not exercise free will. We ought therefore to be able to extract from them the proper definition of the term. Let us put the cases in a table:

Free Acts	Unfree Acts
Gandhi fasting because he wanted to free India.	The man fasting in the desert because there was no food.
Stealing bread because one is hungry.	Stealing because one's employer threatened to beat one.
Signing a confession because one wanted to tell the truth.	Signing because the police beat one.
Leaving the office because one wanted one's lunch.	Leaving because forcibly removed.

It is obvious that to find the correct definition of free acts we must discover what characteristic is common to all the acts in the left-hand column, and is, at the same time, absent from all the acts in the right-hand column. This characteristic which all free acts have, and which no unfree acts have, will be the defining characteristic of free will.

Is being uncaused, or not being determined by causes, the characteristic of which we are in search? It cannot be, because although it is true that all the acts in the right-hand column have causes, such as the beating by the police or the absence of food in the desert, so also do the acts in the left-hand column. Mr. Gandhi's fasting was caused by his desire to free India, the man leaving his office by his hunger, and so on. Moreover there is no reason to doubt that these causes of the free acts were in turn caused by prior conditions, and that these were again the results of causes, and so on back indefinitely into the past. Any physiologist can tell us the causes of hunger. What caused Mr. Gandhi's tremendously powerful desire to free India is no doubt more difficult to discover. But it must have had causes. Some of them may have lain in peculiarities of his glands or brain, others in his past experiences, others in his heredity, others in his education. Defenders of free will have usually tended to deny such facts. But to do so is plainly a case of special pleading, which is unsupported by any scrap of evidence. The only reasonable view is that all human actions, both those which are freely done and those which are not, are either wholly determined by causes, or at least as much determined as other events in nature. It may be true, as the physicists tell us, that nature is not as deterministic as was once thought. But whatever degree of determinism prevails in the world, human actions appear to be as much determined as anything else. And if this is so, it cannot be the case that what distinguishes actions freely chosen from those which are not free is that the latter are determined by causes while the former are not. Therefore, being uncaused or being undetermined by causes, must be an incorrect definition of free will.

What, then, is the difference between acts which are freely done and those which are not? What is the characteristic which is present to all the acts in the left-hand column and absent from all those in the right-hand column? Is it not obvious that, although both sets of actions have causes, the causes of those in the left-hand column are *of a different kind* from the causes of those in the right-hand column? The free acts are all caused by desires, or motives, or by some sort of internal psychological states of the agent's mind. The unfree acts, on the other hand, are all caused by physical forces or physical conditions, outside the agent. Police arrest means physical force exerted from the outside; the absence of food in the desert is a physical condition of the outside world. We may therefore frame the following rough definitions. *Acts freely done are those whose immediate causes are psychological states in the agent. Acts not freely done are those whose immediate causes are states of affairs external to the agent.*

It is plain that if we define free will in this way, then free will certainly exists, and the philosopher's denial of its existence is seen to be what it is—nonsense. For it is obvious that all those actions of men which we should ordinarily attribute to the exercise of their free will, or of which we should say that they freely chose to do them, are in fact actions which have been caused by their own desires, wishes, thoughts, emotions, impulses, or other psychological states.

CHAPTER **21**

*O*n *Liberty*

John Stuart Mill

The argument here is not about "free will" but about how much free-dom individuals should have in a well-ordered society. Should you have the freedom to deny proper medical care to your children or to harm yourself by using drugs? Should you have the freedom to do what every-one else thinks is morally wrong? What limits should there be on one's right to oppose the government?

John Stuart Mill (1806–1873), the greatest British philosopher of the nineteenth century, considers questions like these in *On Liberty* (1859). He defends what writers now call "Mill's Harm Principle"— the idea that one's freedom should be restricted only for the protection of others. This selection is taken from chapter 1 of *On Liberty*. Those who would like to read the whole chapter can find it on Jonathan Bennett's website, earlymoderntexts.com. On that site, Professor Bennett has rewritten a number of great philosophical works with an eye to making them easier to understand.

The subject of this essay is not the so-called "liberty of the will," so unfortunately opposed to the misnamed doctrine of philosophical necessity; but civil, or social liberty: the nature and limits of the power which can be legitimately exercised by society over the individual. . . .

Source: From the first chapter of Mill's *On Liberty* (1859). In a few places, I have altered Mill's language by substituting a common word for an obscure word.

The object of this essay is to assert one very simple principle, as entitled to govern absolutely the dealings of society with the individual in the way of compulsion and control, whether the means used be physical force in the form of legal penalties or the moral coercion of public opinion. That principle is that the sole end for which mankind are warranted, individually or collectively, in interfering with the liberty of action of any of their number is self-protection. That the only purpose for which power can be rightfully exercised over any member of a civilized community, against his will, is to prevent harm to others. His own good, either physical or moral, is not a sufficient warrant. He cannot rightfully be compelled to do or forbear because it will be better for him to do so, because it will make him happier, because, in the opinions of others, to do so would be wise or even right. These are good reasons for protesting to him, or reasoning with him, or persuading him, or begging him, but not for compelling him or visiting him with any evil in case he do otherwise. To justify that, the conduct from which it is desired to deter him must be calculated to produce evil to someone else. The only part of the conduct of anyone for which he is amenable to society is that which concerns others. In the part which merely concerns himself, his independence is, of right, absolute. Over himself, over his own body and mind, the individual is sovereign.

It is, perhaps, hardly necessary to say that this doctrine is meant to apply only to human beings in the maturity of their faculties. We are not speaking of children or of young persons below the age which the law may fix as that of manhood or womanhood. Those who are still in a state to require being taken care of by others must be protected against their own actions as well as against external injury. For the same reason we may leave out of consideration those backward states of society in which the race itself may be considered as in its nonage. The early difficulties in the way of spontaneous progress are so great that there is seldom any choice of means for overcoming them; and a ruler full of the spirit of improvement is warranted in the use of any expedients that will attain an end perhaps otherwise unattainable. Despotism is a legitimate mode of government in dealing with barbarians, provided the end be their improvement and the means justified by actually effecting that end. Liberty, as a principle, has no application to any state of things anterior to the time when mankind have become capable of being improved by free and equal discussion. Until then, there is nothing for them but implicit obedience to an Akbar or a Charlemagne, if they are so fortunate as to find one. But as soon as mankind have attained the capacity of being guided to their own improvement by conviction or persuasion (a period long since reached in all nations with whom we need here concern ourselves), compulsion, either in the direct form or in that of pains and penalties for noncompliance, is no longer admissible as a means to their own good, and justifiable only for the security of others.

It is proper to state that I forego any advantage which could be derived to my argument from the idea of abstract right as a thing independent of utility. I regard utility as the ultimate appeal on all ethical questions; but it must be utility in the largest sense, grounded on the permanent interests of man as a progressive being. Those interests, I contend, authorize the subjection of individual spontaneity to external control only in respect to those actions of each which concern the interest of other people. If anyone does an act hurtful to others, there is a *prima facie* case for punishing him by law or, where legal penalties are not safely applicable, by general disapprobation. There are also many positive acts for the benefit of others which he may rightfully be compelled to perform, such as to give evidence in a court of justice, to bear his fair share in the common defense or in any other joint work necessary to the interest of the society of which he enjoys the protection, and to perform certain acts of individual beneficence, such as saving a fellow creature's life or interposing to protect the defenseless against ill usage—things which whenever it is obviously a man's duty to do he may rightfully be made responsible to society for not doing. A person may cause evil to others not only by his actions but by his inaction, and in either case he is justly accountable to them for the injury. The latter case, it is true, requires a much more cautious exercise of compulsion than the former. To make anyone answerable for doing evil to others is the rule; to make him answerable for not preventing evil is, comparatively speaking, the exception. Yet there are many cases clear enough and grave enough to justify that exception. . . .

But there is a sphere of action in which society, as distinguished from the individual, has, if any, only an indirect interest: comprehending all that portion of a person's life and conduct which affects only himself or, if it also affects others, only with their free, voluntary, and undeceived consent and participation. When I say only himself, I mean directly and in the first instance; for whatever affects himself may affect others through himself. . . . This, then, is the appropriate region of human liberty. It comprises, first, the inward domain of

consciousness, demanding liberty of conscience in the most compre-
hensive sense, liberty of thought and feeling, absolute freedom of
opinion and sentiment on all subjects, practical or speculative, scientific, moral, or theological. The liberty of expressing and publishing
opinions may seem to fall under a different principle, since it belongs
to that part of the conduct of an individual which concerns other
people, but, being almost of as much importance as the liberty of
thought itself and resting in great part on the same reasons, is practically inseparable from it. Secondly, the principle requires liberty of
tastes and pursuits, of framing the plan of our life to suit our own
character, of doing as we like, subject to such consequences as may
follow, without impediment from our fellow creatures, so long as
what we do does not harm them, even though they should think our
conduct foolish, perverse, or wrong. Thirdly, from this liberty of each
individual follows the liberty, within the same limits, of combination
among individuals; freedom to unite for any purpose not involving
harm to others: the persons combining being supposed to be of full
age and not forced or deceived.

No society in which these liberties are not, on the whole,
respected is free, whatever may be its form of government; and none
is completely free in which they do not exist absolute and unquali-
fied. The only freedom which deserves the name is that of pursuing
our own good in our own way, so long as we do not attempt to deprive
others of theirs or impede their efforts to obtain it. Each is the proper
guardian of his own health, whether bodily *or* mental and spiritual.
Mankind are greater gainers by allowing each other to live as seems
good to themselves than by compelling each to live as seems good to
the rest.

K*nowledge*

CHAPTER 22

Meditations I and II

René Descartes

René Descartes (1596–1650) is often called "The Father of Modern Philosophy." Almost four hundred years ago, Descartes laid out the basic questions about knowledge and human nature that have occupied us ever since.

Descartes' classic works include his *Discourse on Method* (1637) and *Principles of Philosophy* (1644). The selection below comes from his most famous book, *Meditations on First Philosophy* (1641). Those who would like to read the whole book can find it on Jonathan Bennett's Web site, earlymoderntexts.com. On that site, Professor Bennett has rewritten a number of great philosophical works with an eye to making them more accessible.

First Meditation

Concerning Things That Can Be Doubted. There is no novelty to me in the reflection that, from my earliest years, I have accepted many false opinions as true, and that what I have concluded from such badly assured premises could not but be highly doubtful and uncertain. From the time that I first recognized this fact, I have realized that if I wished to have any firm and constant knowledge in the sciences, I would have to undertake, once and for all, to set aside all the opinions which I had previously accepted among my beliefs and start

Source: This selection includes all of Descartes' First Meditation and most of the Second, which were originally published in 1641. It is reprinted from *Meditations on First Philosophy,* trans. Laurence J. Lafleur (New York: Macmillan, 1951), pp. 17–29.

again from the very beginning. But this enterprise appeared to me to be of very great magnitude, and so I waited until I had attained an age so mature that I could not hope for a later time when I would be more fitted to execute the project. Now, however, I have delayed so long that henceforward I should be afraid that I was committing a fault if, in continuing to deliberate, I expended time which should be devoted to action.

The present is opportune for my design; I have freed my mind of all kinds of cares; I feel myself, fortunately, disturbed by no passions; and I have found a serene retreat in peaceful solitude. I will therefore make a serious and unimpeded effort to destroy generally all my former opinions. In order to do this, however, it will not be necessary to show that they are all false, a task which I might never be able to complete; because, since reason already convinces me that I should abstain from the belief in things which are not entirely certain and indubitable no less carefully than from the belief in those which appear to me to be manifestly false, it will be enough to make me reject them all if I can find in each some ground for doubt. And for that it will not be necessary for me to examine each one in particular, which would be an infinite labor; but since the destruction of the foundation necessarily involves the collapse of all the rest of the edifice, I shall first attack the principles upon which all my former opinions were founded.

Everything which I have thus far accepted as entirely true and assured has been acquired from the senses or by means of the senses. But I have learned by experience that these senses sometimes mislead me, and it is prudent never to trust wholly those things which have once deceived us.

But it is possible that, even though the senses occasionally deceive us about things which are barely perceptible and very far away, there are many other things which we cannot reasonably doubt, even though we know them through the senses—as, for example, that I am here, seated by the fire, wearing a winter dressing gown, holding this paper in my hands, and other things of this nature. And how could I deny that these hands and this body are mine, unless I am to compare myself with certain lunatics whose brain is so troubled and befogged by the black vapors of the bile that they continually affirm that they are kings while they are paupers, that they are clothed in gold and purple while they are naked; or imagine that their head is made of clay, or that they are gourds, or that their body is glass? But this is ridiculous; such men are fools, and I would be no less insane than they if I followed their example.

Nevertheless, I must remember that I am a man, and that consequently I am accustomed to sleep and in my dreams to imagine the same things that lunatics imagine when awake, or sometimes things which are even less plausible. How many times has it occurred that the quiet of the night made me dream of my usual habits: that I was here, clothed in a dressing gown, and sitting by the fire, although I was in fact lying undressed in bed! It seems apparent to me now, that I am not looking at this paper with my eyes closed, that this head that I shake is not drugged with sleep, that it is with design and deliberate intent that I stretch out this hand and perceive it. What happens in sleep seems not at all as clear and as distinct as all this. But I am speaking as though I never recall having been misled, while asleep, by similar illusions! When I consider these matters carefully, I realize so clearly that there are no conclusive indications by which waking life can be distinguished from sleep that I am quite astonished, and my bewilderment is such that it is almost able to convince me that I am sleeping.

So let us suppose now that we are asleep and that all these details, such as opening the eyes, shaking the head, extending the hands, and similar things, are merely illusions; and let us think that perhaps our hands and our whole body are not such as we see them. Nevertheless, we must at least admit that these things which appear to us in sleep are like painted scenes and portraits which can only be formed in imitation of something real and true, and so, at the very least, these types of things—namely, eyes, head, hands, and the whole body—are not imaginary entities, but real and existent. For in truth painters, even when they use the greatest ingenuity in attempting to portray sirens and satyrs in bizarre and extraordinary ways, nevertheless cannot give them wholly new shapes and natures, but only invent some particular mixture composed of parts of various animals; or even if perhaps their imagination is sufficiently extravagant that they invent something so new that nothing like it has ever been seen, and so their work represents something purely imaginary and absolutely false, certainly at the very least the colors of which they are composed must be real.

And for the same reason, even if these types of things—namely, a body, eyes, head, hands, and other similar things—could be imaginary, nevertheless, we are bound to confess that there are some other still more simple and universal concepts which are true and existent, from the mixture of which, neither more nor less than in the case of the mixture of real colors, all these images of things are formed in our minds, whether they are true and real or imaginary and fantastic.

Of this class of entities is corporeal [i.e., material or physical] nature in general and its extension, including the shape of extended things, their quantity, or size and number, and also the place where they are, the time that measures their duration, and so forth. That is why we will perhaps not be reasoning badly if we conclude that physics, astronomy, medicine, and all the other sciences which follow from the consideration of composite entities are very dubious and uncertain; whereas arithmetic, geometry, and the other sciences of this nature, which treat only of very simple and general things without concerning themselves as to whether they occur in nature or not, contain some element of certainty and sureness. For whether I am awake or whether I am asleep, two and three together will always make the number five, and the square will never have more than four sides; and it does not seem possible that truths so clear and so apparent can ever be suspected of any falsity or uncertainty.

Nevertheless, I have long held the belief that there is a God who can do anything, by whom I have been created and made what I am. But how can I be sure but that he has brought it to pass that there is no earth, no sky, no extended bodies, no shape, no size, no place, and that nevertheless I have the impressions of all these things and cannot imagine that things might be other than as I now see them? And furthermore, just as I sometimes judge that others are mistaken about those things which they think they know best, how can I be sure but that God has brought it about that I am always mistaken when I add two and three or count the sides of a square, or when I judge of something else even easier, if I can imagine anything easier than that? But perhaps God did not wish me to be deceived in that fashion, since he is said to be supremely good. But if it was repugnant to his goodness to have made me so that I was always mistaken, it would seem also to be inconsistent for him to permit me to be sometimes mistaken, and nevertheless I cannot doubt that he does permit it.

At this point there will perhaps be some persons who would prefer to deny the existence of so powerful a God, rather than to believe that everything else is uncertain. Let us not oppose them for the moment, and let us concede according to their point of view that everything which I have stated here about God is fictitious. Then in whatever way they suppose that I have reached the state of being that I now have, whether they attribute it to some destiny or fate or refer it to chance, or whether they wish to explain it as the result of a continual interplay of events or in any other manner; nevertheless, since to err and be mistaken is a kind of imperfection, to whatever degree less powerful they consider the author to whom they attribute my origin, in that degree it will be more probable that I am so imperfect that I am always mistaken. To this reasoning, certainly, I have nothing to reply; and I am at last constrained to admit that there is nothing in what I formerly believed to be true which I cannot somehow doubt, and this not for lack of thought and attention, but for weighty and well-considered reasons. Thus I find that, in the future, I should withhold and suspend my judgment about these matters, and guard myself no less carefully from believing them than I should from believing what is manifestly false if I wish to find any certain and assured knowledge in the sciences.

It is not enough to have made these observations; it is also necessary that I should take care to bear them in mind. For these customary and long-standing beliefs will frequently recur in my thoughts, my long and familiar acquaintance with them giving them the right to occupy my mind against my will and almost to make themselves masters of my beliefs. I will never free myself of the habit of deferring to them and having faith in them as long as I consider that they are what they really are—that is, somewhat doubtful, as I have just shown, even if highly probable—so that there is much more reason to believe than to deny them. That is why I think that I would not do badly if I deliberately took the opposite position and deceived myself in pretending for some time that all these opinions are entirely false and imaginary, until at last I will have so balanced my former and my new prejudices that they cannot incline my mind more to one side than the other, and my judgment will not be mastered and turned by bad habits from the correct perception of things and the straight road leading to the knowledge of the truth. For I feel sure that I cannot overdo this distrust, since it is not now a question of acting, but only of meditating and learning.

I will therefore suppose that, not a true God, who is very good and who is the supreme source of truth, but a certain evil spirit, not less clever and deceitful than powerful, has bent all his efforts to deceiving me. I will suppose that the sky, the air, the earth, colors, shapes, sounds, and all other objective things that we see are nothing but illusions and dreams that he has used to trick my credulity. I will consider myself as having no hands, no eyes, no flesh, no blood, nor any senses, yet falsely believing that I have all these things. I will remain resolutely attached to this hypothesis; and if I cannot attain the knowledge of any truth by this method, at any rate it is in my power to suspend my judgment. That is why I shall take great care not to accept any falsity among my beliefs and shall prepare my mind so well for all the ruses of this great deceiver that, however powerful and artful he may be, he will never be able to mislead me in anything.

But this undertaking is arduous, and a certain laziness leads me insensibly into the normal paths of ordinary life. I am like a slave who, enjoying an imaginary liberty during sleep, begins to suspect that his liberty is only a dream; he fears to wake up and conspires with his pleasant illusions to retain them longer. So insensibly to myself I fall into my former opinions; and I am slow to wake up from this slumber for fear that the labors of waking life which will have to follow the tranquillity of this sleep, instead of leading me into the daylight of the knowledge of the truth, will be insufficient to dispel the darkness of all the difficulties which have just been raised.

Second Meditation

Of the Nature of the Human Mind, and That It Is More Easily Known Than the Body. Yesterday's Meditation has filled my mind with so many doubts that it is no longer in my power to forget them. Nor do I yet see how I will be able to resolve them; I feel as though I were suddenly thrown into deep water, being so disconcerted that I can neither plant my feet on the bottom nor swim on the surface. I shall nevertheless make every effort to conform precisely to the plan commenced yesterday and put aside every belief in which I could imagine the least doubt, just as though I knew that it was absolutely false. And I shall continue in this manner until I have found something certain, or at least, if I can do nothing else, until I have learned with certainty that there is nothing certain in this world. Archimedes, to move the earth from its orbit and place it in a new position, demanded nothing more than a fixed and immovable fulcrum; in a similar manner I shall have the right to entertain high hopes if I am fortunate enough to find a single truth which is certain and indubitable.

I suppose, accordingly, that everything that I see is false; I convince myself that nothing has ever existed of all that my deceitful memory recalls to me. I think that I have no senses; and I believe that body, shape, extension, motion, and location are merely inventions of my mind. What then could still be thought true? Perhaps nothing else, unless it is that there is nothing certain in the world.

But how do I know that there is not some entity, of a different nature from what I have just judged uncertain, of which there cannot be the least doubt? Is there not some God or some other power who gives me these thoughts? But I need not think this to be true, for possibly I am able to produce them myself. Then, at the very least, am I not an entity myself? But I have already denied that I had any senses or any body. However, at this point I hesitate, for what follows from that? Am I so dependent upon the body and the senses that I could not exist without them? I have just convinced myself that nothing whatsoever existed in the world, that there was no sky, no earth, no minds, and no bodies; have I not thereby convinced myself that I did not exist? Not at all; without doubt I existed if I was convinced or even if I thought anything. Even though there may be a deceiver of some sort, very powerful and very tricky, who bends all his efforts to keep me perpetually deceived, there can be no slightest doubt that I exist, since he deceives me; and let him deceive me as much as he will, he can never make me be nothing as long as I think that I am something. Thus, after having thought well on this matter, and after examining all things with care, I must finally conclude and maintain that this proposition: *I am, I exist,* is necessarily true every time that I pronounce it or conceive it in my mind.

But I do not yet know sufficiently clearly what I am, I who am sure that I exist. So I must henceforth take very great care that I do not incautiously mistake some other thing for myself, and so make an error even in that knowledge which I maintain to be more certain and more evident than all other knowledge that I previously had. That is why I shall now consider once more what I thought myself to be before I began these last deliberations. Of my former opinions I shall reject all that are rendered even slightly doubtful by the arguments that I have just now offered, so that there will remain just that part alone which is entirely certain and indubitable.

What then have I previously believed myself to be? Clearly, I believed that I was a man. But what is a man? Shall I say a rational animal? Certainly not, for I would have to determine what an "animal" is and what is meant by "rational"; and so, from a single question, I would find myself gradually enmeshed in an infinity of others more difficult and more inconvenient, and I would not care to waste the little time and leisure remaining to me in disentangling such difficulties. I shall rather pause here to consider the ideas which previously arose naturally and of themselves in my mind whenever I considered what I was. I thought of myself first as having a face, hands, arms, and all this mechanism composed of bone and flesh and members, just as it appears in a corpse, and which I designated by the name of "body." In addition, I thought of the fact that I consumed nourishment, that I walked, that I perceived and thought, and I ascribed all these actions to the soul. But either I did not stop to consider what this soul was or else, if I did, I imagined that it was something very rarefied and subtle, such as a wind, a flame, or a very much expanded air which penetrated into and was infused throughout my grosser components. As for what body was, I did not realize that there could be any doubt about it, for I thought that I recognized its nature very distinctly. If I had wished to explain it according to the notions that I then entertained, I would have described it somewhat in this way: By "body" I understand all that can be bounded by some figure; that can be located in some place and occupy space in such a way that every other body is excluded from it; that can be perceived by touch or sight or hearing or taste or smell; that can be moved in various ways, not by itself but by some other object by which it is touched and from which it receives an impulse. For to possess the power to move itself, and also to feel or to think, I did not believe at all that these are attributes of corporeal nature; on the contrary, rather, I was astonished to see a few bodies possessing such abilities.

But I, what am I, on the basis of the present hypothesis that there is a certain spirit who is extremely powerful and, if I may dare to say so, malicious and tricky, and who uses all his abilities and efforts in order to deceive me? Can I be sure that I possess the smallest fraction of all those characteristics which I have just now said belonged to the nature of body? I pause to consider this attentively. I pass and repass in review in my mind each one of all these things—it is not necessary to pause to take the time to list them—and I do not find any one of them which I can pronounce to be part of me. Let us move on to the attributes of the soul and see if any of these are in me. Is it characteristic of me to consume nourishment and to walk? But if it is true that I do not have a body, these also are nothing but figments of the imagination. To perceive? But once more, I cannot perceive without the body, except in the sense that I have thought I perceived various things during sleep, which I recognized upon waking not to have been really perceived. To think? Here I find the answer. Thought is an attribute that belongs to me; it alone is inseparable from my nature.

I am, I exist—that is certain; but for how long do I exist? For as long as I think; for it might perhaps happen, if I totally ceased thinking, that I would at the same time completely cease to be. I am now admitting nothing except what is necessarily true. I am therefore, to speak precisely, only a thinking being, that is to say, a mind, an understanding, or a reasoning being, which are terms whose meaning was previously unknown to me.

I am something real and really existing, but what thing am I? I have already given the answer: a thing which thinks. And what more? I will stimulate my imagination to see if I am not something else beyond this. I am not this assemblage of members which is called a human body; I am not a rarefied and penetrating air spread throughout all these members; I am not a wind, a flame, a breath, a vapor, or anything at all that I can imagine and picture to myself—since I have supposed that all that was nothing, and since, without abandoning this supposition, I find that I do not cease to be certain that I am something.

But perhaps it is true that those same things which I suppose not to exist because I do not know them are really no different from the self which I do know. As to that I cannot decide; I am not discussing that question at the moment, since I can pass judgment only upon those things which are known to me: I know that I exist and I am seeking to discover what I am, that "I" that I know to be. Now it is very certain that this notion and knowledge of my being, thus precisely understood, does not depend on things whose existence is not yet known to me; and consequently and even more certainly, it does not depend on any of those things that I can picture in my imagination. And even these terms, "picture" and "imagine," warn me of my error. For I would be imagining falsely indeed were I to picture myself as something; since to imagine is nothing else than to contemplate the shape or image of a bodily entity, and I already know both that I certainly exist and that it is altogether possible that all these images, and everything in general which is involved in the nature of body, are only dreams and illusions. From this I see clearly that there was no more sense in saying that I would stimulate my imagination to learn more distinctly what I am than if I should say: I am now awake, and I see something real and true; but because I do not yet perceive it sufficiently clearly, I will go to sleep on purpose, in order that my dreams will show it to me with more truth and evidence. And thus I know manifestly that nothing of all that I can understand by means of the imagination is pertinent to the knowledge which I have of myself, and that I must remember this and prevent my mind from thinking in this fashion, in order that it may clearly perceive its own nature.

But what then am I? A thinking being. What is a thinking being? It is a being which doubts, which understands, which conceives, which affirms, which denies, which wills, which rejects, which imagines also, and which perceives. It is certainly not a trivial matter if all these

244 THE TRUTH ABOUT THE WORLD

things belong to my nature. But why should they not belong to it? Am I not that same person who now doubts almost everything, who nevertheless understands and conceives certain things, who is sure of and affirms the truth of this one thing alone, who denies all the others, who wills and desires to know more about them, who rejects error, who imagines many things, sometimes even against my will, and who also perceives many things, as through the medium of the senses or the organs of the body? Is there anything in all that which is not just as true as it is certain that I am and that I exist, even though I were always asleep and though the one who created me directed all his efforts to deluding me? And is there any one of these attributes which can be distinguished from my thinking or which can be said to be separable from my nature? For it is so obvious that it is I who doubt, understand, and desire, that nothing could be added to make it more evident. And I am also certainly the same one who imagines; for once more, even though it could happen that the things I imagine are not true, nevertheless this power of imagining cannot fail to be real, and it is part of my thinking. Finally I am the same being which perceives— that is, which observes certain objects as though by means of the sense organs, because I do really see light, hear noises, feel heat. Will it be said that these appearances are false and that I am sleeping? Let it be so; yet at the very least it is certain that it seems to me that I see light, hear noises, and feel heat. This much cannot be false, and it is this, properly considered, which in my nature is called perceiving, and that, again speaking precisely, is nothing else but thinking.

As a result of these considerations, I begin to recognize what I am somewhat better and with a little more clarity and distinctness than heretofore. But nevertheless it still seems to me, and I cannot keep myself from believing, that corporeal things, images of which are formed by thought and which the senses themselves examine, are much more distinctly known than that indescribable part of myself which cannot be pictured by the imagination. Yet it would truly be very strange to say that I know and comprehend more distinctly things whose existence seems doubtful to me, that are unknown to me and do not belong to me, than those of whose truth I am persuaded, which are known to me, and which belong to my real nature—to say, in a word, that I know them better than myself. But I see well what is the trouble: my mind is a vagabond who likes to wander and is not yet able to stay within the strict bounds of truth.

CHAPTER 23

*D*oes Matter Exist?

George Berkeley

Bishop George Berkeley (1685–1753) believed that "matter" does not exist. All that exists are minds and their ideas. Our perceptions are not perceptions "of" things; they are just perceptions. Berkeley's views struck his contemporaries as so odd that many of them thought he was joking.

Berkeley is usually considered to be the greatest Irish philosopher ever. His works include *An Essay towards a New Theory of Vision* (1709), *A Treatise concerning the Principles of Human Knowledge* (1710), and *Three Dialogues between Hylas and Philonous* (1713).

1. It is evident to any one who takes a survey of the *objects of human knowledge,* that they are either *ideas* actually imprinted on the senses; or else such as are perceived by attending to the passions and operations of the mind; or lastly, *ideas* formed by help of memory and imagination—either compounding, dividing, or barely representing those originally perceived in the aforesaid ways. By sight I have the ideas of light and colours, with their several degrees and variations. By touch I perceive hard and soft, heat and cold, motion and resistance; and of all these more and less either as to quantity or degree. Smelling furnishes me with odours; the palate with tastes; and hearing conveys sounds to the mind in all their variety of tone and composition.

Source: George Berkeley, *A Treatise concerning the Principles of Human Knowledge* (1710). I have updated the spelling in a few places.

And as several of these are observed to accompany each other, they come to be marked by one name, and so to be reputed as one *thing*. Thus, for example, a certain colour, taste, smell, figure, and consistence having been observed to go together, are accounted one distinct thing, signified by the name apple; other collections of ideas constitute a stone, a tree, a book, and the like sensible things; which as they are pleasing or disagreeable excite the passions of love, hatred, joy, grief, and so forth.

2. But, besides all that endless variety of ideas or objects of knowledge, there is likewise Something which knows or perceives them; and exercises divers operations, as willing, imagining, remembering, about them. This perceiving, active being is what I call *mind, spirit, soul,* or *myself.* By which words I do not denote any one of my ideas, but a thing entirely distinct from them, wherein they exist, or, which is the same thing, whereby they are perceived; for the existence of an idea consists in being perceived.

3. That neither our thoughts, nor passions, nor ideas formed by the imagination, exist without the mind is what everybody will allow. And to me it seems no less evident that the various sensations or ideas imprinted on the Sense, however blended or combined together (that is, whatever objects they compose), cannot exist otherwise than in a mind perceiving them. I think an intuitive knowledge may be obtained of this, by any one that shall attend to what is meant by the term *exist* when applied to sensible things. The table I write on I say exists; that is, I see and feel it: and if I were out of my study I should say it existed; meaning thereby that if I was in my study I might perceive it, or that some other spirit actually does perceive it. There was an odour, that is, it was smelt; there was a sound, that is, it was heard; a colour or figure, and it was perceived by sight or touch. This is all that I can understand by these and the like expressions. For as to what is said of the *absolute* existence of unthinking things, without any relation to their being perceived, that is to me perfectly unintelligible. Their *esse* is *percipi;* nor is it possible they should have any existence out of the minds or thinking things which perceive them.

4. It is indeed an opinion strangely prevailing amongst men, that houses, mountains, rivers, and in a word all sensible objects, have an existence, natural or real, distinct from their being perceived by the understanding. But, with how great an assurance and acquiescence soever this Principle may be entertained in the world, yet whoever shall find in his heart to call it in question may, if I mistake not, perceive it to involve a manifest contradiction. For, what are the

forementioned objects but the things we perceive by sense? and what do we perceive besides our own ideas or sensations? and is it not plainly repugnant that any one of these, or any combination of them, should exist unperceived? . . .

17. If we inquire into what the most accurate philosophers declare themselves to mean by *material substance,* we shall find them acknowledge they have no other meaning annexed to those sounds but the idea of Being in general, together with the relative notion of its supporting accidents. The general idea of Being appears to me the most abstract and incomprehensible of all other; and as for its supporting accidents, this, as we have just now observed, cannot be understood in the common sense of those words: it must therefore be taken in some other sense, but what that is they do not explain. So that when I consider the two parts or branches which make the signification of the words *material substance,* I am convinced there is no distinct meaning annexed to them. But why should we trouble ourselves any farther, in discussing this material *substratum* or support of figure and motion and other sensible qualities? Does it not suppose they have an existence without the mind? And is not this a direct repugnancy, and altogether inconceivable?

18. But, though it were possible that solid, figured, moveable substances may exist without the mind, corresponding to the ideas we have of bodies, yet how is it possible for us to know this? Either we must know it by Sense or by Reason. As for our senses, by them we have the knowledge only of our sensations, ideas, or those things that are immediately perceived by sense, call them what you will: but they do not inform us that things exist without the mind, or unperceived, like to those which are perceived. This the materialists themselves acknowledge.—It remains therefore that if we have any knowledge at all of external things, it must be by reason inferring their existence from what is immediately perceived by sense. But what reason can induce us to believe the existence of bodies without the mind, from what we perceive, since the very patrons of Matter themselves do not pretend there is any necessary connection betwixt them and our ideas? I say it is granted on all hands (and what happens in dreams, frenzies, and the like, puts it beyond dispute) that it is possible we might be affected with all the ideas we have now, though no bodies existed without resembling them. Hence it is evident the supposition of external bodies is not necessary for the producing of our ideas; since it is granted they are produced sometimes, and might possibly be produced always, in the same order we see them in at present, without their concurrence.

19. But, though we might possibly have all our sensations without them, yet perhaps it may be thought easier to conceive and explain the manner of their production, by supposing external bodies in their likeness rather than otherwise; and so it might be at least probable there are such things as bodies that excite their ideas in our minds. But neither can this be said. For, though we give the materialists their external bodies, they by their own confession are never the nearer knowing how our ideas are produced; since they own themselves unable to comprehend in what manner body can act upon spirit, or how it is possible it should imprint any idea in the mind. Hence it is evident the production of ideas or sensations in our minds, can be no reason why we should suppose Matter or corporeal substances; since that is acknowledged to remain equally inexplicable with or without this supposition. If therefore it were possible for bodies to exist without the mind, yet to hold they do so must needs be a very precarious opinion; since it is to suppose, without any reason at all, that God has created innumerable beings that are entirely useless, and serve to no manner of purpose.

20. In short, if there were external bodies, it is impossible we should ever come to know it; and if there were not, we might have the very same reasons to think there were that we have now. Suppose—what no one can deny possible—an intelligence, without the help of external bodies, to be affected with the same train of sensations or ideas that you are, imprinted in the same order and with like vividness in his mind. I ask whether that intelligence has not all the reason to believe the existence of Corporeal Substances, represented by his ideas, and exciting them in his mind, that you can possibly have for believing the same thing? Of this there can be no question. Which one consideration were enough to make any reasonable person suspect the strength of whatever arguments he may think himself to have, for the existence of bodies without the mind. . . .

23. But, say you, surely there is nothing easier than for me to imagine trees, for instance, in a park, or books existing in a closet, and nobody by to perceive them. I answer, you may so, there is no difficulty in it. But what is all this, I beseech you, more than framing in your mind certain ideas which you call *books* and *trees,* and at the same time omitting to frame the idea of any one that may perceive them? But do not you yourself perceive or think of them all the while? This therefore is nothing to the purpose: it only shows you have the power of imagining, or forming ideas in your mind; but it does not show that you can conceive it possible the objects of your thought may exist

without the mind. To make out this, it is necessary that you conceive them existing unconceived or unthought of; which is a manifest repugnancy. When we do our utmost to conceive the existence of external bodies, we are all the while only contemplating our own ideas. But the mind, taking no notice of itself, is deluded to think it can and does conceive bodies existing unthought of, or without the mind, though at the same time they are apprehended by, or exist in, itself. A little attention will discover to any one the truth and evidence of what is here said, and make it unnecessary to insist on any other proofs against the existence of *material substance.*

24. It is very obvious, upon the least inquiry into our own thoughts, to know whether it be possible for us to understand what is meant by the *absolute existence of sensible objects in themselves,* or *without the mind.* To me it is evident those words mark out either a direct contradiction, or else nothing at all. And to convince others of this, I know no readier or fairer way than to entreat they would calmly attend to their own thoughts; and if by this attention the emptiness or repugnancy of those expressions does appear, surely nothing more is requisite for their conviction. It is on this therefore that I insist, to wit, that the *absolute existence of unthinking things* are words without a meaning, or which include a contradiction. This is what I repeat and inculcate, and earnestly recommend to the attentive thoughts of the reader.

CHAPTER 24

The Lure of Radical Skepticism

Michael Huemer

As human beings, we can't help but believe that a world exists outside of our own thoughts and feelings. We believe that there are snow cones and street signs and other people like us. Nobody can deny that we think this way. However, radical skeptics deny that we have any good reason to hold these beliefs; according to them, our belief in the existence of a world outside of our own minds is *unjustified*. Here Michael Huemer lays out the four strongest arguments for that view. Answering these arguments is central to epistemology, which is the study of the nature of knowledge.

Michael Huemer is Associate Professor of Philosophy at the University of Colorado at Boulder. His books include *Ethical Intuitionism* (2005) and *Skepticism and the Veil of Perception* (2001), from which this selection is taken.

Philosophical skeptics hold that one cannot know anything about the external world. The phrase "the external world" (a.k.a. "the objective world") refers to everything that exists outside of one's own mind. So, according to the skeptic, you cannot know how many fingers you have, if any. You cannot know whether the book you seem to be reading from really exists, or if it is just a convincing illusion. You also cannot

Source: This is chapter 2 of Michael Huemer, *Skepticism and the Veil of Perception* (Lanham, MD: Rowman & Littlefield Publishers, Inc., 2001). Notes have been omitted. Copyright © 2001 by Michael Huemer. Reprinted with permission of Rowman & Littlefield.

know anything about the minds of other people—you cannot know whether there are any other conscious beings in the world, nor, if there are, what kinds of thoughts they might be having. You can only know, at most, what is going on in your own mind. Every person (assuming there are more than one person) is in the same situation—that is, each person knows only of his own mind.

As an aside, notice that the skeptic does not say you only know what is going on *in your head.* He says you only know what is going on in your *mind.* "Heads," just like fingers and books and brains, are objects in the alleged physical world of whose existence we can never be certain. You think you have a head only because you think you can see and feel it; but what you really, directly experience is only a mental representation of a head (just as, in the case of a finger, you experience a mental representation of the finger), which could be an illusion. For all you know, you might be only a disembodied spirit, subject to a massive hallucination of existing in the physical world.

Notice also that skepticism is not the same thing as idealism. The skeptic need not *deny* the existence of an external world, as the idealist does. Rather, the skeptic maintains that we *do not know* there is an external world. To use an analogy, the skeptic is like the agnostic, whereas the idealist is like the atheist. This puts the skeptic in a stronger position than the idealist, for this reason: the skeptic does not need to prove that our beliefs about physical objects are false or even probably false; the skeptic only needs to create some reasonable doubt about those beliefs.

Even so, the skeptic's position seems extravagant. Is there a serious doubt, for example, about whether rocks exist? People who harbor such doubts for too long are liable to end up in mental institutions. Why, then, does this position merit serious discussion? For now, I will simply say that skepticism deserves serious philosophical attention because of the arguments that have been developed on its behalf. In philosophy, it is not good enough merely to find your opponents' views absurd and dismiss them. Even if you are right (one might say, especially if you are right), the important thing is to understand why. In the present case, this means understanding the lines of thought that lead to skepticism, and knowing precisely where they go wrong. This turns out to be a much more difficult task than it sounds.

I shall present four skeptical arguments below. Each of these arguments purports to show, at a minimum, that there is no good reason for thinking external objects exist. In fact, the first two arguments try to show even more: that there is no good reason for believing anything whatsoever. My aim in this chapter, playing devil's advocate, is to present the skeptic's case in its strongest form. . . .

1. The Infinite Regress Argument

The first argument goes as follows. In order for me to *know* something to be true, I must have an adequate reason for believing it. This is one of the things that distinguishes knowledge from mere belief. To take an example from Richard Fumerton, suppose I announce that the world is going to come to an end in the year 2100. You ask me, "How do you know that?" What you are asking for is a *reason* (specifically, some *evidence*) for believing that the world will come to an end in the year 2100. Now suppose I say, "Oh, it's just a whimsical hunch I have. I don't really have any reason for thinking that's true." In that case, you could conclude that, although I may *believe* that the world is coming to an end in the year 2100, I certainly do not *know* that it is. Beliefs like that—beliefs held for no reason—are typically referred to as "arbitrary assumptions."

In addition, in order for my reason to be adequate, it too must be something that I know to be the case. Again, suppose I announce that the world will end in the year 2100. This time, when asked why I believe this, I say, "I believe the world will come to an end in the year 2100, because the Plutonians are going to launch a lethal nuclear strike against us in that year." When asked how I know about the Plutonians' plans, however, I reply that I don't know any such thing; it was just a whimsical hunch. Once again, you would conclude that I do not know that the world is going to end in the year 2100, since the reason I gave for this hypothesis was inadequate.

These requirements on knowledge create the threat of an infinite regress. For suppose I claim to know some proposition, A. You ask me my reason for believing it. It turns out that my reason for believing A is another proposition, B. You ask me my reason for believing B, which turns out to be a further proposition, C. You ask me my reason for believing C. . . . It is clear that this cannot go on forever. I cannot actually have an infinitely long chain of reasons standing behind my original assertion A. Nor is it permissible for me to rely on circular reasoning. For instance, suppose that, when asked my reason for believing A, I say I believe A because I believe A. In that case, I have not really given any (legitimate) reason for believing A. Nor are matters improved if I say B is my reason for believing A, and A is my reason for believing B. Nor, again, will matters be better if I simply expand the circle to include more beliefs; no exercise in circular reasoning will help me gain knowledge, however many steps the circle contains.

There is one remaining possibility, then. Every chain of reasoning must have a beginning point. In other words, all of my beliefs must rest, sooner or later, on propositions that I believe *for no reason.* Now, how can I know whether these starting beliefs are true? From what we have said above, it is clear that I cannot. By definition, I have no argument or evidence for my starting beliefs—if I did, then they would not be "starting beliefs." But without an assurance of the truth of my starting assumptions, the derivation, however rigorous, of other propositions from them is worthless. This is an obvious point, but it bears stressing. After all, any proposition whatsoever can be derived from *some* premises or other. The mere fact that I can derive my belief that A from some assumptions does nothing whatever to establish the truth of A; if it did, one could also establish the negation of A by *its* derivability from certain, other assumptions.

In general, conclusions are only as good as the premises they are based on. So if I do not know my starting premises to be true, then even more surely I do not know my conclusions to be true. Therefore, I cannot know anything.

This argument can be summarized as follows:

1. In order to know something, I must have a good reason for believing it.
2. Any chain of reasons must have one of the following structures: Either
   (a) it is an infinite series,
   (b) it is circular, or
   (c) it begins with a belief for which there are no further reasons. But,
3. I cannot have an infinitely long chain of reasoning for any of my beliefs.
4. Circular reasoning cannot produce knowledge.
5. Nor can I gain knowledge by structure 2c, for
   (a) I would not know my starting beliefs to be true (from 1), and
   (b) I cannot gain knowledge by deriving it from assumptions that I do not know to be true.
6. Therefore, I cannot know anything.

What is wrong with the above argument? The majority of philosophers and others who hear the argument say that it is premise (1) which is mistaken. They say that there are certain self-evident, or *foundational*, propositions. A foundational proposition, by definition, is one that we can know to be true *without* having a reason for it, and the people who believe in such things are called "foundationalists." According to most foundationalists, propositions such as "2 = 2" and "I am now conscious" would be good examples of foundational propositions. I do not have to give an argument, or engage in a process of reasoning, to know that I am conscious, or that the number 2 is equal to itself. I merely think about these propositions and thereupon find their truth immediately obvious.

The skeptic, of course, will deny the existence of self-evident propositions. But why? Obviously, the skeptic cannot say, "It is self-evident that self-evident propositions do not exist." To be consistent, he will have to produce an *argument* against the idea of self-evident propositions. What argument can he give?

Well, the skeptic can argue that the foundationalist has no way of distinguishing *self-evident* propositions from merely *arbitrary* propositions. A self-evident proposition, we have said, is one that we need have no reason for in order to be fully justified (or rational) in accepting it. An arbitrary proposition, on the other hand, is a proposition that we have no reason for and would be wholly unjustified in believing. For instance, suppose I suddenly decide, completely out of the blue, that I think there is a twelve-headed purple dragon living on Venus. This would be an arbitrary belief. The foundationalist must explain what *differentiates* a foundational proposition like "2 = 2" from an arbitrary proposition like "There is a twelve-headed purple dragon on Venus." That is, he must identify some feature of the foundational proposition that the arbitrary proposition lacks, and that explains why the foundational proposition is justified. Let "F" denote this feature.

Assume, then, that I have a belief, A, which is a legitimate foundational belief. And assume that I have another belief, B, which is merely arbitrary. By hypothesis, A has F, while B lacks F. Now, either I am *aware* of feature F, or I am not. But if I were completely unaware of feature F, then how could its presence serve to make it rational for me to accept A? If the presence of F is to explain why I am rational (or justified) in accepting A but not rational in accepting B, it must be something that I am aware of (in the one case, but not in the other). Otherwise, A and B will be, *from my point of view,* equally good (or equally arbitrary) assumptions. In that case, given the information available to me, it would be equally reasonable for me to accept one as to accept the other.

So the foundationalist position will have to be that it is reasonable for me to accept A, because I am aware that A has feature F. But then A is not a foundational proposition after all, because I *do* have a reason for accepting A—namely, that A has F. Thus, foundationalism is reduced to absurdity: from the supposition that A is legitimately foundational, we can derive the conclusion that A is not foundational after all. Therefore, the very idea of a foundational proposition is self-contradictory. Therefore, it appears, the skeptic's argument stands.

2. The Problem of the Criterion

I have on my desk an epistemologically interesting toy called "the Magic Eight Ball." It is a plastic ball painted like an eight ball, and it is meant to be used as follows. You ask the eight ball a yes/no question. Then you turn it over and see an answer float up to a window in the bottom. Answers include the likes of "Yes, definitely," "Very doubtful," and "Cannot predict now."

Now, imagine there were a community in which use of the eight ball was an accepted method of arriving at conclusions. Suppose you meet one of these eight-ball reasoners, and you ask him why he believes that the eight ball is a reliable informant. He swiftly takes out his Magic Eight Ball, says, "Are you reliable?" and turns it over. At this point, if the answer "No" floats up to the window, then the eight-ball reasoner is in trouble. But suppose a definite "Yes" answer appears, and the eight-ball reasoner triumphantly declares that the reliability of the eight ball has been established. Would this be legitimate?

Evidently not. You would no doubt object, rightly, that there is a problem of circularity here. If we already knew the eight ball was reliable, then we would be justified in accepting the answers it produces. But if the eight ball is unreliable, then we should not trust its answers. And if we don't know whether it is reliable, then we likewise should not trust its answers *until* its reliability has been established. The method of eight-ball reasoning presupposes that we know the eight ball to be reliable, in the sense that it would not be reasonable to use the method unless we already knew (or at least had reason to believe) it to be a reliable method. Therefore, we certainly cannot use eight-ball reasoning to establish that the eight ball is reliable.

Now consider an analogous case. Suppose some skeptic comes along and asks you why you believe the senses to be reliable. Why do you think that, when you seem to see, hear, or feel things, this is a reliable indicator of the way things really are, in the external world? How would you respond?

Here is one thing you might try. You go to an eye doctor to have your eyes examined. He gives you a series of tests, and at the end he assures you that your eyesight is perfect. Then you go to another doctor to take some hearing tests. He assures you that you have excellent hearing. (You might have difficulty finding doctors to test your taste, smell, and sense of touch, but let's pass over that difficulty.) You then explain to the skeptic that the reliability of your senses has been established. Would this be legitimate?

Apparently not. You would be engaging in just the same sort of circular reasoning that the benighted eight-ball reasoner used, for you can only collect the results of your tests by using your senses. You may seem to hear the doctors tell you that your hearing and eyesight are normal, but how do you know they are really saying that? Indeed, if you were in doubt as to the reliability of your senses in general, you could not even be sure that the doctors really existed, let alone that they were reliable informants.

So you will have to use some other method to verify the reliability of your senses—you will have to rely on some cognitive faculty other than the senses. But—here is the problem—whatever method you try to use to verify that your senses are reliable, the skeptic can always ask why you believe *that* method to be reliable. For instance, suppose you wanted to prove the reliability of the senses through the exercise of pure reason (though I have no idea how such a proof would go). In that case, the skeptic could ask why you think reason itself is reliable. You could not use reason to establish the reliability of reason, nor could you use the five senses to establish the reliability of reason, again on pain of circularity. So you will need to find yet a third belief-forming method. At which point the skeptic will question the reliability of this third method as well. At some point, and probably sooner rather than later, you will have to either resort to circular reasoning or else give up on answering the skeptic's question. But this means that ultimately you cannot establish the reliability of your cognitive faculties. And all of your beliefs are formed through one or another of your cognitive faculties, whether it be through the five senses, or reason, or memory, or introspection. Since you cannot know whether any of your belief-forming methods is reliable, it seems, you cannot know whether any of your beliefs is true. In short, you are in the same position as the eight-ball reasoner. The eight-ball-generated beliefs were all unjustified since the eight-ball reasoner could not (noncircularly) establish that the eight ball was reliable. Similarly, all of your beliefs are unjustified since you cannot (noncircularly) establish that your belief-forming methods in general are reliable.

This argument can be summarized as follows:

1. All my beliefs are formed by some method.
2. I am justified in accepting a belief formed by method M only if I *first* know that M is reliable.
3. I do not have an infinite series of belief-forming methods.
4. Thus, all my beliefs must rest on beliefs formed by methods whose reliability has not first been established. (from 1 and 3)
5. Therefore, none of my beliefs are justified. (from 2 and 4)

This argument is similar to the argument of section 1. Again we have a threat of infinite regress or circularity, though this time it would be a series of belief-forming methods, rather than a series of beliefs. Once we rule out both the infinite regress and the circularity possibilities, the only remaining possibility is that I have belief-forming methods whose reliability is not established by any method. This is analogous to the beliefs of section 1 that are not supported by any reasons. I pointed out that even the most impeccable derivation of a conclusion from such assumptions would do nothing to establish the truth of the conclusion, given that we have no reason to accept the starting assumptions. Similarly, even the most scrupulous exercise of method M, whatever that may be, will do nothing whatsoever to establish the truth of any conclusion, given that we have no reason to think M itself is reliable. As a result, it seems, we have no way of knowing anything whatever.

3. How Can You Get Outside Your Head?

Most of the things we think we know, including everything we think we know about the physical world, we learn through sensory perception, which includes sight, hearing, taste, touch, and smell. Of course, this does not mean that everything we know about the physical world is something we actually observe. A lot of what we know of the physical world is the result of scientific theorizing or inference, but those theories and inferences are ultimately *based on* observations. For instance, we know of the existence of atoms through inferences from the observed results of experiments. Similarly, I know that the Battle of Hastings took place in 1066, not because I personally observed it, but because I read that in a history book—but I knew what the book said only because I could *see the book*. In that sense, my belief was acquired through the exercise of my senses.

If you think about it, then, you will probably realize that everything you think you know about the external world is dependent on your senses. So in order to determine how much we really know about the physical world, we must first ask what the senses really tell us about the physical world. This question can be separated into two sub-issues: First, what is it that the senses make us *directly aware* of? Second, what can be *inferred* from what we are thus directly aware of?

The skeptical argument we are about to consider seeks to establish, first, that the senses do not make us directly aware of the physical world; and second, that no conclusions about the physical world can be inferred from what we are directly aware of either. It will follow that we can have no knowledge of the physical world.

To put that another way: the skeptic will seek to show, first, that direct realism is false. Second, he will try to show that indirect realism is false as well. It will then be clear that we have no knowledge of the physical world, since we do not know about it directly, and we do not know about it indirectly either.

. . . There are, actually, quite a few arguments against direct realism, but for now, let us stick to the argument from double vision. As you recall, we considered a case in which, though there is only one physical finger in front of you, you seem to see two fingerlike things. This was supposed to show that what you are immediately aware of is mental images, rather than the physical finger. The reasoning can be summarized as follows:

1. As your focus shifts to the background, the fingerlike thing you are seeing splits in two.
2. No physical object splits in two at this time.
3. Therefore, the thing you are seeing is not a physical object.

If the thing you are seeing is not a physical object, the next natural candidate is that it is a mental image (what else could it plausibly be?). These mental images are traditionally called "sense data," so that is what I will call them here. . . .

Now, given that all you ever directly perceive is your own sense data, can you infer anything about the external world? At first glance, this doesn't seem too difficult. Your sense data must come from somewhere, and you know that you didn't create them, since you have no direct control over your sense data. (If you did, you could just decide to stop hearing that horrible music your neighbor is playing.) So they must have been caused by external objects. Suppose you are having a sense datum of a tree. The simplest explanation of why you're having this experience—and normally the correct one—is that there is a tree in front of you, which is causing your experience. Granted, it is possible for a person to hallucinate a tree; however, that is not the normal situation, and there is no special reason for thinking you are hallucinating now.

The great skeptic David Hume neatly exposed the problem with this line of thought:

> It is a question of fact, whether the perceptions of the senses be produced by external objects resembling them. How shall this question be determined? By experience surely, as all other questions of a like nature. But here experience is, and must be entirely silent. The mind has never anything present to it but the perceptions, and cannot possibly reach any experience of their connexion with objects. The supposition of such a connexion is, therefore, without any foundation in reasoning.

Hume believed, plausibly enough, that the only way of knowing that A causes B (where A and B are any two types of events) is by having some experience of A and B—specifically, you must observe A being followed by B on a number of occasions. For instance, suppose there's a light switch on the wall in front of me. In order to find out what the switch does, I'll have to try it out. I flip it a few times, notice the light go on and off, and conclude that flipping the switch causes the light to go on or off. If I never observed the flipping of the switch, I would not have been able to know this. Now, it is true that, when I enter a room I've never been in before, I can often predict that the switch on the wall will turn on the lights. However, this is because I am relying on *past* experience with light switches. If I had never had any experience with any light switches, I would have no idea what it would do.

Now, Hume says, for the reasons given above, that we never actually see physical objects, only our representations of them. Therefore, we have certainly not observed the presence of physical objects being followed by the occurrence of sense data. Therefore, we cannot claim to know that physical objects cause sense data. In particular, we could not claim to know that physical trees cause treelike sense data, because we have never actually had any direct experience of a physical tree; all we have seen is the tree-representing sense data. It is as if I saw the lights go on and off periodically, but I never saw the light switch (suppose the switch was located in another room of which I was unaware). In that case, I would never know what was causing the lights to go on or off.

This argument can be summarized as follows:

1. In order to have knowledge of the physical world, we must be able to know that our sense data are caused by physical objects.
2. In order to know that A causes B, one must have experience of A and B.
3. We have no experience of physical objects.
4. Therefore, we do not know that physical objects cause our sense data. (from 2, 3)
5. Therefore, we have no knowledge of the physical world. (from 1, 4)

4. The Brain in a Vat

The scientists are keeping your brain alive in a vat through artificial means—they have mechanical devices to pump blood to and from your brain, along with machines to add oxygen and nutrients to your blood. They have hundreds of tiny electrodes inserted into your brain to recreate the same pattern of electrical stimulation to your sensory cortex as a normal brain in a human body receives. A giant supercomputer does the calculations necessary to figure out exactly how to stimulate your brain. Of course, the scientists will also need a brain scanner, so they can determine when you are trying to move your body in various ways; then the supercomputer will figure out how to modify the pattern of brain stimulations to make it look as if your body is in fact moving the way it should. Thus, you can exercise your free will (if there is such a thing) within the simulated world. Everything appears normal to you. The scientists decide, for amusement, to throw into the scenario a simulated book talking about the brain-in-a-vat scenario, just to see what you'll think. They have a chuckle when you think to yourself, "That's ridiculous; of course I'm not a brain in a vat."

Let's think about what kind of arguments you might give against the brain-in-a-vat (BIV) scenario. In the first place, you might say, the scenario clearly assumes a level of technology beyond anything we possess. Medical science does not have the ability to keep a disembodied brain alive, nor is current computer technology up to simulating an interactive world with anything like the detail of the real world. But what you don't realize is that it is now actually the year 3440, and the scientists simply chose to program a simulation of life in the twenty-first century—when, of course, human science was very primitive. In the real world, human technology is far beyond where it is in your simulated world.

You might think that even so, it would require an enormous computer to do the sorts of calculations required by the BIV scenario. And why would anyone want to expend the resources to build such a machine? But what you don't realize is that enormous technological and economic advances have occurred in the last 1400 years, making it possible to build computers millions of times more powerful than twenty-first-century computers, at a small fraction of the cost.

Is there any evidence to suggest that you are a BIV? No, but if you *were* a BIV there *wouldn't* be any evidence (at least, not that you were aware of). The scientists and their supercomputer control all the "evidence" you receive, which consists in your sensory experiences, and they have chosen not to give you any evidence that you're a BIV. Thus, the lack of evidence supporting the BIV scenario is not evidence *against* it either. That is why, the skeptic says, you simply do not know whether you are a BIV or not.

That is the crux of the matter. Everything you think you know about how the physical world works, about computer technology, about the laws of physics—anything you might try to use to argue against the BIV scenario—depends on sensory experience. All of that information, the skeptic claims, is suspect, since it could have just been fed to you by the scientists who didn't want you to figure out that you are a BIV. No matter what observations you make, a suitably modified BIV scenario can account for them. That is why there cannot, in principle, be any evidence against the BIV scenario.

From this, the skeptic infers that you do not know you are not a brain in a vat. And further, the skeptic infers that you do not know that anything you "observe" is real. And therefore, you do not know anything about the external world at all, since all your beliefs about the external world are based on your alleged observations. In summary:

1. Your sensory experiences are the only evidence you have for propositions about the external world.
2. The BIV scenario predicts that you would be having the same sort of sensory experiences as you are actually having.
3. Therefore, the sensory experiences you are actually having are not evidence that the BIV scenario isn't true. (from 2)

4. Therefore, you have no evidence that the BIV scenario isn't true. (from 1, 3)
5. Therefore, you do not know that you're not a BIV. (from 4)
6. Therefore, you do not know anything about the external world. (from 5)

5. Skepticism and Common Sense

Having just seen four examples of skeptical arguments—what I regard as the four most important skeptical arguments—we are now in a position to define "skepticism" more precisely. I define skepticism as *any philosophical theory that challenges a significant class of common sense beliefs.* Now to explain the terms in that definition.

First, "common sense beliefs." Consider the following propositions, all of which I believe: I am a human being. I have two hands. I have spent my life at or near the surface of the Earth. I have thoughts and feelings. There are other people in the world. They have bodies. They also have thoughts and feelings. The Earth has existed for many years. It generally gets colder in the winter than it is in the summer. 2 is greater than 1. There is a table in front of me now.

I have no serious doubts about any of these propositions. Unless you are either a skeptic or a madman, you have the same or analogous beliefs, and you probably hold them with a similar degree of certainty. I say "analogous" because you may not believe, for example, that there is a table in front of me now. But, when placed in the circumstance of seeing a familiar type of physical object (as I am now), you believe that that object is there. Generally, when you have the same kind of grounds for a proposition that I have for any of the propositions in the list above, you accept that proposition without reservations, as would any normal human being.

I call these things "common sense beliefs." Common sense beliefs generally have these characteristics:

i. They are accepted by almost everyone (except some philosophers and some madmen), regardless of what culture or time period one belongs to.
ii. They tend to be taken for granted in ordinary life. For instance, when I sit down at my table, I *take it for granted* that the table is real; I don't even think about it explicitly, because for me, there is no *issue* about whether the table exists.

iii. If a person believes a contrary of one of these propositions, then it is a sign of insanity. For instance, that I am a human being is, for me, a common sense belief. An example of a *contrary* proposition would be the proposition that I am a chicken. If I thought I was a chicken, that would be a sign of insanity.

The remark in (i) about philosophers and madmen sounds flippant, but it is quite accurate nonetheless. In the context of a philosophical discussion, people will sometimes express doubts about common sense beliefs, but, if sane, this is the *only* time they have such doubts. In real life, philosophical skeptics do not bump into walls because they don't trust their senses, or stick their hands on hot stoves because past experience gives no justification for future predictions, or kick other people because there's no reason to think other people are sentient. A variety of possible explanations for this could be proposed, such as: the skeptic just finds it more fun to *pretend* that there's a real world, that other people are conscious, and so on; or the skeptic is just trying to indirectly modify his own sense data, and he has discovered certain correlations between his own acts of will and changes in his sense data (though this wouldn't work for the inductive skeptic). But in actual fact, the explanation is that in ordinary life, outside of philosophical discussions, the skeptic thinks pretty much like the rest of us, taking for granted the things the rest of us do.

This doesn't prove that skepticism is false; at most it proves that skeptics are hypocritical. But it indicates an interesting characteristic of the beliefs I call "common sense." Most beliefs are not like this; people who question a given opinion do not usually find themselves constantly slipping into taking that opinion for granted. People who think there is no God, for example, do not find themselves praying or planning for the afterlife when they exit philosophical debate. People who think abortion is murder do not find themselves having abortions or in any other way thinking or acting as if abortion were permissible. But the people who say that we have no reason to think physical objects exist do nonetheless, in their everyday lives, take the reality of the physical objects around them for granted. And this marks an interesting difference between, on the one hand, things like the belief that there is a God or the belief that abortion is permissible, and on the other hand, the things I'm calling "common sense beliefs."

Second, what do I mean by a "challenge" to a belief? Where *P* is some proposition, a "challenge" to *P* is a claim that could not rationally be accepted in conjunction with *P*, in that it would be inherently self-defeating to do so. Consider the following propositions, all of which are self-defeating in the sense I intend:

It is raining, but I don't believe it.

It is raining, but that's not true.

It is raining, but I have no reason to think so.

It is raining, but the reasons I have for believing that are false.

It is raining, but I don't know whether it is or not.

It would be *inherently* irrational (independent of what evidence I have) for me to accept any of these propositions, since in order for me to justifiably believe the first half, the second half of each sentence would have to be unjustified. So the second conjunct of each of these five propositions is a "challenge" to my belief that it is raining.

Third, why do I say, "a *significant class* of common sense beliefs"? Suppose someone enters this room and is in doubt about whether there is really a table here. He doesn't have doubts about physical objects in general; he just thinks there is something funny about *this particular* (alleged) table. Well, that is not what we call "skepticism" in philosophy. A philosophical skeptic makes some kind of general claim—for instance, that nothing about the physical world can be known; or that no prediction about any future event can ever be justified.

My definition of "skepticism" differs from those of most philosophers, so I should say a word about that. If asked what skepticism is, most philosophers will say something like "the view that no one can know anything." But my definition fits better with the way philosophers actually use the word when they label various positions "skeptical." Without going into too much detail, I note that my definition applies to inductive skepticism, moral skepticism, and skepticism about the past (none of which says that no one can know *anything*), and it explains why Hume (who spoke mainly about having *reasons* for believing things, rather than about *knowledge*) is considered a skeptic.

6. Skepticism and Internal Justification

There are many possible forms of skepticism under my definition. This is for two reasons: first, because there are different kinds of common sense beliefs that one might be skeptical about (e.g., beliefs about the past, about the physical world, about other people's minds), and second, because there are several different ways to challenge a belief. Some skeptics argue that our common sense beliefs are not true. Others argue that common sense beliefs are not *known* to be true. Others argue that common sense beliefs are *unjustified.*

This last is what I call "radical skepticism." It is important to understand what radical skepticism entails, because it is the form of skepticism the preceding arguments support and the form I will be responding to. To say a proposition is "justified" is to say, roughly, that there is good reason (or good evidence) to believe it, or that it would be rational to believe it. However, justification comes in degrees, so a proposition can be *slightly* justified, *highly* justified, and so on. The radical skeptic I will be confronting holds that (some significant class of) common sense beliefs are *not at all* justified, which is to say: there is no reason to believe they are true; it is no more rational to think they are true than to think they are false. According to one theory of probability, this is the same as to say the beliefs are no more *likely* to be true than false.

There are some skeptics (nonradical ones) who argue *merely* that we cannot be absolutely certain that our common sense beliefs are true, that there is at least *some* chance, however remote, that we could be wrong. This kind of skepticism (if it counts as such) is not very interesting, since it requires at most a minor revision in our beliefs. You could grant this skeptic his point and still hold on to all your common sense beliefs (though not with absolute certainty). In contrast, you could not grant *radical* skepticism and then go on thinking pretty much as you always had. You could not accept that *P* is no more likely to be true than false, but then just go on believing *P*. This would be self-defeating, like saying, "It's raining outside, but it's just as likely that it's not raining as that it is." For this reason, I focus on answering radical skepticism.

The first two skeptical arguments above (sections 1 and 2) support radical skepticism *about everything:* if sound, they would show that we have no justification for believing anything. The third and fourth (sections 3 and 4) support radical skepticism *about the external world:* that is, if sound, they would show that we have no justification for our beliefs about the external world; they would not show anything about the rest of our beliefs, however—they don't say, for example, that we cannot know about our sense data.

I need to make one more point about what "radical skepticism" is. The radical skeptic is concerned with what philosophers call the "internalist" sense of justification. Internalist justification is justification from one's own point of view, as opposed to justification from (so to speak) the omniscient, third-person perspective. I explain this distinction with an anecdote.

In John Steinbeck's novel, *The Pearl,* the protagonist, a fisherman, discovers an enormous pearl. He thinks that the pearl will bring wealth and comfort to his family for a long time to come, as soon as he sells it. But throughout the rest of the story, the fisherman is beset by people trying to trick or cheat him, highwaymen trying to rob him, and so on. By the end of the novel, it has become clear that the pearl was far more trouble than it was worth.

An English teacher of mine once posed the following essay question about the story: "True or false: When the fisherman discovered the pearl, he should have just thrown it back into the ocean." Many students answered "true," citing the many troubles it would have saved the fisherman and his family. But the teacher claimed the answer was "false," because the fisherman had no way of knowing about those troubles in advance. As far as *he* could tell, the pearl was going to make him and his family rich. It would have been ridiculous to throw it back into the ocean!

What's the right answer? Well, (*pace* the English teacher) the question was ambiguous. *From the fisherman's point of view*—that is, given the information available to *him*—he should have done just as he did, try to sell the pearl. On the other hand, from the point of view of the omniscient observer—that is, given *all* the facts about the case—the fisherman should have thrown the pearl back into the ocean. Throwing the pearl back is the action that would in fact have had the best results; in that sense, he "should" have done that. But taking the pearl and trying to sell it is the course of action that, in the light of his information at the time, it was most reasonable for the fisherman to take; in that sense, he "should" have done that.

The point of this example: When I talk about what beliefs are "justified," I do not mean what things it is reasonable to believe given a total knowledge of all the facts (which would collapse the reasonable into the true). Rather, I mean what things it is reasonable for a person to believe, given their situation at the time. This is what I mean by "justification from the first-person perspective."

Another word for what is justified, or *should* be done or believed, from the first-person perspective, is "rational." If the teacher had asked, "True or false: When the fisherman found the pearl, it would have been rational for him to just throw it back into the ocean," then the question would have been unambiguous, the correct answer being "false."

Justification from the first-person perspective is what matters to us. The reason is that we have only our own perspective from which to decide what to believe. We never have the omniscient point of view, and we never have anyone else's point of view. If I am to decide what to believe, I have to do it on the basis of the information I have; I can't do it on the basis of information *you* have and I don't. Similarly, when *you* want to decide what to believe, you have to do it on the basis of *your* information, not mine.

Radical skepticism, as I define it, holds that our common sense beliefs are not rational, that is, not justified from the first-person point of view. This might seem strange, since surely there is no doubt that we *believe* our common sense beliefs to be justified. But "*x* is justified from our point of view" does not mean "we believe that *x* is justified." It means "*x* is rational for us." The "from our point of view" modifier simply indicates that rationality does not require taking account of things we had no reasonable way of knowing about. If *x* results from confusion, fallacious reasoning, or arbitrary assumptions, then *x* is *not* justified, regardless of the fact that we may think it is. As we have seen, the external-world skeptic thinks all our beliefs about the external world rest on mere assumption.

*E*thics

CHAPTER 25

*E*thics and Human Feeling

David Hume

David Hume (1711–1776) believed that our conduct should be guided by a general feeling of goodwill toward all human beings. But he did not think this could be proved by reason. Instead, whether we come to embrace such an ethic depends on whether we have beneficent feelings.

Hume's writings on morality include *Essays: Moral and Political* (two volumes, 1742) and *An Enquiry concerning the Principles of Morals* (1751). *A Treatise of Human Nature* (1740) was Hume's masterpiece.

Those who affirm that virtue is nothing but a conformity to reason; that there are eternal fitnesses and unfitnesses of things, which are the same to every rational being that considers them; that the immutable measures of right and wrong impose an obligation, not only on human creatures, but also on the Deity himself: All these systems concur in the opinion, that morality, like truth, is discerned merely by ideas, and by their juxtaposition and comparison. In order, therefore, to judge of these systems, we need only consider, whether it be possible, from reason alone, to distinguish betwixt moral good and evil, or whether there must concur some other principles to enable us to make that distinction.

If morality had naturally no influence on human passions and actions, it would be in vain to take such pains to inculcate it; and

Source: David Hume, *A Treatise of Human Nature* (1740), bk. 3, pt. 1, sec. 1; and *An Enquiry concerning the Principles of Morals* (1751), app. 1. In a few places I have updated the language.

nothing would be more fruitless than that multitude of rules and precepts, with which all moralists abound. Philosophy is commonly
divided into *speculative* and *practical;* and as morality is always comprehended under the latter division, 'tis supposed to influence our passions and actions, and to go beyond the calm and indolent judgments
of the understanding. And this is confirmed by common experience,
which informs us, that men are often governed by their duties, and are
deterred from some actions by the opinion of injustice, and impelled
to others by that of obligation.

Since morals, therefore, have an influence on the actions and
affections, it follows, that they cannot be derived from reason; and that
because reason alone, as we have already proved, can never have any
such influence. Morals excite passions, and produce or prevent
actions. Reason of itself is utterly impotent in this particular. The rules
of morality, therefore, are not conclusions of our reason.

. . . Take any action allowed to be vicious: Willful murder, for
instance. Examine it in all lights, and see if you can find that matter of
fact, or real existence, which you call *vice.* In whichever way you take
it, you find only certain passions, motives, volitions and thoughts.
There is no other matter of fact in the case. The vice entirely escapes
you, as long as you consider the object. You never can find it, till you
turn your reflection into your own breast, and find a sentiment of disapprobation, which arises in you, towards this action. Here is a matter
of fact; but 'tis the object of feeling, not of reason. It lies in yourself,
not in the object. So that when you pronounce any action or character to be vicious, you mean nothing, but that from the constitution of
your nature you have a feeling or sentiment of blame from the con-
templation of it.

. . . I cannot forbear adding to these reasonings an observation,
which may, perhaps, be found of some importance. In every system of
morality, which I have hitherto met with, I have always remarked, that
the author proceeds for some time in the ordinary way of reasoning,
and establishes the being of a God, or makes observations concerning
human affairs; when of a sudden I am surprised to find, that instead
of the usual copulations of propositions, *is,* and *is not,* I meet with no
proposition that is not connected with an *ought,* or an *ought not.* This
change is imperceptible; but is, however, of the last consequence. For
as this *ought,* or *ought not,* expresses some new relation or affirmation,
'tis necessary that it should be observed and explained; and at the
same time that a reason should be given, for what seems altogether
inconceivable, how this new relation can be a deduction from others,

which are entirely different from it. But as authors do not commonly use this precaution, I shall presume to recommend it to the readers; and am persuaded, that this small attention would subvert all the vulgar systems of morality, and let us see, that the distinction of vice and virtue is not founded merely on the relations of objects, nor is perceived by reason. . . .

Examine the crime of *ingratitude,* for instance, which has place wherever we observe good-will expressed and known, together with good-offices performed, on the one side, and a return of ill-will or indifference with ill-offices or neglect on the other: anatomize all these circumstances and examine, by your reason alone, in what consists the demerit or blame. You never will come to any issue or conclusion.

Reason judges either of *matter of fact* or of *relations.* Enquire then, *first,* where is that matter of fact which we here call *crime;* point it out, determine the time of its existence, describe its essence or nature, explain the sense or faculty to which it discovers itself. It resides in the mind of the person who is ungrateful. He must, therefore, feel it and be conscious of it. But nothing is there, except the passion of ill-will or absolute indifference. You cannot say that these, of themselves, always and in all circumstances are crimes. No, they are only crimes when directed towards persons who have before expressed and displayed goodwill towards us. Consequently, we may infer that the crime of ingratitude is not any particular individual *fact,* but arises from a complication of circumstances which, being presented to the spectator, excites the *sentiment* of blame by the particular structure and fabric of his mind.

This representation, you say, is false. Crime, indeed, consists not in a particular *fact,* of whose reality we are assured by *reason,* but it consists in certain *moral relations,* discovered by reason, in the same manner as we discover by reason the truths of geometry or algebra. But what are the relations, I ask, of which you here talk? In the case stated above, I see first good-will and good-offices in one person, then ill-will and ill-offices in the other. Between these, there is a relation of *contrariety.* Does the crime consist in that relation? But suppose a person bore me ill-will or did me ill-offices, and I, in return, were indifferent towards him, or did him good-offices. Here is the same relation of *contrariety,* and yet my conduct is often highly laudable. Twist and turn this matter as much as you will, you can never rest the morality on relation, but must have recourse to the decisions of sentiment.

When it is affirmed that two and three are equal to the half of ten, this relation of equality I understand perfectly. I conceive that, if ten be divided into two parts, of which one has as many units as the other, and if any of these parts be compared to two added to three, it will contain as many units as that compound number. But when you draw thence a comparison to moral relations, I own that I am altogether at a loss to understand you. A moral action, a crime, such as ingratitude, is a complicated object. Does the morality consist in the relation of its parts to each other? How? After what manner? Specify the relation: be more particular and explicit in your propositions, and you will easily see their falsehood.

No, say you, the morality consists in the relation of actions to the rule of right; and they are denominated good or ill, according as they agree or disagree with it. What then is this rule of right? In what does it consist? How is it determined? By reason, you say, which examines the moral relations of actions. So that moral relations are determined by the comparison of action to a rule. And that rule is determined by considering the moral relations of objects. Is not this fine reasoning?

All this is metaphysics, you cry. That is enough; there needs nothing more to give a strong presumption of falsehood. Yes, reply I, here are metaphysics surely; but they are all on your side, who advance an abstruse hypothesis which can never be made intelligible, nor quadrate with any particular instance or illustration. The hypothesis which we embrace is plain. It maintains that morality is determined by sentiment. It defines virtue to be *whatever mental action or quality gives to a spectator the pleasing sentiment of approbation;* and vice the contrary. We then proceed to examine a plain matter of fact, to wit, what actions have this influence. We consider all the circumstances in which these actions agree, and thence endeavour to extract some general observations with regard to these sentiments. If you call this metaphysics and find anything abstruse here, you need only conclude that your turn of mind is not suited to the moral sciences.

CHAPTER 26

*O*ur Sense of Right and Wrong

C. S. Lewis

C. S. Lewis (1898–1963), a beloved defender of Christian faith, argued that in grasping the moral law we understand something about what the world is really like. The world is not the cold, impersonal place pictured by science; it also includes moral standards that bind all human beings together.

Lewis wrote dozens of books, mostly novels and short stories. His more philosophical works include *The Problem of Pain* (1940), *Surprised by Joy* (1955), and *Mere Christianity* (1952), from which this selection is taken.

The Law of Human Nature

Every one has heard people quarrelling. Sometimes it sounds funny and sometimes it sounds merely unpleasant; but however it sounds, I believe we can learn something very important from listening to the kind of things they say. They say things like this: 'How'd you like it if anyone did the same to you?'—'That's my seat, I was there first'—'Leave him alone, he isn't doing you any harm'—'Why should you shove in first?'—'Give me a bit of your orange, I gave you a bit of mine'—'Come on, you promised.' People say things like that every day, educated people as well as uneducated, and children as well as grown-ups.

Source: C. S. Lewis, "The Law of Human Nature," from *Mere Christianity*. Copyright © C. S. Lewis Pte. Ltd. 1942, 1943, 1944, 1952. Extract reprinted by permission.

Now what interests me about all these remarks is that the man who makes them is not merely saying that the other man's behaviour does not happen to please him. He is appealing to some kind of standard of behaviour which he expects the other man to know about. And the other man very seldom replies: 'To hell with your standard.' Nearly always he tries to make out that what he has been doing does not really go against the standard, or that if it does there is some special excuse. He pretends there is some special reason in this particular case why the person who took the seat first should not keep it, or that things were quite different when he was given the bit of orange, or that something has turned up which lets him off keeping his promise. It looks, in fact, very much as if both parties had in mind some kind of Law or Rule of fair play or decent behaviour or morality or whatever you like to call it, about which they really agreed. And they have. If they had not, they might, of course, fight like animals, but they could not quarrel in the human sense of the word. Quarrelling means trying to show that the other man is in the wrong. And there would be no sense in trying to do that unless you and he had some sort of agreement as to what Right and Wrong are; just as there would be no sense in saying that a footballer had committed a foul unless there was some agreement about the rules of football.

Now this Law or Rule about Right and Wrong used to be called the Law of Nature. Nowadays, when we talk of the 'laws of nature' we usually mean things like gravitation, or heredity, or the laws of chemistry. But when the older thinkers called the Law of Right and Wrong 'the Law of Nature,' they really meant the Law of Human Nature. The idea was that, just as all bodies are governed by the law of gravitation, and organisms by biological laws, so the creature called man also had his law—with this great difference, that a body could not choose whether it obeyed the law of gravitation or not, but a man could choose either to obey the Law of Human Nature or to disobey it.

We may put this in another way. Each man is at every moment subjected to several different sets of law but there is only one of these which he is free to disobey. As a body, he is subjected to gravitation and cannot disobey it; if you leave him unsupported in mid-air, he has no more choice about falling than a stone has. As an organism, he is subjected to various biological laws which he cannot disobey any more than an animal can. That is, he cannot disobey those laws which he shares with other things; but the law which is peculiar to his human nature, the law he does not share with animals or vegetables or inorganic things, is the one he can disobey if he chooses.

This law was called the Law of Nature because people thought that every one knew it by nature and did not need to be taught it. They did not mean, of course, that you might not find an odd individual here and there who did not know it, just as you find a few people who are colour-blind or have no ear for a tune. But taking the race as a whole, they thought that the human idea of decent behaviour was obvious to every one. And I believe they were right. If they were not, then all the things we said about the war were nonsense. What was the sense in saying the enemy were in the wrong unless Right is a real thing which the Nazis at bottom knew as well as we did and ought to have practised? If they had had no notion of what we mean by right, then, though we might still have had to fight them, we could no more have blamed them for that than for the colour of their hair.

I know that some people say the idea of a Law of Nature or decent behaviour known to all men is unsound, because different civilisations and different ages have had quite different moralities.

But this is not true. There have been differences between their moralities, but these have never amounted to anything like a total difference. If anyone will take the trouble to compare the moral teaching of, say, the ancient Egyptians, Babylonians, Hindus, Chinese, Greeks and Romans, what will really strike him will be how very like they are to each other and to our own. Some of the evidence for this I have put together in the appendix of another book called *The Abolition of Man;* but for our present purpose I need only ask the reader to think what a totally different morality would mean. Think of a country where people were admired for running away in battle, or where a man felt proud of double-crossing all the people who had been kindest to him. You might just as well try to imagine a country where two and two made five. Men have differed as regards what people you ought to be unselfish to—whether it was only your own family, or your fellow countrymen, or every one. But they have always agreed that you ought not to put yourself first. Selfishness has never been admired. Men have differed as to whether you should have one wife or four. But they have always agreed that you must not simply have any woman you liked.

But the most remarkable thing is this. Whenever you find a man who says he does not believe in a real Right and Wrong, you will find the same man going back on this a moment later. He may break his promise to you, but if you try breaking one to him he will be complaining 'It's not fair' before you can say Jack Robinson. A nation may say treaties don't matter; but then, next minute, they spoil their case by saying that the particular treaty they want to break was an unfair one. But if treaties do not matter, and if there is no such thing as Right and Wrong—in other words, if there is no Law of Nature—what is the difference between a fair treaty and an unfair one? Have they not let the cat out of the bag and shown that, whatever they say, they really know the Law of Nature just like anyone else?

It seems, then, we are forced to believe in a real Right and Wrong. People may be sometimes mistaken about them, just as people sometimes get their sums wrong; but they are not a matter of mere taste and opinion any more than the multiplication table. Now if we are agreed about that, I go on to my next point, which is this. None of us are really keeping the Law of Nature. If there are any exceptions among you, I apologise to them. They had much better read some other book, for nothing I am going to say concerns them. And now, turning to the ordinary human beings who are left:

I hope you will not misunderstand what I am going to say. I am not preaching, and Heaven knows I do not pretend to be better than anyone else. I am only trying to call attention to a fact; the fact that this year, or this month, or, more likely, this very day, we have failed to practise ourselves the kind of behaviour we expect from other people. There may be all sorts of excuses for us. That time you were so unfair to the children was when you were very tired. That slightly shady business about the money—the one you have almost forgotten—came when you were very hard-up. And what you promised to do for old So-and-so and have never done—well, you never would have promised if you had known how frightfully busy you were going to be. And as for your behaviour to your wife (or husband) or sister (or brother) if I knew how irritating they could be, I would not wonder at it—and who the dickens am I, anyway? I am just the same. That is to say, I do not succeed in keeping the Law of Nature very well, and the moment anyone tells me I am not keeping it, there starts up in my mind a string of excuses as long as your arm. The question at the moment is not whether they are good excuses. The point is that they are one more proof of how deeply, whether we like it or not, we believe in the Law of Nature. If we do not believe in decent behaviour, why should we be so anxious to make excuses for not having behaved decently? The truth is, we believe in decency so much—we feel the Rule of Law pressing on us so—that we cannot bear to face the fact that we are breaking it, and consequently we try to shift the responsibility. For you notice that it is only for our bad behaviour that we find all these explanations. It is only our bad temper that we put down to being tired or worried or hungry; we put our good temper down to ourselves.

These, then, are the two points I wanted to make. First, that human beings, all over the earth, have this curious idea that they ought to behave in a certain way, and cannot really get rid of it. Secondly, that they do not in fact behave in that way. They know the Law of Nature; they break it. These two facts are the foundation of all clear thinking about ourselves and the universe we live in.

CHAPTER 27

The Virtues

Martha C. Nussbaum

Martha C. Nussbaum (1947–) of the University of Chicago began her career as a classical scholar before writing on a wide range of topics in moral, legal, and political theory. Here she defends the Aristotelian conception of the virtues as an alternative to the more popular ideas of utility and the social contract.

Nussbaum's many books include *The Fragility of Goodness* (1986), *From Disgust to Humanity: Sexual Orientation and Constitutional Law* (2011), and *Not for Profit: Why Democracy Needs the Humanities* (2011).

All Greeks used to go around armed with swords.
— Thucydides, *History of the Peloponnesian War*

The customs of former times might be said to be too simple and barbaric. For Greeks used to go around armed with swords; and they used to buy wives from one another; and there are surely other ancient customs that are extremely stupid. (For example, in Cyme there is a law about homicide, that if a man prosecuting a charge can produce a certain number of witnesses from among his own relations, the defendant will automatically be convicted of murder.) In general, all human beings seek not the way of their ancestors, but the good.
— Aristotle, *Politics* 1268a39 ff.

One may also observe in one's travels to distant countries the feelings of recognition and affiliation that link every human being to every other human being.
— Aristotle, *Nicomachean Ethics* 1155a21–22

Source: From "Non-Relative Virtues: An Aristotelian Approach," *Midwest Studies in Philosophy* 13, *Ethical Theory: Character and Virtue*, pp. 32–39. Copyright © 1988 by the University of Notre Dame. Reprinted by permission of Blackwell Publishing, Ltd.

I

The virtues are attracting increasing interest in contemporary philosophical debate. From many different sides one hears of a dissatisfaction with ethical theories that are remote from concrete human experience. Whether this remoteness results from the utilitarian's interest in arriving at a universal calculus of satisfactions or from a Kantian concern with universal principles of broad generality, in which the names of particular contexts, histories, and persons do not occur, remoteness is now being seen by an increasing number of moral philosophers as a defect in an approach to ethical questions. In the search for an alternative approach, the concept of virtue is playing a prominent role. So, too, is the work of Aristotle, the greatest defender of an ethical approach based on the concept of virtue. For Aristotle's work seems, appealingly, to combine rigor with concreteness, theoretical power with sensitivity to the actual circumstances of human life and choice in all their multiplicity, variety, and mutability.

But on one central point there is a striking divergence between Aristotle and contemporary virtue theory. To many current defenders of an ethical approach based on the virtues, the return to the virtues is connected with a turn toward relativism—toward, that is, the view that the only appropriate criteria of ethical goodness are local ones, internal to the traditions and practices of each local society or group that asks itself questions about the good. The rejection of general algorithms and abstract rules in favor of an account of the good life based on specific modes of virtuous action is taken, by writers as otherwise diverse as Alasdair MacIntyre, Bernard Williams, and Philippa Foot,[1] to be connected with the abandonment of the project of rationally justifying a single norm of flourishing life for and to all human beings and with a reliance, instead, on norms that are local both in origin and in application.

The positions of all of these writers, where relativism is concerned, are complex; none unequivocally endorses a relativist view. But all connect virtue ethics with a relativist denial that ethics, correctly understood, offers any trans-cultural norms, justifiable with reference to reasons of universal human validity, with reference to which we may appropriately criticize different local conceptions of the good. And all suggest that the insights we gain by pursuing ethical questions in the Aristotelian virtue-based way lend support to relativism.

For this reason it is easy for those who are interested in supporting the rational criticism of local traditions and in articulating an idea of ethical progress to feel that the ethics of virtue can give them little help. If the position of women, as established by local traditions in many parts of the world, is to be improved, if traditions of slave holding and racial inequality, if religious intolerance, if aggressive and warlike conceptions of manliness, if unequal norms of material distribution are to be criticized in the name of practical reason, this criticizing (one might easily suppose) will have to be done from a Kantian or utilitarian viewpoint, not through the Aristotelian approach.

This is an odd result, where Aristotle is concerned. For it is obvious that he was not only the defender of an ethical theory based on the virtues, but also the defender of a single objective account of the human good, or human flourishing. This account is supposed to be objective in the sense that it is justifiable with reference to reasons that do not derive merely from local traditions and practices, but rather from features of humanness that lie beneath all local traditions and are there to be seen whether or not they are in fact recognized in local traditions. And one of Aristotle's most obvious concerns is the criticism of existing moral traditions, in his own city and in others, as unjust or repressive, or in other ways incompatible with human flourishing. He uses his account of the virtues as a basis for this criticism of local traditions: prominently, for example, in Book II of the *Politics*, where he frequently argues against existing social forms by pointing to ways in which they neglect or hinder the development of some important human virtue.[2] Aristotle evidently believes that there is no incompatibility between basing an ethical theory on the virtues and defending the singleness and objectivity of the human good. Indeed, he seems to believe that these two aims are mutually supportive.

Now the fact that Aristotle believes something does not make it true. (Though I have sometimes been accused of holding that position!) But it does, on the whole, make that something a plausible *candidate* for the truth, one deserving our most serious scrutiny. In this case, it would be odd indeed if he had connected two elements in ethical thought that are self-evidently incompatible, or in favor of whose connectedness and compatibility there is nothing interesting to be said. The purpose of this paper is to establish that Aristotle does indeed have an interesting way of connecting the virtues with a search for ethical objectivity and with the criticism of existing local norms, a way that deserves our serious consideration as we work on these questions. Having described the general shape of the Aristotelian approach, we can then begin to understand some of the objections that might be brought against such a non-relative account of the virtues, and to imagine how the Aristotelian could respond to those objections.

II

The relativist, looking at different societies, is impressed by the variety and the apparent non-comparability in the lists of virtues she encounters. Examining the different lists, and observing the complex connections between each list and a concrete form of life and a concrete history, she may well feel that any list of virtues must be simply a reflection of local traditions and values, and that, virtues being (unlike Kantian principles or utilitarian algorithms) concrete and closely tied to forms of life, there can in fact be no list of virtues that will serve as normative for all these varied societies. It is not only that the specific forms of behavior recommended in connection with the virtues differ greatly over time and place, it is also that the very areas that are singled out as spheres of virtue, and the manner in which they are individuated from other areas, vary so greatly. For someone who thinks this way, it is easy to feel that Aristotle's own list, despite its pretensions to universality and objectivity, must be similarly restricted, merely a reflection of one particular society's perceptions of salience and ways of distinguishing. At this point, relativist writers are likely to quote Aristotle's description of the "great-souled" person, the *megalopsuchos*, which certainly contains many concrete local features and sounds very much like the portrait of a certain sort of Greek gentleman, in order to show that Aristotle's list is just as culture-bound as any other.[3]

But if we probe further into the way in which Aristotle in fact enumerates and individuates the virtues, we begin to notice things that cast doubt upon the suggestion that he has simply described what is admired in his own society. First of all, we notice that a rather large number of virtues and vices (vices especially) are nameless, and that, among the ones that are not nameless, a good many are given, by Aristotle's own account, names that are somewhat arbitrarily chosen by Aristotle, and do not perfectly fit the behavior he is trying to describe.[4] Of such modes of conduct he writes, "Most of these are nameless, but we must try . . . to give them names in order to make our account clear and easy to follow" (*NE* 1108a16–19). This does not sound like the procedure of someone who is simply studying local traditions and singling out the virtue names that figure most prominently in those traditions.

What *is* going on becomes clearer when we examine the way in which he does, in fact, introduce his list. For he does so, in the

Nicomachean Ethics,[5] by a device whose very straightforwardness and simplicity has caused it to escape the notice of most writers on this topic. What he does, in each case, is to isolate a sphere of human experience that figures in more or less any human life, and in which more or less any human being will have to make *some* choices rather than others, and act in *some* way rather than some other. The introductory chapter enumerating the virtues and vices begins from an enumeration of these spheres (*NE* 2.7); and each chapter on a virtue in the more detailed account that follows begins with "Concerning X . . ." or words to this effect, where "X" names a sphere of life with which all human beings regularly and more or less necessarily have dealings.[6] Aristotle then asks: What is it to choose and respond well within that sphere? What is it, on the other hand, to choose defectively? The "thin account" of each virtue is that it is whatever it is to be stably disposed to act appropriately in that sphere. There may be, and usually are, various competing specifications of what acting well, in each case, in fact comes to. Aristotle goes on to defend in each case some concrete specification, producing, at the end, a full or "thick" definition of the virtue.

Here are the most important spheres of experience recognized by Aristotle, along with the names of their corresponding virtues:[7]

Sphere	Virtue
1. Fear of important damages, esp. death	courage
2. Bodily appetites and their pleasures	moderation
3. Distribution of limited resources	justice
4. Management of one's personal property, where others are concerned	generosity
5. Management of personal property, where hospitality is concerned	expansive hospitality
6. Attitudes and actions with respect to one's own worth	greatness of soul
7. Attitude to slights and damages	mildness of temper
8. "Association and living together and the fellowship of words and actions"	
a. truthfulness in speech	truthfulness
b. social association of a playful kind	easy grace (contrasted with coarseness, rudeness, insensitivity)

c. social association more generally	nameless, but a kind of friendliness (contrasted with irritability and grumpiness)
9. Attitude to the good and ill fortune of others	proper judgment (contrasted with enviousness, spitefulness, etc.)
10. Intellectual life	the various intellectual virtues (such as perceptiveness, knowledge, etc.)
11. The planning of one's life and conduct	practical wisdom

There is, of course, much more to be said about this list, its specific members, and the names Aristotle chooses for the virtue in each case, some of which are indeed culture bound. What I want, however, to insist on here is the care with which Aristotle articulates his general approach, beginning from a characterization of a sphere of universal experience and choice, and introducing the virtue name as the name (as yet undefined) of whatever it is to choose appropriately in that area of experience. On this approach, it does not seem possible to say, as the relativist wishes to, that a given society does not contain anything that corresponds to a given virtue. Nor does it seem to be an open question, in the case of a particular agent, whether a certain virtue should or should not be included in his or her life—except in the sense that she can always choose to pursue the corresponding deficiency instead. The point is that everyone makes some choices and acts somehow or other in these spheres: if not properly, then improperly. Everyone has *some* attitude and behavior toward her own death; toward her bodily appetites and their management; toward her property and its use; toward the distribution of social goods; toward telling the truth; toward being kindly or not kindly to others; toward cultivating or not cultivating a sense of play and delight; and so on. No matter where one lives one cannot escape these questions, so long as one is living a human life. But then this means that one's behavior falls, willy nilly, within the sphere of the Aristotelian virtue, in each case. If it is not appropriate, it is inappropriate; it cannot be off the map altogether. People will of course disagree about what the appropriate ways of acting and reacting in fact *are*. But in that case, as Aristotle has set things up, they are arguing about the same thing, and advancing competing specifications of the same virtue. The reference of the virtue term in each case is fixed by the sphere of experience— by what we shall from now on call the "grounding experiences." The thin or "nominal definition" of the virtue will be, in each case, that it is whatever it is that being disposed to choose and respond well consists in, in that sphere. The job of ethical theory will be to search for the best further specification corresponding to this nominal definition, and to produce a full definition.

III

We have begun to introduce considerations from the philosophy of language. We can now make the direction of the Aristotelian account clearer by considering his own account of linguistic indicating (referring) and defining, which guides his treatment of both scientific and ethical terms, and of the idea of progress in both areas.[8]

Aristotle's general picture is as follows. We begin with some experiences—not necessarily our own, but those of members of our linguistic community, broadly construed.[9] On the basis of these experiences, a word enters the language of the group, indicating (referring to) whatever it is that is the content of those experiences. Aristotle gives the example of thunder.[10] People hear a noise in the clouds, and they then refer to it, using the word "thunder." At this point, it may be that nobody has any concrete account of the noise or any idea about what it really is. But the experience fixes a subject for further inquiry. From now on, we can refer to thunder, ask "What is thunder?" and advance and assess competing theories. The thin or, we might say, "nominal definition" of thunder is "That noise in the clouds, whatever it is." The competing explanatory theories are rival candidates for correct full or thick definition. So the explanatory story citing Zeus' activities in the clouds is a false account of the very same thing of which the best scientific explanation is a true account. There is just one debate here, with a single subject.

So too, Aristotle suggests, with our ethical terms. Heraclitus, long before him, already had the essential idea, saying, "They would not have known the name of justice, if these things did not take place."[11] "These things," our source for the fragment informs us, are experiences of injustice—presumably of harm, deprivation, inequality. These experiences fix the reference of the corresponding virtue word. Aristotle proceeds along similar lines. In the *Politics* he insists that only human beings, and not either animals or gods, will have our basic ethical terms and concepts (such as just and unjust, noble and base, good and bad), because the beasts are unable to form the concepts, and gods lack the experiences of limit and finitude that give a concept such as justice its point.[12] In the *Nicomachean Ethics* enumeration of the virtues, he carries the line of thought further, suggesting that the reference of the virtue terms is fixed by spheres of choice, frequently connected with our finitude and limitation, that we encounter in virtue of shared conditions of human existence.[13] The question about virtue usually arises in areas in which human choice is both non-optional and somewhat problematic. (Thus, he stresses, there is no virtue involving the regulation of listening to attractive sounds or seeing pleasing sights.) Each family of virtue and vice or deficiency words attaches to some such sphere. And we can understand progress in ethics, like progress in scientific understanding, to be progress in finding the correct fuller specification of a virtue, isolated by its thin or "nominal" definition. This progress is aided by a perspicuous mapping of the sphere of the grounding experiences. When we understand more precisely what problems human beings encounter in their lives with one another, what circumstances they face in which choice of some sort is required, we will have a way of assessing competing responses to those problems, and we will begin to understand what it might be to act well in the face of them.

Aristotle's ethical and political writings provide many examples of how such progress (or, more generally, such a rational debate) might go. We find argument against Platonic asceticism, as the proper specification of moderation (appropriate choice and response vis-à-vis the bodily appetites) and the consequent proneness to anger over slights, that was prevalent in Greek ideals of maleness and in Greek behavior, together with a defense of a more limited and controlled expression of anger, as the proper specification of the virtue that Aristotle calls "mildness of temper." (Here Aristotle evinces some discomfort with the virtue term he has chosen, and he is right to do so, since it certainly loads the dice heavily in favor of his concrete specification and against the traditional one.[14]) And so on for all the virtues.

In an important section of *Politics* II, part of which forms one of the epigraphs to this paper, Aristotle defends the proposition that laws should be revisable and not fixed, by pointing to evidence that there is progress toward greater correctness in our ethical conceptions, as also in the arts and sciences. Greeks used to think that courage was a matter of waving swords around; now they have (the *Ethics* informs us) a more inward and a more civic and communally attuned understanding of proper behavior toward the possibility of death. Women used to be regarded as property, bought and sold; now this would be thought barbaric. And in the case of justice as well we have, the *Politics* passage claims, advanced toward a more adequate understanding of what is fair and appropriate. Aristotle gives the example of an existing homicide law that convicts the defendant automatically on the evidence of the prosecutor's relatives (whether they actually witnessed anything or not, apparently). This, Aristotle says, is clearly a stupid and unjust law; and yet it once seemed appropriate—and, to a tradition-bound community, must still be so. To hold tradition fixed is then to prevent ethical progress. What human beings want and seek is not conformity with the past, it is the good. So our systems of law should make it possible for them to progress beyond the past, when they have agreed that a change is good. (They should not, however, make change too easy, since it is no easy matter to see one's way to the good, and tradition is frequently a sounder guide than current fashion.)

In keeping with these ideas, the *Politics* as a whole presents the beliefs of the many different societies it investigates not as unrelated local norms, but as competing answers to questions of justice and courage (and so on) with which all the societies (being human) are concerned, and in response to which they are all trying to find what is good. Aristotle's analysis of the virtues gives him an appropriate framework for these comparisons, which seem perfectly appropriate inquiries into the ways in which different societies have solved common human problems.

In the Aristotelian approach it is obviously of the first importance to distinguish two stages of the inquiry: the initial demarcation of the sphere of choice, of the "grounding experiences" that fix the reference of the virtue term; and the ensuing more concrete inquiry into what appropriate choice, in that sphere, *is*. Aristotle does not always do this carefully, and the language he has to work with is often not helpful to him. We do not have much difficulty with terms like "moderation" and "justice" and even "courage," which seem vaguely normative but relatively empty, so far, of concrete moral content. As the approach requires, they can serve as extension-fixing labels under which many competing specifications may be investigated. But we have already noticed the problem with "mildness of temper," which seems to rule out by fiat a prominent contender for the appropriate disposition concerning anger. And much the same thing certainly seems to be true of the relativists' favorite target, *megalopsuchia*, which implies in its very name an attitude to one's own worth that is more Greek than universal. (For example, a Christian will feel that the proper attitude to one's own worth requires understanding one's lowness, frailty, and sinfulness. The virtue of humility requires considering oneself *small*, not great.) What we ought to get at this point in the inquiry is a word for the proper behavior toward anger and offense and a word for the proper behavior toward one's worth that are more truly neutral among the competing specifications, referring only to the sphere of experience within which we wish to determine what is appropriate. Then we could regard the competing conceptions as rival accounts of one and the same thing, so that, for example, Christian humility would be a rival specification of the same virtue whose Greek specification is given in Aristotle's account of *megalopsuchia*, namely, the proper way to behave toward the question of one's own worth.

And in fact, oddly enough, if one examines the evolution in the use of this word from Aristotle through the Stoics to the Christian fathers, one can see that this is more or less what happened, as "greatness of soul" became associated, first, with Stoic emphasis on the supremacy of virtue and the worthlessness of externals, including the body, and, through this, with the Christian denial of the body and of the worth of earthly life.[15] So even in this apparently unpromising case, history shows that the Aristotelian approach not only provided the materials for a single debate but actually succeeded in organizing such a debate, across enormous differences of both place and time.

Here, then, is a sketch for an objective human morality based upon the idea of virtuous action—that is, of appropriate functioning in each human sphere. The Aristotelian claim is that, further developed, it will retain virtue morality's immersed attention to actual human experiences, while gaining the ability to criticize local and traditional moralities in the name of a more inclusive account of the circumstances of human life, and of the needs for human functioning that these circumstances call forth.

Notes

1. A. MacIntyre, *After Virtue* (Notre Dame, Ind., 1981); P. Foot, *Virtues and Vices* (Los Angeles, 1978); B. Williams, *Ethics and the Limits of Philosophy* (Cambridge, Mass., 1985) and Tanner Lectures, Harvard, 1983. See also M. Walzer, *Spheres of Justice* (New York, 1983) and Tanner Lectures, Harvard, 1985.

2. For examples of this, see Nussbaum, "Nature, Function, and Capability: Aristotle on Political Distribution," circulated as a WIDER working paper, and in *Oxford Studies in Ancient Philosophy,* 1988 (supplement), pp. 145–184, and also, in an expanded version, in the Proceedings of the 12th Symposium Aristotelicum.

3. See, for example, Williams, *Ethics and the Limits,* pp. 34–36; Stuart Hampshire, *Morality and Conflict* (Cambridge, Mass., 1983), 150 ff.

4. For "nameless" virtues and vices, see *NE* 1107b1–2, 1107b8, 1107b30–31, 1108a17, 1119a10–11, 1126b20, 1127a12, 1127a14; for recognition of the unsatisfactoriness of names given, see 1107b8, 1108a5–6, 1108a20 ff. The two categories are largely overlapping, on account of the general principle enunciated at 1108a16–19, that where there is no name a name should be given, unsatisfactory or not.

5. It should be noted that this emphasis on spheres of experience is not present in the *Eudemian Ethics,* which begins with a list of virtues and vices. This seems to me a sign that that treatise expresses a more primitive stage of Aristotle's thought on the virtues—whether earlier or not.

6. For statements with *peri,* connecting virtues with spheres of life, see 1115a6–7, 1117a29–30, 1117b25, 27, 1119b23, 1122a19, 1122b34, 1125b26, 1126b13; and *NE* 2.7 throughout. See also the related usages at 1126b11, 1127b32.

7. My list here inserts justice in a place of prominence. (In the *NE* it is treated separately, after all the other virtues, and the introductory list defers it for that later examination.) I have also added at the end of the list categories corresponding to the various intellectual virtues discussed in *NE* 6, and also to *phronesis* or practical wisdom, discussed in 6 as well. Otherwise the order and wording of my list closely follows 2.7, which gives the program for the more detailed analyses of 3.5–4.

8. For a longer account of this, with references to the literature and to related philosophical discussions, see Nussbaum, *The Fragility of Goodness* (Cambridge, Mass., 1986), chap. 8.

9. Aristotle does not worry about questions of translation in articulating this idea.

10. *Posterior Analytics,* 2.8. 93a21 ff.; see *Fragility,* chap. 8.

11. Heraclitus, fragment DK B23; see Nussbaum, "*Psuche* in Heraclitus, II," *Phronesis* 17 (1972): 153–70.

12. See *Politics* 1.2. 1253a1–18; that discussion does not deny the virtues to gods explicitly, but this denial is explicit at *NE* 1145a25–27 and 1178b10 ff.

13. Aristotle does not make the connection with his account of language explicit, but his project is one of defining the virtues, and we would expect him to keep his general view of defining in mind in this context. A similar idea about the virtues, and experience of a certain sort as a possible basis for a non-relative account, is developed, without reference to Aristotle, in a review of P. Foot's *Virtues and Vices* by N. Sturgeon, *Journal of Philosophy* 81 (1984): 326–33.

14. See 1108a5, where Aristotle says that the virtues and the corresponding person are "pretty much nameless," and says "Let us call . . ." when he introduces the names. See also 1125b29, 1126a3–4.

15. See John Procope, *Magnanimity* (1987); also R.-A. Gauthier, *Magnanimité* (Paris, 1951).

CHAPTER 28

Four Applications of the Categorical Imperative

Immanuel Kant

Many people think that Immanuel Kant (1724–1804) was the greatest modern philosopher. Kant believed that morality can be summed up in one ultimate principle, the Categorical Imperative. According to the Categorical Imperative, to act morally is to act from motives that everyone, everywhere could live by.

The following selection is from Kant's "Foundations of the Metaphysics of Morals," the most accessible presentation of his ethical theory.

All imperatives command either hypothetically or categorically. . . .

The hypothetical imperative . . . says only that the action is good to some purpose, possible or actual. . . . The categorical imperative, which declares the action to be of itself objectively necessary without making any reference to a purpose, i.e., without having any other end, holds as an apodictical (practical) principle. . . .

If I think of a hypothetical imperative as such, I do not know what it will contain until the condition is stated [under which it is an imperative]. But if I think of a categorical imperative, I know immediately what it contains. For since the imperative contains besides the

Source: Excerpted from Immanuel Kant, "Foundations of the Metaphysics of Morals" (1785), in *The Critique of Practical Reason and Other Writings in Moral Philosophy,* trans. Lewis White Beck (Chicago: University of Chicago Press, 1949), pp. 73–74, 80–83. Reprinted by permission of the Estate of Lewis White Beck.

law only the necessity of the maxim of acting in accordance with this law, while the law contains no condition to which it is restricted, there is nothing remaining in it except the universality of law as such to which the maxim of the action should conform; and in effect this conformity alone is represented as necessary by the imperative.

There is, therefore, only one categorical imperative. It is: Act only according to that maxim by which you can at the same time will that it should become a universal law.

Now if all imperatives of duty can be derived from this one imperative as a principle, we can at least show what we understand by the concept of duty and what it means, even though it remain undecided whether that which is called duty is an empty concept or not.

The universality of law according to which effects are produced constitutes what is properly called nature in the most general sense (as to form), i.e., the existence of things so far as it is determined by universal laws. [By analogy], then, the universal imperative of duty can be expressed as follows: Act as though the maxim of your action were by your will to become a universal law of nature.

We shall now enumerate some duties. . . .

1. A man who is reduced to despair by a series of evils feels a weariness with life but is still in possession of his reason sufficiently to ask whether it would not be contrary to his duty to himself to take his own life. Now he asks whether the maxim of his action could become a universal law of nature. His maxim, however, is: For love of myself, I make it my principle to shorten my life when by a longer duration it threatens more evil than satisfaction. But it is questionable whether this principle of self-love could become a universal law of nature. One immediately sees a contradiction in a system of nature, whose law would be to destroy life by the feeling whose special office is to impel the improvement of life. In this case it would not exist as nature; hence that maxim cannot obtain as a law of nature, and thus it wholly contradicts the supreme principle of all duty.

2. Another man finds himself forced by need to borrow money. He well knows that he will not be able to repay it, but he also sees that nothing will be loaned him if he does not firmly promise to repay it at a certain time. He desires to make such a promise, but he has enough conscience to ask himself whether it is not improper and opposed to duty to relieve his distress in such a way. Now, assuming he does decide to do so, the maxim of his action would be as follows: When

I believe myself to be in need of money, I will borrow money and promise to repay it, although I know I shall never do so. Now this principle of self-love or of his own benefit may very well be compatible with his whole future welfare, but the question is whether it is right. He changes the pretension of self-love into a universal law and then puts the question: How would it be if my maxim became a universal law? He immediately sees that it could never hold as a universal law of nature and be consistent with itself; rather it must necessarily contradict itself. For the universality of a law which says that anyone who believes himself to be in need could promise what he pleased with the intention of not fulfilling it would make the promise itself and the end to be accomplished by it impossible; no one would believe what was promised to him but would only laugh at any such assertion as vain pretense.

3. A third finds in himself a talent which could, by means of some cultivation, make him in many respects a useful man. But he finds himself in comfortable circumstances and prefers indulgence in pleasure to troubling himself with broadening and improving his fortunate natural gifts. Now, however, let him ask whether his maxim of neglecting his gifts, besides agreeing with his propensity to idle amusement, agrees also with what is called duty. He sees that a system of nature could indeed exist in accordance with such a law, even though man (like the inhabitants of the South Sea Islands) should let his talents rust and resolve to devote his life merely to idleness, indulgence, and propagation—in a word, to pleasure. But he cannot possibly will that this should become a universal law of nature or that it should be implanted in us by a natural instinct. For, as a rational being, he necessarily wills that all his faculties should be developed, inasmuch as they are given to him for all sorts of possible purposes.

4. A fourth man, for whom things are going well, sees that others (whom he could help) have to struggle with great hardships, and he asks, "What concern of mine is it? Let each one be as happy as heaven wills, or as he can make himself; I will not take anything from him or even envy him; but to his welfare or to his assistance in time of need I have no desire to contribute." If such a way of thinking were a universal law of nature, certainly the human race could exist, and without doubt even better than in a state where everyone talks of sympathy and good will or even exerts himself occasionally to practice them while, on the other hand, he cheats when he can and betrays or otherwise violates the rights of man. Now although it is possible that a universal law of nature according to that maxim could exist, it is nevertheless impossible to will that such a principle should hold everywhere as a law of nature. For a will which resolved this would conflict with itself, since instances can often arise in which he would need the love and sympathy of others, and in which he would have robbed himself, by such a law of nature springing from his own will, of all hope of the aid he desires.

The foregoing are a few of the many actual duties, or at least of duties we hold to be actual, whose derivation from the one stated principle is clear. We must be able to will that a maxim of our action become a universal law; this is the canon of the moral estimation of our action generally. Some actions are of such a nature that their maxim cannot even be *thought* as a universal law of nature without contradiction, far from it being possible that one could will that it should be such. In others this internal impossibility is not found though it is still impossible to *will* that their maxim should be raised to the universality of a law of nature, because such a will would contradict itself. We easily see that the former maxim conflicts with the stricter or narrower (imprescriptable) duty, the latter with broader (meritorious) duty. Thus all duties, so far as the kind of obligation (not the object of their action) is concerned, have been completely exhibited by these examples in their dependence on the one principle. . . .

CHAPTER 29

*F*our Ethical Principles

Peter Singer

Peter Singer (1946–) of Princeton University and Melbourne University is the most controversial philosopher writing today. His defense of animal rights, his insistence that affluent people should share their wealth with the poor, and his criticism of the traditional sanctity of life ethic have all aroused protest. In the following selection, Singer briefly sketches some of the principles that led him to these controversial views.

Singer has written over forty books, including *Animal Liberation* (3rd edition, 2002), *The Way We Eat: Why Our Food Choices Matter* (2006, with Jim Mason) and *The Life You Can Save: Acting Now to End World Poverty* (2009).

Had there been no protest rallies at the gates of Princeton University, had the superrich aspiring presidential candidate Steve Forbes not vowed to freeze his donations to his alma mater until it got rid of me, had my appointment as DeCamp Professor of Bioethics at Princeton not turned into what *The New York Times* called the biggest academic commotion since an American university tried to hire the notorious advocate of free love, Bertrand Russell, the book you now have in your hands would not have existed. For without those events the media would barely have noticed my arrival in the United States, my

Source: Singer's *Writings on an Ethical Life* (New York: HarperCollins, 2000), pp. xiii–xviii. Reprinted by permission of HarperCollins Publishers, Inc.

controversial views on a variety of ethical issues would not have become the topic of conversation around the country. . . .

What are the ideas that have caused so much controversy? . . . The momentous issues of civil rights, racial equality, and opposition to the war in Vietnam had made the subject matter of most university ethics courses seem dry and insignificant and to spend time studying them, self-indulgent. There were more important things to do. Students were demanding "relevance," and philosophers began to realize that their area of expertise did, after all, have something to say on how we can find answers to such fundamental and perennially important questions as why racial discrimination is wrong, whether we are under an obligation to obey an unjust law, and what, if anything, can make it right to go to war.

The issue on which I have made my most significant contribution to ethical thinking took a little longer to become prominent. Claims that I am "the most influential living philosopher" generally refer to my work on the ethics of our relations with animals. There is an element of media hype in such claims, of course, but the grain of truth in them is the fact that my book *Animal Liberation* played a significant role in kicking off the modern animal rights movement, and very few living philosophers have had their ideas taken up in that way. In contrast, my views on the obligation of the rich to help the world's poorest people are potentially as significant as my thinking about animals, but they have, unfortunately, had much less influence. The issues raised by the critical work I have done on the idea of the sanctity of human life, including the discussion of euthanasia that has aroused such hostility, are in one respect less important than those two topics, simply because the treatment of animals and maldistribution of wealth affect far more people (or in the case of the animals, sentient beings), and relatively simple changes in those areas could relieve so much suffering. It is my critique of the sanctity of human life that gets the media headlines, however, because it can easily be made to sound quite shocking and there is no problem in finding people who will strenuously oppose it. Hence it provides the controversy on which the media feed.

All of these views have a common core. They rest on four quite simple claims:

1. Pain is bad, and similar amounts of pain are equally bad, no matter whose pain it might be. By "pain" here I would include suffering and distress of all kinds. This does not

mean that pain is the only thing that is bad, or that inflicting pain is always wrong. Sometimes it may be necessary to inflict pain and suffering on oneself or others. We do this to ourselves when we go to the dentist, and we do it to others when we reprimand a child or jail a criminal. But this is justified because it will lead to less suffering in the long run; the pain is still in itself a bad thing. Conversely, pleasure and happiness are good, no matter whose pleasure or happiness they might be, although doing things in order to gain pleasure or happiness may be wrong, for example, if doing so harms others.

2. Humans are not the only beings capable of feeling pain or of suffering. Most nonhuman animals—certainly all the mammals and birds that we habitually eat, like cows, pigs, sheep, and chickens—can feel pain. Many of them can also experience other forms of suffering, for instance, the distress that a mother feels when separated from her child, or the boredom that comes from being locked up in a cage with nothing to do all day except eat and sleep. Of course, the nature of the beings will affect how much pain they suffer in any given situation.

3. When we consider how serious it is to take a life, we should look, not at the race, sex, or species to which that being belongs, but at the characteristics of the individual being killed, for example, its own desires about continuing to live, or the kind of life it is capable of leading.

4. We are responsible not only for what we do but also for what we could have prevented. We would never kill a stranger, but we may know that our intervention will save the lives of many strangers in a distant country, and yet do nothing. We do not then think ourselves in any way responsible for the deaths of these strangers. This is a mistake. We should consider the consequences both of what we do and of what we decide not to do.

To most people these claims are not, in themselves, shocking. In some respects they seem like common sense. But consider the conclusions to which they point. Put together the first and the last, and add in some facts about the suffering caused by extreme poverty in the world's least developed countries, and about our ability to reduce that suffering by donating money to organizations that assist people to lift themselves out of this poverty. Consider, for example, the fact that the sum that buys us a meal in a fine restaurant would be enough to provide basic health care to several children who might otherwise die of easily preventable diseases. It follows from the first of my claims that the suffering of these children, or their parents, is as bad as our own suffering would be in similar circumstances, and it follows from the last claim that we cannot escape responsibility for this suffering by the fact that we have done nothing to bring it about. Where so many are in such great need, indulgence in luxury is not morally neutral, and the fact that we have not killed anyone is not enough to make us morally decent citizens of the world.

From the first and second premises I draw the conclusion that we have no right to discount the interests of nonhuman animals simply because, for example, we like the taste of their flesh. Modern industrialized agriculture treats animals as if they were things, putting them indoors and confining them whenever it turns out to be cheaper to do so, with no regard at all paid to their suffering or distress, as long as it does not mean that they cease to be productive. But we cannot ethically disregard the interests of other beings merely because they are not members of our species. Note that this argument says nothing at all about whether it is wrong to kill nonhuman animals for food. It is based entirely on the suffering that we inflict on farm animals when we raise them by the methods that are standard today.

The third premise is probably the most controversial because we are so used to thinking of the killing of a member of our own species as invariably much more serious than the killing of a member of any other species. But why should that be? Mere difference of species is surely not a morally significant difference. Suppose that there were Martians, just like us in respect of their abilities to think and to care for others, in their sense of justice, and in any other capacities we care to name, but of course, not members of the species *Homo sapiens*. We surely could not claim that it was all right to kill them, simply because of the difference of species. We might, of course, try to find some other differences, of greater moral relevance, between humans and members of other species. If, for example, we think that it is more serious to kill a human being than it is to kill a nonhuman animal, and we hold this view because we believe that every human being—and no other earthly creature—has an immortal soul, then our position is not contrary to the third premise, for it is taking the view that there is a characteristic—possession of an immortal soul—that makes it worse to kill some beings than others, and that happens to be possessed by

all and only members of our species. My disagreement with that position is simply that I see no evidence for belief in an immortal soul, let
alone one that happens to be the exclusive property of our species.

The third premise helps to explain what is true and what is misleading in the common assertion that I think the life of a human
being is of no greater value than the life of an animal. It is true that I
do not think that the fact that the human is a member of the species
Homo sapiens is *in itself* a reason for regarding his or her life as being of
greater value than that of a member of a different species. But, as I
argue in more detail, in *Practical Ethics* and *Rethinking Life and Death*,
human beings typically, though not invariably, do have desires about
going on living that nonhuman animals are not capable of having,
and that does make a difference. Thus, I have no doubt that the
events that we read about all too often in our newspapers, when someone gets a gun and starts randomly killing people in a school, church,
or supermarket, are more tragic than the shooting of a number
of animals in a field would be.

Though the third premise must be part of any full grounding of
my views about why it is worse to kill some beings than others, some
of my claims about euthanasia could be derived from the first and
fourth premises alone, combined with widely accepted medical practice. Many doctors and theologians, including those who are quite
conservative in their moral thinking, agree that when a patient's prospects of a minimally decent quality of life are very poor, and there is
no likelihood of improvement, we are not obliged to do everything we
could to prolong life. For example, if a baby is born with severe dis-
abilities incompatible with an acceptable quality of life, and the baby
then develops an infection, many doctors and theologians would say
that it is permissible to refrain from giving the baby antibiotics. But
these same people think that it would be wrong to allow the doctor to
give the baby a lethal injection. Why? The motives, the intention, and
the outcome may be the same in both cases. If it is sometimes right
deliberately to allow a baby to die when a simple medical intervention
could save its life, then it must also sometimes be right to kill the baby.
To deny this is to refuse to take responsibility for deciding not to act,
even when the consequences of omission and action are the same.

That this final conclusion is contrary to widely shared moral
views, I readily concede. But the aim of practical ethics is not to produce a theory that will match all of our conventional moral responses,
and thus confirm us in the views we already hold. Those responses
come from many different sources. Sometimes they vary according to

the customs of the society that we come from. Even when they are more or less universal among human societies, they may be no more than a reflection of the interests of the dominant group. That was true of justifications of slavery that for centuries were predominant in European slave-holding societies. It remains true, in many parts of the world, of the view that a married woman should obey her husband. It is not too big a step to see the same self-interested factors at work in our common moral views about the ways in which we may use animals. Here, as on many other moral issues, Christianity has for two thousand years been a powerful influence on the moral intuitions of people in Western societies. People do not need to continue to hold religious beliefs to be under the influence of Christian moral teaching. Yet without the religious beliefs—for example, that God created the world, that he gave us dominion over the other animals, that we alone of all of his creation have an immortal soul—the moral teachings just hang in the air, without foundations. If no better foundations can be provided for these teachings, we need to consider alternative views. So it is with the question of euthanasia, which, along with suicide, has in non-Christian societies like ancient Rome and Japan been considered both a reasonable and an honorable way of ending one's life. The shock with which some people react to any suggestion of euthanasia should therefore be not the end of the argument but a spur to reflection and critical scrutiny.

CHAPTER 30

The Debate over Utilitarianism

James Rachels and Stuart Rachels

Traditionally, morality was understood in terms of high-minded, abstract rules laid down by God in Heaven. A good person will follow those rules, it was thought, come what may. A different way of thinking about ethics was developed by the Englishmen Jeremy Bentham (1748–1832), John Stuart Mill (1806–1873), and Henry Sidgwick (1838–1900). This new theory was called utilitarianism. On this theory, morality should be about making people as happy as possible, and all moral rules should aim at that goal.

Today utilitarianism is the most influential theory in ethics. It might also be the most despised. To some people, it represents liberation from the old, arbitrary ways; to others, it represents a simplistic, decadent secularism. In this selection, James Rachels and Stuart Rachels discuss some of the best-known objections to utilitarianism and consider some replies. The authors do not reach any definite conclusions about the theory.

The utilitarian doctrine is that happiness is desirable, and the only thing desirable, as an end; all other things being desirable as means to that end.
—John Stuart Mill, *Utilitarianism* (1861)

Man does not strive after happiness; only the Englishman does that.
—Friedrich Nietzsche, *Twilight of the Idols* (1889)

Source: This is chapter 8 of James Rachels and Stuart Rachels, *The Elements of Moral Philosophy,* 6th edition (New York: McGraw-Hill, 2010), pp. 109–123. Copyright © 2010 by the McGraw-Hill Companies, Inc.

The Classical Version of the Theory

Classical Utilitarianism, the theory of Bentham and Mill, can be summarized in three propositions: (a) Actions are to be judged right or wrong solely by virtue of their consequences; nothing else matters. (b) In assessing consequences, the only thing that matters is the amount of happiness or unhappiness that is created; everything else is irrelevant. (c) Each person's happiness counts the same. Thus, right actions are those that produce the greatest balance of happiness over unhappiness, with each person's happiness counted as equally important.

This theory has profoundly influenced both ethicists and social scientists. Most ethicists, however, reject Utilitarianism, due to a slew of objections. In what follows, we will examine some of these objections and consider whether they succeed. In doing so, we will grapple with some fundamental questions in moral philosophy.

Is Pleasure All That Matters?

The question *What things are good?* is different from the question *What actions are right?* and Utilitarianism answers the second question by reference to the first. Right actions are the ones that produce the most good. But what is good? The utilitarian reply is: happiness. As Mill puts it, "The utilitarian doctrine is that happiness is desirable, and the only thing desirable, as an end; all other things being desirable as means to that end."

But what is happiness? According to the classical utilitarians, happiness is pleasure. Utilitarians understand "pleasure" broadly, to include all mental states that feel good. A sense of accomplishment, a delicious taste, and the heightened awareness that comes at the climax of a suspenseful movie are all examples of pleasure. The idea that pleasure is the one ultimate good—and pain the one ultimate evil—has been known since antiquity as Hedonism. Hedonism has always been attractive because of its simplicity and because it expresses the plausible notion that things are good or bad because of how they make us *feel*. Yet a little reflection seems to reveal flaws in this theory.

Consider these two examples:

- *You think someone is your friend, but he ridicules you behind your back.* No one tells you, so you never know. Is this unfortunate for you? Hedonists would have to say it is not, because you are never caused any pain. Yet we feel there is something bad going on. You are "being made a fool of," even though you are unaware of it and you suffer no unhappiness.

- *A promising young pianist's hands are injured in a car accident so that she can no longer play.* Why is this bad for her? Hedonists would say it is bad because it causes her pain and eliminates a source of joy for her. But suppose she finds something else that she enjoys just as much—suppose, for example, that she gets as much pleasure from watching hockey on TV as she once got from playing the piano. Why is her accident now a tragedy? The hedonist can only say that she will feel frustrated and upset whenever she thinks of what might have been, and her misfortune is that she feels bad. But this explanation gets things backwards. It is not as though, by feeling upset, she has turned a neutral situation into a bad one. On the contrary, the bad situation is what made her unhappy. She could have had a career as a concert pianist, and now she cannot. That is the tragedy. We cannot eliminate the tragedy just by getting her to cheer up and watch hockey.

Both of these examples make the same basic point: We value all sorts of things, such as artistic creativity and friendship, for their own sakes. It makes us happy to have them, but that's not the only reason we value them. It seems like a misfortune to lose them, even if there is no loss of happiness.

For this reason, there are not many hedonists among contemporary philosophers. Those sympathetic to Utilitarianism have therefore sought a way to formulate their view without assuming a hedonistic account of the good. Some, such as the English philosopher G. E. Moore (1873–1958), have tried to compile short lists of things to be regarded as valuable in themselves. Moore suggested that there are three obvious intrinsic goods—pleasure, friendship, and aesthetic enjoyment—and so right actions are those actions that increase the world's supply of these things. Other utilitarians bypass the question of how many things are good in themselves, saying only that right actions are the ones that have the best results, however that is measured. Still others say that we should act so as to maximize the satisfaction of people's *preferences*. I won't discuss the merits and demerits of these varieties of Utilitarianism. I mention them only to note that, although Hedonism has largely been rejected, contemporary utilitarians have not found it difficult to carry on.

Are Consequences All That Matter?

To determine whether an action is right, utilitarians believe that we should look at *what will happen as a result of doing it.* This idea is essential to the theory. If things other than consequences are important in determining what is right, then Utilitarianism is incorrect. Here are three arguments that attack the theory at just this point.

Justice. In 1965, writing in the racially charged climate of the American Civil Rights movement, H. J. McCloskey asks us to consider the following case:

> Suppose a utilitarian were visiting an area in which there was racial strife, and that, during his visit, a Negro rapes a white woman, and that race riots occur as a result of the crime. . . . Suppose too that our utilitarian is in the area of the crime when it is committed such that his testimony would bring about the conviction of [whomever he accuses]. If he knows that a quick arrest will stop the riots and lynchings, surely, as a utilitarian, he must conclude that he has a duty to bear false witness in order to bring about the punishment of an innocent person.

Such an accusation would have bad consequences—the innocent man would be convicted—but there would be enough good consequences to outweigh them: The riots and lynchings would be stopped. The best outcome would be achieved by lying; therefore, according to Utilitarianism, lying is the thing to do. But, the argument continues, it would be wrong to bring about the conviction of an innocent person. Therefore, Utilitarianism, which implies otherwise, must be incorrect.

According to the critics of Utilitarianism, this argument illustrates one of the theory's most serious shortcomings, namely, that it is incompatible with the ideal of justice. Justice requires that we treat people fairly, according to the merits of their particular situations. In McCloskey's example, Utilitarianism requires that we treat someone unfairly. Thus, Utilitarianism cannot be right.

Rights. Here is an example from the U.S. Court of Appeals. In the case of *York v. Story* (1963), arising out of California:

> In October, 1958, appellant [Ms. Angelynn York] went to the police department of Chino for the purpose of filing charges in connection with an assault upon her. Appellee Ron Story, an officer of that police department, then acting under color of his authority as such, advised appellant that it was necessary to take

photographs of her. Story then took appellant to a room in the police station, locked the door, and directed her to undress, which she did. Story then directed appellant to assume various indecent positions, and photographed her in those positions. These photographs were not made for any lawful or legitimate purpose.

Appellant objected to undressing. She stated to Story that there was no need to take photographs of her in the nude, or in the positions she was directed to take, because the bruises would not show in any photograph. . . .

Later that month, Story advised appellant that the pictures did not come out and that he had destroyed them. Instead, Story circulated these photographs among the personnel of the Chino police department. In April, 1960, two other officers of that police department, appellee Louis Moreno and defendant Henry Grote, acting under color of their authority as such, and using police photographic equipment located at the police station, made additional prints of the photographs taken by Story. Moreno and Grote then circulated these prints among the personnel of the Chino police department.

Ms. York brought suit against these officers and won. Her legal rights had clearly been violated. But what of the *morality* of the officers' behavior? Utilitarianism says that actions are defensible if they produce a favorable balance of happiness over unhappiness. This suggests that we compare the amount of unhappiness caused to York with the amount of pleasure the photographs gave to Officer Story and the others. It is at least possible that more happiness than unhappiness was created. In that case, the utilitarian conclusion would be that their actions were morally acceptable. But this seems to be a perverse way of thinking. Why should the pleasure of Story and his friends matter at all? They had no right to treat York in this way, and the fact that they enjoyed doing so hardly seems a relevant defense.

Consider a related case. Suppose a Peeping Tom spied on a woman through her bedroom window and secretly took pictures of her undressed. Further suppose that he did this without being detected and that he used the photographs entirely for his own pleasure, without showing them to anyone. Now, under these circumstances, the only consequence of his action seems to be an increase in his own happiness. No one else, including the woman, is caused any unhappiness at all. How, then, could Utilitarianism deny that the Peeping Tom's actions are right? But it is evident to moral common sense that they are not right. Thus, Utilitarianism appears to be unacceptable.

The key point to be drawn from this argument is that Utilitarianism is at odds with the idea that people have *rights* that may not be trampled on merely because one anticipates good results. In these cases, the woman's right to privacy is violated. But it would not be difficult to think of similar cases in which other rights are at issue—the right to worship freely, the right to speak your mind, or even the right to live. It may happen that good purposes are served, from time to time, by violating these rights. But we do not think that our rights should be set aside so easily. The notion of a personal right is not a utilitarian notion. Quite the opposite: It is a notion that places limits on how an individual may be treated, regardless of the good purposes that might be accomplished.

Backward-Looking Reasons. Suppose you have promised someone you will do something—say, you promised to meet her at the mall this afternoon. But when the time comes to go, you don't want to do it; you need to catch up on some work and you would rather stay home. You try to call her up to cancel, but she isn't answering her cell phone. What should you do? Suppose you judge that the utility of getting your work done slightly outweighs the irritation your friend will experience from being stood up. Appealing to the utilitarian standard, you might conclude that staying home is better than keeping your promise. However, this does not seem correct. The fact that you *promised* imposes an obligation on you that you cannot escape so easily. Of course, if a great deal were at stake—if, for example, you had to rush your mother to the hospital—you would be justified in breaking the promise. But a *small* gain in utility cannot overcome the obligation created by your promise; the obligation should mean something, morally. Thus, Utilitarianism once again seems mistaken.

This criticism is possible because Utilitarianism cares only about the *consequences* of our actions. However, we normally think that considerations about the past are important, too. You made a promise to your friend, and that's a fact about the past. Utilitarianism seems faulty because it excludes such backward-looking reasons.

Once we understand this point, we can think of other examples of backward-looking reasons. The fact that someone committed a crime is a reason to punish him. The fact that someone did you a favor last week may be a reason why you should do her a favor next week. The fact that you did something to hurt someone may be a reason to make it up to him now. These are all facts about the past that are relevant to determining our obligations. But Utilitarianism makes the past irrelevant, and so it seems flawed.

Should We Be Equally Concerned for Everyone?

The last part of Utilitarianism says that we must treat each person's happiness as equally important—or as Mill put it, we must be "as strictly impartial as a disinterested and benevolent spectator." Stated abstractly, this sounds plausible, but it has troublesome implications. One problem is that the requirement of "equal concern" places too great a demand on us; another problem is that it disrupts our personal relationships.

The Charge That Utilitarianism Is Too Demanding. Suppose you are on your way to the movies when someone points out that the money you are about to spend could be used to provide food for starving people or inoculations for third-world children. Surely, those people need food and medicine more than you need to see Brad Pitt and Angelina Jolie. So you forgo your entertainment and donate the money to a charitable agency. But that is not the end of it. By the same reasoning, you cannot buy new clothes, a car, a digital camera, or a PlayStation. Probably you should move into a cheaper apartment. After all, what's more important—that you have these luxuries, or that children have food?

In fact, faithful adherence to the utilitarian standard would require you to give away your resources until you've lowered your standard of living to the level of the neediest people you could help. Or rather, you'd need to leave yourself just enough to maintain your job, so that you can keep on giving. Although we admire people who do this, we do not regard them as simply doing their duty. Instead, we regard them as saintly people whose generosity goes *beyond* the call of duty. Philosophers call such actions *supererogatory*. But Utilitarianism seems unable to recognize this moral category.

The problem is not merely that Utilitarianism would require us to give up most of our material resources. It would also prevent us from carrying on our individual lives. We all have goals and projects that make our lives meaningful. An ethic that requires the subordination of everything to the promotion of the general welfare would force us to abandon those endeavors. Suppose you are a web designer, not getting rich but making a decent living; you have two children whom you love; and on weekends, you like to perform with an amateur theater group. In addition, you enjoy reading history. How could there be anything wrong with this? But judged by the utilitarian standard, you are leading a morally unacceptable life. After all, you could be doing a lot more good if you spent your time in other ways.

The Charge That Utilitarianism Disrupts Our Personal Relationships. In practice, none of us is willing to treat everyone equally, since that would require us to abandon our special relationships with friends and family. We are all deeply partial where our family and friends are concerned. We love them, and we go to great lengths to help them. To us, they are not just members of the great crowd of humanity—they are special. But all this is inconsistent with impartiality. When you are impartial, you miss out on intimacy, love, affection, and friendship.

At this point, Utilitarianism seems to have lost touch with reality. What would it be like to be no more concerned for one's husband or wife than for strangers whom one has never met? The very idea is absurd; not only is it profoundly contrary to normal human emotions, but loving relationships could not even exist apart from special responsibilities and obligations. Again, what would it be like to treat one's children with no greater love than one has for strangers? As John Cottingham puts it, "A parent who leaves his child to burn" because "the building contains someone else whose future contribution to the general welfare promises to be greater, is not a hero; he is (rightly) an object of moral contempt, a moral leper."

The Defense of Utilitarianism

These arguments add up to an overwhelming indictment of Utilitarianism. The theory, which at first seemed so plausible and progressive, now seems indefensible. It seems at odds with justice and individual rights, and it seems unable to account for the place of backward-looking reasons in justifying conduct. It would have us give away most of our possessions and spoil the personal relationships that mean everything to us.

Not surprisingly, the combined weight of these arguments has prompted most philosophers to abandon the theory altogether. Some philosophers, however, continue to believe in Utilitarianism. Three general defenses have been offered.

The First Defense: Denying That the Consequences Would Be Good. The first defense says that the anti-utilitarian arguments make unrealistic assumptions. Most of those arguments share a common strategy. The critic describes a case and then says that Utilitarianism requires a certain action—bearing false witness, violating someone's rights, and so on. But, the critic says, these actions are obviously immoral. Therefore, Utilitarianism is incorrect.

But this strategy succeeds only if we agree that the actions described really would have the best consequences. And why should we agree with that? In the real world, lying under oath does *not* have good consequences. Suppose, in the case described by McCloskey, the "utilitarian" tried to incriminate the innocent man in order to stop the riots. He probably would not succeed; his lie might be found out, and then the situation would be even worse than before. Even if the lie succeeded, the real culprit would remain at large and might commit more crimes. Also, if the guilty party were caught later on, which is always possible, the liar would be in deep trouble, and confidence in the criminal justice system would erode. The moral is that although one might *think* that one can bring about the best consequences by such behavior, one cannot be certain of it. In fact, experience teaches the opposite: Utility is not served by framing innocent people.

The same goes for the other cases cited in the anti-utilitarian arguments. Lying, violating people's rights, breaking one's promises, and severing one's personal relationships all have bad consequences. Only in philosophers' imaginations is it otherwise. In the real world, Peeping Toms are caught, just as Officer Story and his cohorts were caught, and their victims suffer. In the real world, when people lie, their reputations suffer and other people get hurt; and when people break their promises and fail to return favors, they lose their friends.

So that is the first defense. How effective is it? Unfortunately, it contains more bluster than substance. While it is true that *most* acts of false witness and the like have bad consequences, it cannot be said that *all* such acts have bad consequences. At least once in a while, one can bring about a good result by doing something repugnant to moral common sense. Therefore, in at least some real-life cases, Utilitarianism will conflict with common sense. Moreover, even if the anti-utilitarian arguments had to rely exclusively on fictitious examples, those arguments would nevertheless retain their power, for showing that Utilitarianism has unacceptable consequences in hypothetical cases is a valid way of critiquing it. The first defense, then, is weak.

The Second Defense: The Principle of Utility Is a Guide for Choosing Rules, Not Acts. Revising a theory is a two-step process: first, you identify which feature of the theory needs work; second, you change only that feature, leaving the rest of the theory intact. What feature of Classical Utilitarianism is causing the trouble?

The troublesome assumption is that *each individual action* should be evaluated by reference to the Principle of Utility. If on a certain occasion you are tempted to lie, Classical Utilitarianism says that whether it would be wrong depends on the consequences of *telling that particular lie;* whether you should keep a particular promise depends on the consequences of *keeping that particular promise;* and so on for each of the examples we have considered. If what we care about is the consequences of particular actions, then we can always dream up circumstances in which a horrific action will have the best consequences.

Therefore, the new version of Utilitarianism modifies the theory so that individual actions are no longer judged by the Principle of Utility. Instead, we first ask what *set of rules* is optimal, from a utilitarian viewpoint. In other words, what rules should we follow to maximize happiness? Individual acts are then judged right or wrong according to whether they are acceptable or unacceptable by these rules. This new version of the theory is called "Rule-Utilitarianism," to distinguish it from the original theory, now commonly called "Act-Utilitarianism."

Rule-Utilitarianism has an easy answer to the anti-utilitarian arguments. An act-utilitarian would incriminate the innocent man in McCloskey's example because the consequences of *that particular act* would be good. But the rule-utilitarian would not reason in that way. She would first ask, What rules of conduct tend to promote the most happiness? One good rule is "Don't bear false witness against the innocent." That rule is simple, easy to remember, and following it will almost always increase happiness. By appealing to it, the rule-utilitarian can conclude that in McCloskey's example we should not testify against the innocent man.

Analogous reasoning can be used to establish rules against violating people's rights, breaking promises, lying, betraying one's friends, and so on. We should accept such rules because following them, as a regular practice, promotes the general happiness. We no longer judge acts by their utility but by their conformity with these rules. Thus, Rule-Utilitarianism cannot be convicted of violating our moral common sense. In shifting emphasis from the justification of acts to the justification of rules, Utilitarianism has been brought into line with our intuitive judgments.

However, a serious problem with Rule-Utilitarianism arises when we ask whether the ideal rules have *exceptions*. Must the rules be followed no matter what? What if a "forbidden" act would greatly increase the overall good? The rule-utilitarian might give any one of three replies.

First, if she says that in such cases we may violate the rules, it looks like she wants to assess actions on a case-by-case basis. This is Act-Utilitarianism, not Rule-Utilitarianism.

Second, she might suggest that we formulate the rules so that violating them never will increase happiness. For example, instead of using the rule "Don't bear false witness against the innocent," we might use the rule "Don't bear false witness against the innocent, unless doing so would achieve some great good." If we change all of the rules in this way, then Rule-Utilitarianism will be exactly like Act-Utilitarianism in practice; the rules we follow will always tell us to choose the act that promotes the most happiness in our particular circumstances. But now Rule-Utilitarianism does not provide a response to the anti-utilitarian arguments; like Act-Utilitarianism, it tells us to incriminate the innocent, to break our promises, to spy on people in their homes, and so on.

Finally, the rule-utilitarian might stand her ground and say that we should never break the rules, even to promote happiness. J. J. C. Smart (1920–) says that such a person suffers from an irrational "rule wor-ship." Whatever one thinks of that, this version of Rule-Utilitarianism is not really a utilitarian theory. Utilitarians care solely about happiness and about consequences; but this theory, in addition, cares about fol-lowing rules. The theory is thus a mix of Utilitarianism and something else entirely. To paraphrase one writer, this type of Rule-Utilitarianism is like a rubber duck: just as a rubber duck is not a kind of duck, this type of Rule-Utilitarianism is not a kind of Utilitarianism. And so, we cannot defend Utilitarianism by appealing to it.

The Third Defense: "Common Sense" Is Wrong. Finally, some utili-tarians have offered a very different response to the objections. Upon being told that Utilitarianism conflicts with common sense, they respond, "So what?" Looking back at his own defense of Utilitarianism, J. J. C. Smart writes:

> Admittedly utilitarianism does have consequences which are incompatible with the common moral consciousness, but I tended to take the view "so much the worse for the common moral consciousness." That is, I was inclined to reject the com-mon methodology of testing general ethical principles by seeing how they square with our feelings in particular instances.

This breed of utilitarian—hard-nosed and unapologetic—can offer three responses to the anti-utilitarian arguments.

The First Response: All Values Have a Utilitarian Basis. Critics of Utilitarianism say that the theory can't make sense of some of our most important values—such as the value we attach to truth telling, promise keeping, respecting others' privacy, and loving our children. Consider, for example, lying. The main reason not to lie, the critics say, has nothing to do with bad consequences. The reason is that lying is dishonest; it betrays people's trust. That fact has nothing to do with the utilitarian calculation of benefits. Honesty has a value over and above any value that the utilitarian can acknowledge. The same is true of promise keeping, respecting others' privacy, and loving our children.

But according to philosophers such as Smart, we should think about these values one at a time and consider why they're important. When people lie, the lies are often discovered, and those betrayed feel hurt and angry. When people break their promises, they irritate their neighbors and alienate their friends. Someone whose privacy is violated may feel humiliated and want to withdraw from others. When people don't care more about their own children than they do about strangers, their children feel unloved, and one day they too may become unloving parents. All these things reduce happiness. Far from being at odds with the idea that we should be honest, dependable, respectful, and loving to our children, Utilitarianism explains why those things are good.

Moreover, apart from the utilitarian explanation, these duties would seem inexplicable. What could be stranger than the idea that lying is wrong "in itself," apart from any harm it causes? And how could people have a "right to privacy" unless respecting that right brought about some benefit? On this way of thinking, Utilitarianism is not incompatible with common sense; on the contrary, Utilitarianism justifies the commonsense values we have.

The Second Response: Our Gut Reactions Can't Be Trusted When Cases Are Exceptional. Although some cases of injustice serve the common good, those cases are exceptions. Lying, promise breaking, and violations of privacy usually lead to unhappiness, not happiness. This observation forms the basis of another utilitarian response.

Consider again McCloskey's example of the person tempted to bear false witness. Why do we immediately and instinctively believe it to be wrong to bear false witness against an innocent person? The reason, some say, is that throughout our lives we have seen lies lead to misery and misfortune. Thus, *we instinctively condemn all lies, even ones that do not lead to misery and misfortune.* But when we condemn lies that are beneficial, our intuitive faculties are misfiring. Experience has taught us to condemn lies because they reduce happiness. Now, however, we are condemning lies that increase happiness. When confronting unusual cases, such as McCloskey's, perhaps we should trust the Principle of Utility more than our gut instincts.

The Third Response: We Should Focus on *All* the Consequences. When we're asked to consider a "despicable" action that maximizes happiness, the action is often presented in a way that encourages us to focus on its bad effects, and not on its good effects. If instead we focus on *all* the effects of the act, Utilitarianism seems more plausible.

Consider yet again the McCloskey example. McCloskey says it would be wrong to convict an innocent man because that would be unjust. But what about the *other* innocent people who will be hurt if the rioting and lynchings continue? What about the pain that will be endured by those who are beaten and tormented by the mob? What about the deaths that will occur if the man doesn't lie? Children will lose their parents, and parents will lose their children. Of course, we never want to face a situation like this. But if we must choose between securing the conviction of one innocent person and allowing the deaths of several innocent people, is it so unreasonable to think that the first option is preferable?

And consider again the objection that Utilitarianism is too demanding because it tells us to use our resources to feed starving children rather than using those resources to eat at restaurants. If we focus our thoughts on those who would starve, do the demands of Utilitarianism seem so unreasonable? Isn't it self-serving of us to say that Utilitarianism is "too demanding," rather than saying that we should feed starving children?

This strategy works better for some cases than for others. Consider the Peeping Tom. The unapologetic utilitarian will tell us to consider the pleasure *he* gets from spying on unsuspecting women. If he gets away with it, what harm has been done? Why should his action be condemned? Most people will condemn his behavior, despite the utilitarian arguments. Utilitarianism, as Smart suggests, cannot be fully reconciled with common sense.

Nevertheless, some philosophers think that Act-Utilitarianism is a perfectly defensible doctrine that does not need to be modified. Even so, it must be said that Utilitarianism is a radical doctrine that challenges many commonsense assumptions. In this respect, it does what good philosophy always does—it makes us think about things that we take for granted.

Concluding Thoughts

If we consult what Smart calls our "common moral consciousness," many considerations other than utility seem morally important. But Smart is right to warn us that "common sense" cannot be trusted. That may turn out to be Utilitarianism's greatest contribution. The deficiencies of moral common sense become obvious if we think for only a moment. Many white people once felt that there was an important difference between whites and blacks, so that the interests of whites were somehow more important. Trusting the "common sense" of their day, they might have insisted that an adequate moral theory should accommodate this "fact." Today, no one worth listening to would say such a thing, but who knows how many other irrational prejudices are still part of our moral common sense? At the end of his classic study of race relations, *An American Dilemma,* Nobel Laureate Gunnar Myrdal (1898–1987) reminds us:

> There must be still other countless errors of the same sort that no living man can yet detect, because of the fog within which our type of Western culture envelops us. Cultural influences have set up the assumptions about the mind, the body, and the universe with which we begin; pose the questions we ask; influence the facts we seek; determine the interpretation we give these facts; and direct our reaction to these interpretations and conclusions.

Could it be, for example, that future generations will look back in disgust at the way affluent people in the 21st century enjoyed their comfortable lives while third-world children died of easily preventable diseases? Or at the way we confined and slaughtered helpless animals? If so, they might note that utilitarian philosophers were ahead of their time in condemning such things.

CHAPTER 31

The Experience Machine

Robert Nozick

Robert Nozick (1938–2002) was Joseph Pellegrino University Professor of Philosophy at Harvard University. The following selection is from his book *Anarchy, State, and Utopia,* a brilliant and entertaining defense of minimal government. In this excerpt, Nozick uses a thought-experiment to explore questions about what matters to us *other than what our experiences are like.* How we answer these questions will cast light on the ethics of drug use, television watching, and perhaps even sleeping late.

. . . Suppose there were an experience machine that would give you any experience you desired. Superduper neuropsychologists could stimulate your brain so that you would think and feel you were writing a great novel, or making a friend, or reading an interesting book. All the time you would be floating in a tank, with electrodes attached to your brain. Should you plug into this machine for life, preprogramming your life's experiences? If you are worried about missing out on desirable experiences, we can suppose that business enterprises have researched thoroughly the lives of many others. You can pick and choose from their large library or smorgasbord of such experiences, selecting your life's experiences for, say, the next two years. After two years have passed, you will have ten minutes or ten hours out of the tank, to select the experiences of your *next* two years. Of course, while in the tank you won't

Source: Excerpted from Robert Nozick, *Anarchy, State, and Utopia* (1974). Copyright © 1977 Robert Nozick. Reprinted by permission of Basic Books, a member of the Perseus Books Group.

know that you're there; you'll think it's all actually happening. Others can also plug in to have the experiences they want, so there's no need to stay unplugged to serve them. (Ignore problems such as who will service the machines if everyone plugs in.) Would you plug in? *What else can matter to us, other than how our lives feel from the inside?* Nor should you refrain because of the few moments of distress between the moment you've decided and the moment you're plugged. What's a few moments of distress compared to a lifetime of bliss (if that's what you choose), and why feel any distress at all if your decision *is* the best one?

What does matter to us in addition to our experiences? First, we want to *do* certain things, and not just have the experience of doing them. In the case of certain experiences, it is only because first we want to do the actions that we want the experiences of doing them or thinking we've done them. (But *why* do we want to do the activities rather than merely to experience them?) A second reason for not plugging in is that we want to *be* a certain way, to be a certain sort of person. Someone floating in a tank is an indeterminate blob. There is no answer to the question of what a person is like who has long been in the tank. Is he courageous, kind, intelligent, witty, loving? It's not merely that it's difficult to tell; there's no way he is. Plugging into the machine is a kind of suicide. It will seem to some, trapped by a picture, that nothing about what we are like can matter except as it gets reflected in our experiences. But should it be surprising that what *we are* is important to us? Why should we be concerned only with how our time is filled, but not with what we are?

Thirdly, plugging into an experience machine limits us to a man-made reality, to a world no deeper or more important than that which people can construct. There is no *actual* contact with any deeper reality, though the experience of it can be simulated. Many persons desire to leave themselves open to such contact and to a plumbing of deeper significance. This clarifies the intensity of the conflict over psychoactive drugs, which some view as mere local experience machines, and others view as avenues to a deeper reality; what some view as equivalent to surrender to the experience machine, others view as following one of the reasons *not* to surrender!

We learn that something matters to us in addition to experience by imagining an experience machine and then realizing that we would not use it. We can continue to imagine a sequence of machines each designed to fill lacks suggested for the earlier machines. For example, since the experience machine doesn't meet our desire to *be* a certain way, imagine a transformation machine which transforms us into whatever sort of person we'd like to be (compatible with our staying us). Surely one would not use the transformation machine to become as one would wish, and thereupon plug into the experience machine! So something matters in addition to one's experiences *and* what one is like. Nor is the reason merely that one's experiences are unconnected with what one is like. For the experience machine might be limited to provide only experiences possible to the sort of person plugged in. Is it that we want to make a difference in the world? Consider then the result machine, which produces in the world any result you would produce and injects your vector input into any joint activity. We shall not pursue here the fascinating details of these or other machines. What is most disturbing about them is their living of our lives for us. Is it misguided to search for *particular* additional functions beyond the competence of machines to do for us? Perhaps what we desire is to live (an active verb) ourselves, in contact with reality. (And this, machines cannot do *for* us.) Without elaborating on the implications of this, which I believe connect surprisingly with issues about free will and causal accounts of knowledge, we need merely note the intricacy of the question of what matters *for people* other than their experiences. . . .

CHAPTER 32

The Meaning of Life

Richard Taylor

Richard Taylor (1919–2003) taught at Brown University, Columbia University, and the University of Rochester in upstate New York. Professor Taylor was known both for his books on metaphysics and for his books on beekeeping. In *Good and Evil: A New Direction* (2000), Taylor endorsed a radically subjectivist view of ethics but concluded with this reflection on the meaning of life.

The question whether life has any meaning is difficult to interpret, and the more one concentrates his critical faculty on it the more it seems to elude him, or to evaporate as any intelligible question. One wants to turn it aside, as a source of embarrassment, as something that, if it cannot be abolished, should at least be decently covered. And yet I think any reflective person recognizes that the question it raises is important, and that it ought to have a significant answer.

If the idea of meaningfulness is difficult to grasp in this context, so that we are unsure what sort of thing would amount to answering the question, the idea of meaninglessness is perhaps less so. If, then, we can bring before our minds a clear image of meaningless existence, then perhaps we can take a step toward coping with our original question by seeing to what extent our lives, as we actually find them, resemble that image, and draw such lessons as we are able to from the comparison.

Meaningless Existence

A perfect image of meaninglessness, of the kind we are seeking, is found in the ancient myth of Sisyphus. Sisyphus, it will be remembered, betrayed divine secrets to mortals, and for this he was condemned by the gods to roll a stone to the top of a hill, the stone then immediately to roll back down, again to be pushed to the top by Sisyphus, to roll down once more, and so on again and again, *forever*. Now in this we have the picture of meaningless, pointless toil, of a meaningless existence that is absolutely *never* redeemed. It is not even redeemed by a death that, if it were to accomplish nothing more, would at least bring this idiotic cycle to a close. If we were invited to imagine Sisyphus struggling for a while and accomplishing nothing, perhaps eventually falling from exhaustion, so that we might suppose him then eventually turning to something having some sort of promise, then the meaninglessness of that chapter of his life would not be so stark. It would be a dark and dreadful dream, from which he eventually awakens to sunlight and reality. But he does not awaken, for there is nothing for him to awaken to. His repetitive toil is his life and reality, and it goes on forever, and it is without any meaning whatever. Nothing ever comes of what he is doing, except simply, more of the same. Not by one step, nor by a thousand, nor by ten thousand does he even expiate by the smallest token the sin against the gods that led him into this fate. Nothing comes of it, nothing at all.

This ancient myth has always enchanted men, for countless meanings can be read into it. Some of the ancients apparently thought it symbolized the perpetual rising and setting of the sun, and others the repetitious crashing of the waves upon the shore. Probably the commonest interpretation is that it symbolizes man's eternal struggle and unquenchable spirit, his determination always to try once more in the face of overwhelming discouragement. This interpretation is further supported by that version of the myth according to which Sisyphus was commanded to roll the stone *over* the hill, so that it would finally roll down the other side, but was never quite able to make it.

I am not concerned with rendering or defending any interpretation of this myth, however. I have cited it only for the one element it does unmistakably contain, namely, that of a repetitious, cyclic activity that never comes to anything. We could contrive other images of this that would serve just as well, and no myth-makers are needed to supply the materials of it. Thus, we can imagine two persons transporting a stone—or even a precious gem, it does not matter—back and forth, relay style. One carries it to a near or distant point where it is received by the other; it is returned to its starting point, there to be recovered by the first, and the process is repeated over and over. Except in this relay nothing counts as winning, and nothing brings the contest to any close, each step only leads to a repetition of itself. Or we can imagine two groups of prisoners, one of them engaged in digging a prodigious hole in the ground that is no sooner finished than it is filled in again by the other group, the latter then digging a new hole that is at once filled in by the first group, and so on and on endlessly.

Now what stands out in all such pictures as oppressive and dejecting is not that the beings who enact these roles suffer any torture or pain, for it need not be assumed that they do. Nor is it that their labors are great, for they are no greater than the labors commonly undertaken by most men most of the time. According to the original myth, the stone is so large that Sisyphus never quite gets it to the top and must groan under every step, so that his enormous labor is all for naught. But this is not what appalls. It is not that his great struggle comes to nothing, but that his existence itself is without meaning. Even if we suppose, for example, that the stone is but a pebble that can be carried effortlessly, or that the holes dug by the prisoners are but small ones, not the slightest meaning is introduced into their lives. The stone that Sisyphus moves to the top of the hill, whether we think of it as large or small, still rolls back every time, and the process is repeated forever. Nothing comes of it, and the work is simply pointless. That is the element of the myth that I wish to capture.

Again, it is not the fact that the labors of Sisyphus continue forever that deprives them of meaning. It is, rather, the implication of this: that they come to nothing. The image would not be changed by our supposing him to push a different stone up every time, each to roll down again. But if we supposed that these stones, instead of rolling back to their places as if they had never been moved, were assembled at the top of the hill and there incorporated, say, in a beautiful and enduring temple, then the aspect of meaninglessness would disappear. His labors would then have a point, something would come of them all, and although one could perhaps still say it was not worth it, one could not say that the life of Sisyphus was devoid of meaning altogether. Meaningfulness would at least have made an appearance, and we could see what it was.

That point will need remembering. But in the meantime, let us note another way in which the image of meaninglessness can be altered by making only a very slight change. Let us suppose that the gods, while condemning Sisyphus to the fate just described, at the same time, as an afterthought, waxed perversely merciful by implanting in him a strange and irrational impulse; namely, a compulsive impulse to roll stones. We may if we like, to make this more graphic, suppose they accomplish this by implanting in him some substance that has this effect on his character and drives. I call this perverse, because from our point of view there is clearly no reason why anyone should have a persistent and insatiable desire to do something so pointless as that. Nevertheless, suppose that is Sisyphus' condition. He has but one obsession, which is to roll stones, and it is an obsession that is only for the moment appeased by his rolling them—he no sooner gets a stone rolled to the top of the hill than he is restless to roll up another.

Now it can be seen why this little afterthought of the gods, which I called perverse, was also in fact merciful. For they have by this device managed to give Sisyphus precisely what he wants—by making him want precisely what they inflict on him. However it may appear to us, Sisyphus' fate now does not appear to him as a condemnation, but the very reverse. His one desire in life is to roll stones, and he is absolutely guaranteed its endless fulfillment. Where otherwise he might profoundly have wished surcease, and even welcomed the quiet of death to release him from endless boredom and meaninglessness, his life is now filled with mission and meaning, and he seems to himself to have been given an entry to heaven. Nor need he even fear death, for the gods have promised him an endless opportunity to indulge his single purpose, without concern or frustration. He will be able to roll stones *forever*.

What we need to mark most carefully at this point is that the picture with which we began has not really been changed in the least by adding this supposition. Exactly the same things happen as before. The only change is in Sisyphus' view of them. The picture before was the image of meaningless activity and existence. It was created precisely to be an image of that. It has not lost that meaninglessness, it has now gained not the least shred of meaningfulness. The stones still roll back as before, each phase of Sisyphus' life still exactly resembles all the others, the task is never completed, nothing comes of it, no temple ever begins to rise, and all this cycle of the same pointless thing over and over goes on forever in this picture as in the other. The *only* thing that has happened is this: Sisyphus has been reconciled to it, and indeed more, he has been led to embrace it. Not, however, by reason or persuasion, but by nothing more rational than the potency of a new substance in his veins.

The Meaninglessness of Life

I believe the foregoing provides a fairly clear content to the idea of meaninglessness and, through it, some hint of what meaningfulness, in this sense, might be. Meaninglessness is essentially endless pointlessness, and meaningfulness is therefore the opposite. Activity, and even long, drawn-out and repetitive activity, has a meaning if it has some significant culmination, some more or less lasting end that can be considered to have been the direction and purpose of the activity. But the descriptions so far also provide something else; namely, the suggestion of how an existence that is objectively meaningless, in this sense, can nevertheless acquire a meaning for him whose existence it is.

Now let us ask: Which of these pictures does life in fact resemble? And let us not begin with our own lives, for here both our prejudices and wishes are great, but with the life in general that we share with the rest of creation. We shall find, I think, that it all has a certain pattern, and that this pattern is by now easily recognized.

We can begin anywhere, only saving human existence for our last consideration. We can, for example, begin with any animal. It does not matter where we begin, because the result is going to be exactly the same.

Thus, for example, there are caves in New Zealand, deep and dark, whose floors are quiet pools and whose walls and ceilings are covered with soft light. As one gazes in wonder in the stillness of these caves it seems that the Creator has reproduced there in microcosm the heavens themselves, until one scarcely remembers the enclosing presence of the walls. As one looks more closely, however, the scene is explained. Each dot of light identifies an ugly worm, whose luminous tail is meant to attract insects from the surrounding darkness. As from time to time one of these insects draws near it becomes entangled in a sticky thread lowered by the worm, and is eaten. This goes on month after month, the blind worm lying there in the barren stillness waiting to entrap an occasional bit of nourishment that will only sustain it to another bit of nourishment until. . . . Until what? What great thing awaits all this long and repetitious effort and makes it worthwhile? Really nothing. The larva just transforms itself finally to a tiny winged adult that lacks even mouth parts to feed and lives only a day or two. These adults, as soon as they have mated and laid eggs, are themselves caught in the threads and are devoured by the cannibalist worms, often without having ventured into the day, the only point to their existence having now been fulfilled. This has been going on for millions of years, and to no end other than that the same meaningless cycle may continue for another millions of years.

All living things present essentially the same spectacle. The larva of a certain cicada burrows in the darkness of the earth for seventeen years, through season after season, to emerge finally into the daylight for a brief flight, lay its eggs, and die—this all to repeat itself during the next seventeen years, and so on to eternity. We have already noted, in another connection, the struggles of fish, made only that others may do the same after them and that this cycle, having no other point than itself, may never cease. Some birds span an entire side of the globe each year and then return, only to ensure that others may follow the same incredibly long path again and again. One is led to wonder what the point of it all is, with what great triumph this ceaseless effort, repeating itself through millions of years, might finally culminate, and why it should go on and on for so long, accomplishing nothing, getting nowhere. But then one realizes that there is no point to it at all, that it really culminates in nothing, that each of these cycles, so filled with toil, is to be followed only by more of the same. The point of any living thing's life is, evidently, nothing but life itself.

This life of the world thus presents itself to our eyes as a vast machine, feeding on itself, running on and on forever to nothing. And we are part of that life. To be sure, we are not just the same, but the differences are not so great as we like to think; many are merely invented, and none really cancels the kind of meaninglessness that we found in Sisyphus and that we find all around, wherever anything lives. We are conscious of our activity. Our goals, whether in any significant sense we choose them or not, are things of which we are at least partly aware and can therefore in some sense appraise. More significantly, perhaps, men have a history, as other animals do not, such that each generation does not precisely resemble all those before. Still, if we can in imagination disengage our wills from our lives and disregard the deep interest each man has in his own existence, we shall find that they do not so little resemble the existence of Sisyphus. We toil after goals, most of them—indeed every single one of them—of transitory significance and, having gained one of them, we immediately set forth for the next, as if that one had never been, with this next one being essentially more of the same. Look at a busy street any day, and observe the throng going hither and thither. To what? Some office or shop, where the same things will be done today as were done yesterday, and are done now so they may be repeated tomorrow. And if we think that, unlike Sisyphus, these labors do have a point, that they culminate in something lasting and, independently of our own deep interests in them, very worthwhile, then we simply have not considered the thing closely enough. Most such effort is directed only to the establishment and perpetuation of home and family; that is, to the begetting of others who will follow in our steps to do more of the same. Each man's life thus resembles one of Sisyphus' climbs to the summit of his hill, and each day of it one of his steps; the difference is that whereas Sisyphus himself returns to push the stone up again, we leave this to our children. We at one point imagined that the labors of Sisyphus finally culminated in the creation of a temple, but for this to make any difference it had to be a temple that would at least endure, adding beauty to the world for the remainder of time. Our achievements, even though they are often beautiful, are mostly bubbles; and those that do last, like the sand-swept pyramids, soon become mere curiosities while around them the rest of mankind continues its perpetual toting of rocks, only to see them roll down. Nations are built upon the bones of their founders and pioneers, but only to decay and crumble before long, their rubble then becoming the foundation for others directed to exactly the same fate. The picture of Sisyphus is the picture of existence of the individual man, great or unknown, of nations, of the race of men, and of the very life of the world.

On a country road one sometimes comes upon the ruined hulks of a house and once extensive buildings, all in collapse and spread over with weeds. A curious eye can in imagination reconstruct from what is left a once warm and thriving life, filled with purpose. There was the hearth, where a family once talked, sang, and made plans; there were the rooms, where people loved, and babes were born to a rejoicing mother; there are the musty remains of a sofa, infested with bugs, once bought at a dear price to enhance an ever-growing comfort, beauty, and warmth. Every small piece of junk fills the mind with what once, not long ago, was utterly real, with children's voices, plans made, and enterprises embarked upon. That is how these stones of Sisyphus were rolled up, and that is how they became incorporated into a beautiful temple, and that temple is what now lies before you. Meanwhile other buildings, institutions, nations, and civilizations spring up all around, only to share the same fate before long. And if the question "What for?" is now asked, the answer is clear: so that just this may go on forever.

The two pictures—of Sisyphus and of our own lives, if we look at them from a distance—are in outline the same and convey to the mind the same image. It is not surprising, then, that men invent ways of denying it, their religions proclaiming a heaven that does not crumble, their hymnals and prayer books declaring a significance to life of which our eyes provide no hint whatever.[1] Even our philosophies portray some permanent and lasting good at which all may aim, from the changeless forms invented by Plato to the beatific vision of St. Thomas and the ideals of permanence contrived by the moderns. When these fail to convince, then earthly ideals such as universal justice and brotherhood are conjured up to take their places and give meaning to man's seemingly endless pilgrimage, some final state that will be ushered in when the last obstacle is removed and the last stone pushed to the hilltop. No one believes, of course, that any such state will be final, or even wants it to be in case it means that human existence would then cease to be a struggle; but in the meantime such ideas serve a very real need.

The Meaning of Life

We noted that Sisyphus' existence would have meaning if there were some point to his labors, if his efforts ever culminated in something that was not just an occasion for fresh labors of the same kind. But that is precisely the meaning it lacks. And human existence resembles his in that respect. Men do achieve things—they scale their towers and raise their stones to their hilltops—but every such accomplishment fades, providing only an occasion for renewed labors of the same kind.

But here we need to note something else that has been mentioned, but its significance not explored, and that is the state of mind and feeling with which such labors are undertaken. We noted that if Sisyphus had a keen and unappeasable desire to be doing just what he found himself doing, then, although his life would in no way be changed, it would nevertheless have a meaning for him. It would be

---

[1] A popular Christian hymn, sung often at funerals and typical of many hymns, expresses this thought:

Swift to its close ebbs out life's little day;
Earth's joys grow dim, its glories pass away;
Change and decay in all around I see:
O thou who changest not, abide with me.

an irrational one, no doubt, because the desire itself would be only the product of the substance in his veins, and not any that reason could discover, but a meaning nevertheless.

And would it not, in fact, be a meaning incomparably better than the other? For let us examine again the first kind of meaning it could have. Let us suppose that, without having any interest in rolling stones, as such, and finding this, in fact, a galling toil, Sisyphus did nevertheless have a deep interest in raising a temple, one that would be beautiful and lasting. And let us suppose he succeeded in this, that after ages of dreadful toil, all directed at this final result, he did at last complete his temple, such that now he could say his work was done, and he could rest and forever enjoy the result. Now what? What picture now presents itself to our minds? It is precisely the picture of infinite boredom! Of Sisyphus doing nothing ever again, but contemplating what he has already wrought and can no longer add anything to, and contemplating it for an eternity! Now in this picture we have a meaning for Sisyphus' existence, a point for his prodigious labor, because we have put it there; yet, at the same time, that which is really worthwhile seems to have slipped away entirely. Where before we were presented with the nightmare of eternal and pointless activity, we are now confronted with the hell of its eternal absence.

Our second picture, then, wherein we imagined Sisyphus to have had inflicted on him the irrational desire to be doing just what he found himself doing, should not have been dismissed so abruptly. The meaning that picture lacked was no meaning that he or anyone could crave, and the strange meaning it had was perhaps just what we were seeking.

At this point, then, we can reintroduce what has been until now, it is hoped, resolutely pushed aside in an effort to view our lives and human existence with objectivity; namely, our own wills, our deep interest in what we find ourselves doing. If we do this we find that our lives do indeed still resemble that of Sisyphus, but that the meaningfulness they thus lack is precisely the meaningfulness of infinite boredom. At the same time, the strange meaningfulness they possess is that of the inner compulsion to be doing just what we were put here to do, and to go on doing it forever. This is the nearest we may hope to get to heaven, but the redeeming side of that fact is that we do thereby avoid a genuine hell.

If the builders of a great and flourishing ancient civilization could somehow return now to see archaeologists unearthing the trivial remnants of what they had once accomplished with such effort—see the fragments of pots and vases, a few broken statues, and such tokens of another age and greatness—they could indeed ask themselves what the point of it all was, if this is all it finally came to. Yet, it did not seem so to them then, for it was just the building, and not what was finally built, that gave their life meaning. Similarly, if the builders of the ruined home and farm that I described a short while ago could be brought back to see what is left, they would have the same feelings. What we construct in our imaginations as we look over these decayed and rusting pieces would reconstruct itself in their very memories, and certainly with unspeakable sadness. The piece of a sled at our feet would revive in them a warm Christmas. And what rich memories would there be in the broken crib? And the weed-covered remains of a fence would reproduce the scene of a great herd of livestock, so laboriously built up over so many years. What was it all worth, if this is the final result? Yet, again, it did not seem so to them through those many years of struggle and toil, and they did not imagine they were building a Gibraltar. The things to which they bent their backs day after day, realizing one by one their ephemeral plans, were precisely the things in which their wills were deeply involved, precisely the things in which their interests lay, and there was no need then to ask questions. There is no more need of them now—the day was sufficient to itself, and so was the life.

This is surely the way to look at all of life—at one's own life, and each day and moment it contains; of the life of a nation; of the species; of the life of the world; and of everything that breathes. Even the glow worms I described, whose cycles of existence over the millions of years seem so pointless when looked at by us, will seem entirely different to us if we can somehow try to view their existence from within. Their endless activity, which gets nowhere, is just what it is their will to pursue. This is its whole justification and meaning. Nor would it be any salvation to the birds who span the globe every year, back and forth, to have a home made for them in a cage with plenty of food and protection, so that they would not have to migrate any more. It would be their condemnation, for it is the doing that counts for them, and not what they hope to win by it. Flying these prodigious distances, never ending, is what it is in their veins to do, exactly as it was in Sisyphus' veins to roll stones, without end, after the gods had waxed merciful and implanted this in him.

A human being no sooner draws his first breath than he responds to the will that is in him to live. He no more asks whether it will be worthwhile, or whether anything of significance will come of it, than the worms and the birds. The point of his living is simply to be living, in the manner that it is his nature to be living. He goes through his life building his castles, each of these beginning to fade into time as the next is begun; yet, it would be no salvation to rest from all this. It would be a condemnation, and one that would in no way be redeemed were he able to gaze upon the things he has done, even if these were beautiful and absolutely permanent, as they never are. What counts is that one should be able to begin a new task, a new castle, a new bubble. It counts only because it is there to be done and he has the will to do it. The same will be the life of his children, and of theirs; and if the philosopher is apt to see in this a pattern similar to the unending cycles of the existence of Sisyphus, and to despair, then it is indeed because the meaning and point he is seeking is not there—but mercifully so. The meaning of life is from within us, it is not bestowed from without, and it far exceeds in both its beauty and permanence any heaven of which men have ever dreamed or yearned for.